Museum Cataloging in the Computer Age

Museum

Cataloging

in the

Computer Age

Robert G. Chenhall

AMERICAN ASSOCIATION FOR STATE AND LOCAL HISTORY
Nashville, Tennessee, 1975

The publication of this book was
made possible in part by a grant from
The National Endowment for the Arts

Library of Congress Cataloguing-in-Publication Data
Chenhall, Robert G   1923–
  Museum cataloging in the computer age.

  1. Museum registration methods. 2. Electronic data processing—Museums. I. Title.
AM139.C48   1975   069′.52′02854   74–16439
ISBN 0–910050–12–0

Author and publisher make grateful acknowledgment to the publishers of the following, in which adaptations of parts of this book have appeared in articles by Robert G. Chenhall.

"The Mythical Magic Black Box" appeared in *Museum News* 53, No. 1 (September 1974):30–33. Copyright © 1974 by *Museum News*.

"Museums, Catalogs, and Computer Nets" appeared in *EDUCOM Bulletin* 9, No. 3 (Fall 1974):7–11. Copyright © 1974 by *EDUCOM Bulletin*.

Computers in Anthropology and Archaeology. IBM Corporation No. GE20–0384–0, copyright © 1971 by IBM.

Figures 3 and 4 appeared in *Computers in Anthropology and Archaeology,* copyright © 1971 by IBM.

Figure 50 accompanied the article "Museum Computer Network: The Third Phase," by David Vance in *Museum News* 51, No. 8 (April 1973):24–27. Copyright © 1973 by *Museum News*.

Contents

Preface

THIS BOOK began as an archaeological data bank instruction manual. The Archaeological Data Bank Conference, which the Wenner-Gren Foundation for Anthropological Research sponsored at the University of Arkansas in the spring of 1971, clearly indicated that there was a need for some kind of publication to give the layman a better understanding of data banks—what they are, how they work, when they are and are not useful, and what it takes to create them. The writing of a book to meet this need was begun that summer.

On March 29, 1972, though, the form, content, and audience to whom the book is addressed changed considerably. It was on that date, at a meeting in Hershey, Pennsylvania, that the idea for the Museum Data Bank Coordinating Committee was proposed, and since then the Committee and the book have been closely connected.

The Museum Data Bank Coordinating Committee is a working committee for the collection and dissemination of technically competent advice on the use of computers in museums, and one of its major activities has been to oversee the writing of this book. The MDBCC is sponsored by the National Museum Act (administered by the Smithsonian Institution). This has made it possible to employ the firm of Ernst & Ernst to prepare some of the computer system descriptions in chapter 6, and it has given the author uninterrupted blocks of time for writing. In addition, the MDBCC has been a never-ending reservoir of sound advice. The statement of museum catalog content standards that appears here as chapter 4 is the only "official" pronouncement of the MDBCC, but the Committee members have played a large part in the development of the entire manuscript.

The membership of the MDBCC is an interesting combination of hard-headed museum administrators and working scientists. The background disciplines represented are: anthropology (2), art history (2), botany (2), computer science (3), entomology (1), history (1), and paleontology (1). The result is a committee with widely diverse points of view but a common dedication to the future of computerized data banks in museums and museum-related disciplines. The members of the MDBCC, in addition to the author, are: Reginald Creighton, Smithsonian Institution: Dr. Richard H. Foote, U.S. Dept. of Agriculture; Dr. Jack Heller, SUNY at Stony Brook; Dr. William Klein, Missouri Botanical Garden; Harriet Krauss, Computer Consultant; Dr. James F. Mello, National Museum of Natural History; Frederick Schmid, Smithsonian Institution; Dr. David Scott, National Gallery of Art; Stanwyn Shetler, National Museum of Natural History; Holman J. Swinney, Margaret Woodbury Strong Museum; and David Vance, Museum Computer Network, Inc.

On September 30, 1974, the National Museum Act grant which has supported the MDBCC came to an end. However, the work of the committee will continue with only a slight change in name. From October 1 on, the MDBCC will be known as the MDBC—the Museum Data Bank Committee.

To the members of the MDBCC and to the National Museum Act Council I am deeply grateful. In addition, I want to thank Sandra Scholtz, my chief assistant, for her continued willingness to talk over these strange ideas of mine, and Judy Husted for patiently typing and retyping the manuscript. The analysis, synthesis, and evaluation of the information contained here are my own. Regardless of the help he may receive from others, the final responsibility for any book must be the author's alone.

1

Computers and Museums: Past, Present, and Future

THE IDEA that a computer can be an effective aid to the cataloging of museum collections is no more than ten years old. Whether or not the computer can be an economical cataloging device has yet to be demonstrated. A number of museums are now working on it, but for each employee who heartily endorses the idea, there are probably two more who would share the scepticism expressed recently by the director of one of the nation's largest museums: "When you can show me how I can do this cataloging function cheaper using a computer, then I will listen. But, I doubt that it will ever happen."

The main problem in trying to deal with this type of scepticism, of course, is the lack of factual information from which to arrive at any kind of a reasoned conclusion. It is safe to say that every museum director would like to have a good catalog of his collections; and, on the surface of it, the computer looks as if it would be a useful aid to obtaining such a catalog. But, what *is* a computer catalog anyway? How does it work? What does it cost to obtain and operate the necessary computer programs? How do these costs compare with the costs of maintaining a *good* manual catalog? How do they compare with the costs of not maintaining a catalog at all? Finally, what is a catalog? What should it be?

This book is not going to resolve all questions of this kind that every museum administrator may face. However, it will provide enough information to help in answering some of them. It is based upon the premise that the computer is an intimate part of the day-to-day lives of most of us, and that it will become an even more intimate part of our lives in the future. If this premise is valid, then there is no longer any reason to question the fact that someday most museums will use computers as routinely as banks do today. The important questions then center around the *when* and *how* of museum computer use.

All the great ideas of mankind—the ideas of lasting merit—have a right place in time and only one right place in time. This has been expressed by numerous philosophers over the years. Santayana, for example, said, "That which is virtue in season is madness out of season, as when an old man makes love." [1] Another way of expressing the same thought is the right thing at the wrong time becomes the wrong thing. [2]

The best examples of good ideas at the wrong time are probably the flying machines and the submarines of Leonardo da Vinci. As we know now, his ideas were basically sound, but the technology necessary to convert them into reality was not available until the nineteenth and twentieth centuries. Technology, though, was not the whole story. It was important, certainly, but the timeliness of great ideas is also a function of the felt need for the results of the new concepts. The intellectual milieu in which great ideas are first expressed is often quite different from the times when they finally become widely quoted, accepted by large numbers of people, and acted upon.

Consider, for example, that great decade in Western European history, the years from 1850 to 1860. The intellectual ferment of that particular moment in time resulted in the *acceptance* of more new ideas—ideas that had been around for 30, 50, or 100 years—than any comparable period in man's history with the possible exception of the last ten or fifteen years. Uniformitarianism (which had been expressed in print in the 1830s) paved the way, for it set aside once and for all the idea that the Earth had been created by a series of catastrophes, beginning (according to Archbishop Ussher) in the year 4004 B.C. But this was quickly followed with the acceptance of the thought that if the Earth was old, man could be old also. The stone tools that had been found in association with ancient gravels could really have been man-made as claimed by Boucher de Perthe for many years; the concept of evolution could be a reality; and so on. The decade from 1850 to 1860 was one of the best times in all of history for a person to have new ideas accepted and acted upon.

In our generation, new ideas are almost a daily occurrence. The prisoners of war in North Vietnam came back to a world quite different from the one they left. Especially in a field like computers, where innovations are the way of life, ten years is a long time. In order to establish a perspective on what this book is all about, it is perhaps worthwhile to consider what was being done with computers and museum collections ten years ago, then to forecast where computers are going to be ten years from now, and finally, to assess what this means in terms of actions that museum directors and others can or should be taking today in order to prepare themselves and their organizations for the future.

It is difficult for most people to realize the extent of the changes that have taken place in the last ten years both in computer technology and in the impact of that technology upon our lives. Ten years ago we were really just beginning to emerge from the era of mechanical punched card machines. The computer in most widespread use was the IBM 1401, and most programming for this computer was an attempt to duplicate the repetitive accounting functions that had been done previously with mechanical card sorters and tabulators. A few banks were encoding checks with magnetic ink so that they could sort them faster, but they were having lots of problems with the sorting equipment and particularly with the nonstandard sizes of checks.

In 1966 Ling-Temco-Vought had what was claimed to be the largest computer center in the world. At that time Helmuth Naumer, Executive Director of the Fort Worth Museum of Science and History, convinced L-T-V that it would be economically worthwhile to invest whatever time might be required of systems analysts and programmers to develop a computer system for the museum profession. The plan was that L-T-V would eventually get their money back by leasing terminals to individual museums throughout the country. Naumer made several attempts to interest museum directors in this plan, but he received almost no support or encouragement from his peers *even though the initial developmental work would have been done by L-T-V free of charge.* Naumer had an idea that was ahead of its time.

At about the same time—1967—I experienced something that was in many ways exactly the same. Chester A. Thomas, who was then director of the Southwestern Archeological Research Center of the National Park Service in Globe, Arizona, foresaw the possibilities of computer science for control of the many archaeological, historical, and natural history collections at the different parks and monuments and wanted to set up a pilot study using the collections at Globe. Many of the Service's archaeologists agreed that this was a worthwhile project, but by the time it reached Washington, "budget cuts" eliminated the proposal.

It is easy to be critical with twenty-twenty hindsight, but we must remember two things about the situation as it existed then:

1. Technology to support such ideas was just beginning to be available in 1966 and 1967. The so-called third generation of computers was first announced in 1963. The kinds of applications suggested by these illustrations were at that time truly innovative.

2. Much more important, though, was the fact that very few people had the vision to see the extreme impact that computers would have on all aspects of our lives or how common large-scale computers would become within a very few years. Established institutions such as the National Park Service and our national museum organizations have never been, and probably should not be, the pacesetters or visionaries in our society, and there is no reason why we could expect the leaders of these institutions to be immediately responsive to untried innovations.

In any case, the past is behind us. Let us see if we can predict what is going to happen in the *next* ten years with computers and museums, for this is the only way to determine what action is appropriate today. In the last chapter of this book considerable attention will be directed to the future of computerized museum catalogs. In order to give the reader some incentive to read what lies ahead of that chapter, it is necessary that he have at least a partial preview.

The changes in computer technology that are likely to occur within the next ten years are not, for the most part, changes that will be readily apparent to the typical user. There will be great advances made in the efficiency (i.e., the cost) of converting information into machine-readable form. As just one example, I expect that optical character readers (machines designed to read typewritten material and convert it directly into computer input) will be as commonplace in ten years as key punches are now. This, however, is computer technology in only a peripheral sense. As far as the computer itself is concerned, most of us will not be aware of the changes. These will include greatly increased storage capacity even in relatively small computers; a continued emphasis on miniaturization, which will mean units of smaller physical size to accomplish the work larger computers do today; a continued increase in the speed by which operations are performed; new and improved programming languages making it possible for programmers to give instructions to the machine after only a few hours of training; and finally, a much greater availability of computers to anyone who has a valid need for them. As far as the typical user is concerned, these changes will not be readily apparent, but they will all add up to one thing: a greatly reduced cost of computer services.

The biggest change in the next ten years will not be in the area of computer technology at all. Rather it will be in the organization of facilities that, technically at least, are available today. Within the next ten years the widespread knowledge of computers will lead to many new ideas about how to use them effectively and efficiently for all kinds of applications, including many that we cannot envision today. Most of the early (and costly) mistakes will have been made by then so that efficient and practical uses in museums will be commonplace. This will not happen automatically. It will come about only when and as major museums, national museum organizations, and key individuals who compose the ongoing leadership of the museum community are willing to take the time to (1) learn enough about computers so that they neither accept them as magic black boxes that will do everything nor reject them because they are not, and (2) learn enough about the real information needs of museums, including but not limited to cataloging needs, to be able to state with assurance what is wanted when and as the facilities become available.

This book is designed to provide a starting point for museum personnel in both these areas. Some of the chapters (specifically chapters 3, 5, and 6) are designed to provide the background in computer technology that a museum administrator should have. Others (chapters 2 and 4) deal with the problems of cataloging in a way that is largely independent of computers. Uses of computers in museums other than for cataloging are considered only briefly (in chapter 3). However, the approach taken to the solving of the cataloging problem can readily be extended to any other information problem that a museum administrator might face.

2

Documenting the Collection: A Universal Problem

FOR THE purposes of the accreditation program of the American Association of Museums, a museum is defined as

an organized and permanent, non-profit institution, essentially educational or aesthetic in purpose, with professional staff, which owns and utilizes tangible objects, cares for them, and exhibits them to the public on some regular schedule.[3]

A somewhat shorter dictionary definition states that a museum is any place or building in which works of artistic, historical, or scientific value are cared for and exhibited.[4] The word *works* usually implies the output of an artist or an artisan, as for example, in "the works of Verdi." However, museums are also repositories for the works of nature (e.g., geological, botanical, paleontological specimens) that are considered to be of scientific value. In most instances the works of artistic, historic, and scientific value cared for in museums are the physical objects themselves that have been produced by either man or nature. But even this has exceptions. For example, maritime museums, architectural museums, and archaeological museums are concerned with classes of physical objects that often cannot be physically transported to a central building for care and display. In cases such as these, the "works" that are cared for and exhibited may consist not of the objects themselves but of models, photographic representations, maps, drawings, blueprints, and diagrams. Museums are truly many faceted.

When a museum is small, it is possible to maintain an adequate control over the collections, regardless of the nature of the objects, by physical inspection and memory. For example, if one owns a collection of not over 30 or 40 dolls, or bells, or old automobiles, or any other class of objects, and has these objects on display, he probably could remember where and when each was acquired and a good deal of its known history. He would be able to note immediately upon looking at the collection whether or not one of the objects was missing, and he could readily place side by side any of them that were related either historically or physically. However, when a collection numbers in the thousands, perhaps with some objects on display and others in storage, control by visual inspection and memory becomes a problem. *Some* form of written record is necessary just to maintain a physical control over the collection, to say nothing of providing historic and descriptive information about the individual objects that might be usable for research or other purposes.

Most museum administrators would not argue about the desirability of adequate collection documentation. The question of what constitutes adequate documentation, though, elicits a wide variety of opinions.

Registration, Accessioning, and Cataloging

Carl Guthe has given us a clear statement on the importance of record keeping and the kinds of records that should be maintained in a small history museum. He suggests that the significance of an object

lies not in itself alone but also in the information relating to it. Everything that is known about it, whether fact, tradition, or hearsay, should be recorded in permanent form. The object and its written record must be so clearly connected that there can be no possible doubt concerning its identity. . . .

It is, of course, impossible to prepare a complete identifying document for each object and to insure that it will be physically attached to the object permanently. Museums long ago began using identification symbols. A single number in a series, attached to both the object itself and to its written record, will provide a permanent identity of the physical object with information relating to it. . . .

The assignment of this identifying number to an object constitutes registering it in the museum's collections. This process is often referred to erroneously as "cataloging," a faulty usage which is apt to cause confusion between two distinct procedures.[5]

As Guthe points out, registration is not the same as accessioning, and an accession number cannot serve as the registration number, even though in some systems the registration numbers may be subsidiary series within the series of accession numbers.[6] Both registration and accessioning, however, are significantly different from cataloging.

To register an object is to assign to it an individual place in a list or register of the materials in the collection in such a manner that it cannot be confused with any other object listed.

To catalog an object is to assign it to one or more categories of an organized classification system so that it and its record may be associated with other objects similar or related to it.[7]

It is important to recognize this distinction between registration and cataloging and not to try to accomplish both functions at the same time. If an attempt is made to create a complex coding system so that a series of numerals and letters can be placed on each object to tell something about it—the geographic area where it originated, the tribe or culture who made it, the materials out of which it is made, its probable function, and so on—the likelihood is very great that this "cataloging" system will be considered as a substitute for, not an addition to, an adequate registration system that establishes the positive identity of each specimen with a unique registration number. On the other hand, if the system of accessioning and registration is emphasized to the extent that all documentation of the collections is maintained in accession number and/or registration number sequence, then it will not matter how detailed and complete the descriptions of the objects may be, the records appropriate to a particular problem will not be locatable except by a serial search through the entire file.

Registration, accessioning, and cataloging are three separate, though related, activities. The first two can only be carried out manually, and the methods used will not be much different from the smallest to the largest of museums. Cataloging, however, is something quite different. As George Bowditch says, in a simple but accurate statement, "The purpose of cataloging is to retrieve information."[8]

The methods of cataloging described by Guthe for a small history museum[9] are not really adequate for more than a few hundred objects, and such a system breaks down completely when a collection numbers in the tens of thousands. The truth is that *most museums do not have any cataloging system at all.* (Many do not have an adequate registration system either, but that is another problem.) Individual curators usually develop record-keeping systems that allow them to locate objects in the portion of the collection that is their own area of specialization, and the aggregate of these individual records may be referred to as a cataloging system in the Director's Annual Report, but this does not constitute a unified, museum-wide method for retrieving the information necessary to determine the quantity and variety of different classes of objects in the collections.

The preparation of a museum catalog by any method involves considerable time and energy. Some museum administrators would claim that a catalog is not an indispensable part of the object documentation, even though it might be a useful finding aid with some collections. A good case can be made, though, for the fact that *any documentation of the objects in a collection must be cross-indexed as many ways as possible or the information contained in the records will not be usable.* A catalog is such a cross-index—one that covers not just categories of data that demand attention (e.g., donor names) but numerous areas of provenance, taxonomic classification, and descriptive data as well.

What Is a Museum Catalog?

In the preceding discussion numerous references have been made to catalogs and the function of cataloging. The question may well be asked: Just what *is* a museum catalog? Is it the entire collection documentation arranged in some sequence other than in registration number order? Or is it merely an index to the documentation on each object? If it is an index, is it a single or a multiple index to the documentation on each object—that is, is there a separate index for each category of data about the collection? Can it be simply a card file analogous to the subject heading file in a library, or must it be something more complicated? The answer, of course, is that a museum catalog *can* be any of these, and it usually has some elements of all of them in it.

The simplest form of museum catalog is not significantly different from the 3-by-5-inch-card catalog which is used by most libraries as a means of locating books. Each card usually contains a registration number that is also placed on the object as a means of positive identification; a brief statement to identify what the object is; a number of statements about the history of the object, where it was found (or acquired), who owns it, the artist or artisan who created it; and perhaps some descriptive data: materials, techniques used in making the object, dimensions, a typological classification, and so on.

The problems in creating and using a card file museum catalog are also similar to the problems that libraries encounter with such systems, namely: (1) deciding upon the best classification system to use in filing the cards so as to meet the multiple (and often unknown) objectives of potential users when they eventually search the file, and (2) maintaining a reasonable consistency, both interpersonal and intrapersonal (i.e., among and within catalogers in the classificatory terms that are placed at the top of the catalog cards as a basis for filing. The question of whether to place an object in one category or another (e.g., Is a beaded Iroquois dress to be classified as "bead-work" or "clothing"?) can be partially resolved in the same way that libraries approach the problem, namely, by having multiple cards for the same object. Multiple cards may be typed as needed and filed in a single index file, or complex systems may involve multiple cards both for different index files and within some of the files.

There are two major problems in using a card file type catalog:

1. The labor involved in preparing, filing, and controlling card files with more than three or four cards per object usually cannot be justified in terms of the use made of the added files. There are ways by which the second and additional cards can be typed semi-automatically at maximum typewriter speeds (e.g., with paper tape attachments for machines such as the Friden Flexowriter). However, even with these aids, the costs of preparing more than four cards per object are hard to justify, for there is still the labor to file and control the cards, plus the cost of card stock, filing cabinets, office space, etc. With no more than three or four cards per object, the categories of data by which an object can be located are limited, and multiple category searches are extremely slow. If one wished to search out all the dolls, for example, that were made during the last quarter of the nineteenth century, the only way to locate them would be to thumb through all the cards under the heading "Dolls." How serious this limitation may be depends upon the number of items in the collection (i.e., the length of time it would take to search through all the cards on "Dolls") and the number of requests there might be for information that is not compatible with one of the card file arrangements. There is no way of providing general answers to questions such as these.

2. The second problem with a card file type catalog is the matter of data redundancy: because it is usually cheaper to duplicate a single master card than to retype additional cards for specific purposes, all the cards usually carry all the information on an object. Multiple cards normally are the same card with a different heading typed on the top margin for filing purposes. This may or may not be considered a problem in a small museum. However, any information system (and a museum catalog is a specialized example of an informa-

tion system) should be designed so as to accomplish explicitly stated purposes in the most efficient manner possible. *All* catalog records do not need to carry *all* the known information about an object. The most efficient records contain *only* the information necessary to accomplish the purposes of that particular record.

The question of purpose begins to get at the basic cataloging problem. There is no way to answer the question of what a catalog is (or even what it should be) except in terms of the purpose or purposes for which it is created. Most museum administrators, for example, would not argue the fact that a donor record is one of the most important parts of collection documentation. But a donor record *is* a catalog. It is an index to the collections arranged according to the single category of information about each object: the name of the individual who gave it to the museum. There are valid reasons why a catalog arranged by donor name is important. In a particular museum, if this is the only catalog of importance, then a 3-by-5-inch-card file with each card containing the name of the donor, the registration number, and a brief description of the object is all that is required. However, if one begins to think of a catalog in terms of multiple retrieval purposes—that is, for the retrieval of the documentation about objects in accordance with several categories of information (artist name; date of manufacture; city, state, or nation where the object originated, etc.)—then he must think in terms of several card files or he must think about some other type of catalog system, perhaps one that utilizes a computer.

The advantages and the problems in developing a computerized museum catalog will be discussed in detail in the following chapters. However, it is important to recognize that a computer will not answer the question of what a museum catalog is or even the subsidiary questions of whether a catalog is the entire documentation rearranged or just indexes to that documentation. These are questions that should be looked at in terms of the information needs of each particular museum. Decide what is wanted first; *then* look at alternate ways by which the information needs of the several parties involved can be met most efficiently.

There is one facet of computerized cataloging that needs to be recognized at this early stage of considering one's information needs, however. Technically, it is possible today to create computer files that contain every scrap of documentation that a museum could possibly have about an object, including not only all the written material but photographs, diagrams, and maps as well. This is *possible* with the technology that is available today, but do not plan your museum documentation around the replacement of your present files with a computer file, for this is *not economically feasible.* Furthermore, it probably will not be economically feasible at any time in the foreseeable future.

Many museum administrators, perhaps most, will recognize the validity of the statement above as far as photographs, diagrams, and maps are concerned. The important point, though—and it is a point that is often overlooked even by relatively sophisticated computer system analysts and programmers—is the fact that a computerized museum catalog will only be an effective and efficient tool if all documentation is carefully screened in terms of "need to know" *before* it is entered into a computer file. It is technically possible to include all verbal documentation in a computerized museum catalog, but most often it is not economically feasible to do so. One may agree completely with Guthe [10] that everything known about an object "whether fact, tradition, or hearsay" should be recorded. But it does not all have to be recorded in the computer. Storing large quantities of data in a computer costs money; searching a large computer file costs more than searching a small computer file; sorting small computer files is much less expensive than sorting large computer files.

An excellent example, which finally gets back to the question of what a museum catalog is, is provided by the National Register of Historic Places. The form for placing a site on the National Register comprises five 8½-by-11-inch pages and contains spaces for recording many categories of data about a site. Some of the questions are in multiple choice, checklist form, others require short answers. A few questions, however, take lengthy paragraphs to answer, and provision is made for continuation sheets if necessary. The statement of significance is one of these. There is nothing wrong with these forms per se. The only question is, What should a *catalog* of historic places include? The first reaction of most persons is to include everything. It is just as easy, though, to find the lengthy paragraph on significance in a filing cabinet as it is to look up the same paragraph in a book of computer print-out, and a great deal of money is required to place this information in computer print-out form.

A computer catalog does not ordinarily contain anything that has not been previously recorded elsewhere. Rather, it is a reorganization of the collection documentation, arranged so that the categories of information desired most often are readily available. Sometimes, if the documentation on each object is not too lengthy, it is most efficient to have the entire documentation contained in the catalog record (whether on cards or in a computer file) and to sort the entire record according to the different data categories when specific information is needed. When the documentation on each object is as extensive as it must, of necessity, be with the National Register of Historic Places, though, it is most efficient to consider the catalog as an index to the typewritten site files. This may be either a single index of key words or a multiple index to a number of the different categories of data about the sites. In a well-constructed catalog (index) system questions can often be answered by consulting just the catalog, but such an approach means going back to the filing cabinet to obtain the full documentary record on each object. This really is not a great inconvenience if from the catalog you have previously determined with some certainty the records that are wanted and you know that they are all filed in registration number sequence.

Collection Management Information Needs and Research Information Needs

All of us seem to have a penchant for nice, neat packages in which all those things that we think "belong together" can be found together. A husband is irritated when his wife places his screwdriver in the kitchen drawer rather than returning it to his tool box "where it belongs." Mothers are angry with their children when they leave clothes on the floor instead of hanging them up in the closet "where they belong." *And* museum people seem to feel that there should be one and only one place where all the documentary data about any object in their collections can be found. Most of the time this desire for orderliness is probably a good trait, but if we stop to consider our activities in terms of the most efficient expenditure of time and energy, it may be that there should be a screwdriver left in the kitchen drawer, that some of the clothes (those the child is going to wear the next morning) could well be left on the chair or the floor, and that all museum documentation does not need to be in the same place.

In the previous section it was pointed out that in some cases it may be more efficient to maintain complete documentation for museum objects in a filing cabinet and consider the catalog as an index rather than to enter every scrap of information in the catalog. A problem that is closely related to this is the difference in the information needs of those who are responsible for collections management, and those who may be doing research with a collection. In particular, consideration must be given to whether or not it is desirable to record all research findings in a museum catalog.

When researching a museum collection, the researcher will usually examine the objects carefully and record a series of observations about the objects *that have not been previously recorded.* Very often these observations either consist of or include the very kinds of discrete facts that the curator has long wanted for his catalog of that collection. At the same time the researcher may be planning to do correlational or other kinds of statistical studies with the recorded observations—the kinds of studies that today are regularly performed on a computer—and he may have in his research budget sufficient funds to record all the objects for computer entry. The alert curator will immediately see this as an opportunity to obtain his catalog simply by duplicating the researcher's computer file. With some kinds of objects this procedure may be satisfactory. However, there are two possible problems that must be carefully considered:

1. The researcher's file may contain a kind of detailed, esoteric information for which there is only the most remote possibility that a need might ever arise again, and a catalog should not be burdened with excess baggage (again the problem of inefficiency created by excessive record sizes).

2. The researcher's file often does *not* contain all the information desired by the curator for collection management purposes.

Most research people are cooperative in matters of this kind—they appreciate the inconvenience created by the very fact of their using the collections. Usually they will be glad to add a few observations to satisfy a curator's needs if it is discussed with them early in the program. A research file may provide the information from which a good catalog can be created, but it is seldom that the two files will be (or should be) identical.

The approach taken in the recording of the human skeletal material at the University of Arkansas Museum clearly illustrates what can be accomplished by a program of cooperation between museum personnel and research personnel. David Wolf, a physical anthropologist, is making detailed observations on each extant bone of the more than 1,400 skeletons in the museum's collection for the purpose of asking a lengthy series of questions, such as the correlation of particular anatomical traits with different age groupings, the frequency of different traits among the populations that were excavated from various locations, and so on. Most of these research questions require statistical analysis of one kind or another in order to draw meaningful conclusions about the prehistoric populations from which the skeletons came. The skeletons have not been cataloged previously by the university museum, and it appears desirable to obtain such a catalog at the same time that the research observations are being made. However, (1) there are far too many observations being made on each skeleton for the entire research file to be entered as the museum's catalog, (2) the research observations are too specialized in nature to be wanted in the museum's catalog, and (3) some of the observations desired for cataloging purposes were not originally included in the list of research observations.

Because it would obtain a catalog from the project, the museum was willing to provide some personnel to assist in the recording and analysis of the skeletal collection. In exchange for this the researcher added to his list of observations those which the museum wanted for cataloging purposes. The data are recorded in a format that can be entered directly into the museum's catalog input program, even though there are only a small number of data categories actually recorded as input to the museum's catalog. The balance of the data (that required by the researcher) is recorded in the same way and run through a special computer program to convert it to a suitable form for input to SPSS (the Statistical Package for the Social Sciences). It is planned that when the research is completed, the entire file of observations will be transferred to a magnetic tape and stored in the museum's vault, where it will be available if it is ever needed for further research studies. In the meantime, on the catalog record derived from the research project for each of the skeletons in the collection a suitable entry is made under the heading of "additional data" to indicate the file name of the magnetic tape containing the entire set of observations.

The significance of this discussion, of course, lies in the fact that the information concerning any given object in a museum collection is not the same for a curator qua collections management custodian as for a curator (or anyone else) qua researcher, *even though both may use a computer in their work*. Through cooperation the needs of both usually can be met more efficiently than if each attempted to do the work independently of the other. However, data that are to be used for research should be formatted and processed in a manner that will accomplish the objectives of the research most efficiently, whether or not a good catalog record is provided as a by-product of the research project. The cataloging effort will not be seriously impaired by this approach. The worst that can happen is that the catalog data included in the research observations will have to be manually extracted from a computer listing, perhaps to be reentered in another computer format. But a good research project can be damaged beyond repair if the researcher is forced to modify his observational categories to conform to the structure of a generalized cataloging system. To repeat, though, cooperation will usually accomplish both purposes.

The Universal Catalog Problem

By this point it will be apparent that the word *catalog* can have a number of meanings and that the real problem is not just one of mechanics. There are two kinds of decisions that museums must make: (a) What textual information do we generate about the objects in our collections? and (b) How do we arrange this information so that we can use it to do what we want? Much of this book is devoted to a consideration of techniques for arranging and finding needed data—that is, part (b) above—but this can never be separated from the more basic question of who needs what information about the collections and for what purposes.

The answers to these questions depend to some extent upon the nature of the objects in the collections. A botanical collection, for example, requires categories of catalog data somewhat different from a historical collection, and both vary in certain respects from an art collection catalog. Even more important than the nature of the collection, though, are the informational needs that the catalog is designed to satisfy—the purposes or objectives for which the catalog is created. It cannot be emphasized too strongly that an explicit statement of purpose should be written out, discussed by all museum personnel who may have anything to do with the catalog (this may be a surprisingly large part of the staff), and as nearly as possible agreed upon before any attempt is made to delineate what should go into the catalog. In practice it is all too often assumed (particularly if a computerized catalog is in the offing) that the catalog should contain all the written documentation. Even when this is not the case, directors and registrars (and consultants) often seem to assume that "everyone" knows what the needs are when in fact *information needs are not well defined in most museums.*

In order to illustrate this decision-making process, let us assume that we have been given the responsibility to develop a catalog for a history museum that has a collection of 50,000 objects. The size of the collection is not too important, for we are not immediately concerned with *how* the catalog will be maintained (on cards, in a computer, etc.) but rather with *what* information it should contain.

Our discussions with museum personnel reveal the following information needs:

1. The director specifies only that the overall objective will be to maintain a catalog for collection management purposes. The catalog should contain finding aids that may be utilized at times by persons doing research with the collections, but the catalog itself is not to be cluttered with the data from particular research projects.

2. The treasurer's responsibility for the collections is primarily one of protection. His information needs are for two kinds of records: *(a)* a catalog of the collections for insurance purposes and *(b)* a catalog of the collections for security purposes. The first should contain information such as appraisal value, date of most recent appraisal, etc., and should be organized by major categories of objects. The second catalog should be a file organized by physical location.

3. The registrar, of course, maintains the original documentation records in registration number sequence and finds this satisfactory for most of his needs. However, he is presently maintaining separate files by donor name and by accession number.

4. The curators have gotten together and agreed that collection management does mean being able to find both objects and object documentation that might be appropriate to a particular display or to any reasonable public request. To accomplish this, they would *like* to have to have ten different catalogs, with the collections classified according to: major object category; subject represented; artist, artisan, or author; maker, manufacturer, or printer; recognized typological name; materials or media; country where the object was created or manufactured; the named temporal period during which the object was created; and the earliest and latest probable calendric dates when the object was made.

What is needed, then, is the ability to access the documentation on each object in the collection in accordance with fourteen different systems of classification in addition to the original documentation in registration number sequence. These needs can be summarized in the form shown in table 1. Remember that this is only a hypothetical summary of information needs. It is entirely possible that other categories of information would be required on some of these files and that many of the categories shown here would not be wanted in all the files. For example, a file organized by artists' names might contain only the earliest and latest probable dates, a brief description, and the registration number. The point is that all information needs should be written down and then summarized in some manner such as this.

Note that this summary of information needs does not include all the categories of data to be found on the original documentation. Things such as the title of a work of art, biographical data about an artist or artisan, techniques, specific provenance, dimensions, are all important information about the object, but they are not information that is needed or wanted, necessarily, in any of the catalogs. Remember, *a catalog is a finding device.* It should contain all those categories of data that might be required for a major (or a minor) sort of the records. It should also contain enough additional data to enable one to decide whether or not this is an object for which he is searching (e.g., a brief description or the title of a painting), and in some cases it should contain additional data that will be wanted in the form of printed listings (e.g., appraisal value or donors' addressses), but it is neither economical nor necessary to include detailed descriptions, dimensions, and everything else in the catalog record on every item. Some information needs can be satisfied entirely by reference to a catalog, but there is nothing that says all information needs must be satisfied this way. It is very easy to go back to the original documentation for information if one knows the registration numbers of the objects that will probably satisfy his needs.

The universal museum cataloging problem? It is the problem of first deciding what information needs your museum really has and then determining the documentation and the organization of that documentation that is necessary to meet those needs.

Table 1

Summary of Information Needs for a Hypothetical History Museum

Data category	Latest Date	Earliest Date	Period of Origin	Country of Origin	Materials File	Type File	Maker File	Artist File	Subject File	Object File	Accession File	Donor File	Location File	Appraisal File
Registration number	★	★	★	★	★	★	★	★	★	★	★★★	★	★	★★★
Brief description or title	★	★	★	★	★	★	★	★	★	★	★	★	★	
Object category	★	★	★	★	★	★	★	★	★	★★★	★	★	★	
Subject represented	★	★	★	★	★	★	★	★	★★★	★				
Artist, artisan, or author	★	★	★	★	★	★	★	★★★	★	★				
Maker, manufacturer, or printer	★	★	★	★	★	★	★★★	★	★	★				
Typological class	★	★	★	★	★	★★★	★	★	★	★				
Materials or media	★	★	★	★	★★★	★	★	★	★	★				
Country of origin	★	★	★	★★★	★	★	★	★	★	★				
Period of origin	★	★	★★★	★	★	★	★	★	★	★				
Earliest probable date	★	★★★	★	★	★	★	★	★	★	★				
Latest probable date	★★★	★	★	★	★	★	★	★	★	★				
Donor name												★★★		
Donor address												★		
Appraisal value														★
Date of appraisal														★
Date acquired											★	★	★	
Additional information on file	★	★	★	★	★	★	★	★	★	★				
Storage location	★	★	★	★	★	★	★	★	★	★			★★★	

★★★ = Primary classificatory data category; ★ = Other data categories desired in this file

3

Why Use a Computer?

The information needs of the hypothetical history museum discussed in the last chapter are complex enough so that it is unlikely they would ever be met with a manual cataloging system. What usually happens is that some (or most) of the needs are compromised with a shrug of the shoulders, saying in effect, "There's nothing that can be done about it." The purpose of this chapter is to show that something can be done about it, to show how a computerized museum catalog can actually resolve these kinds of information needs without forcing someone in the organization to accept less than the information he really wants.

Some of this, of necessity, will require that the reader know a little about what a computer is and how it functions. Anyone who has had an introductory course on computer programming can probably skip the first section. But for the uninitiated layman, it is hoped that this will provide a sufficient introduction to the subject to make the flow charts in the latter part of the chapter and in chapter 6 understandable.

An Introduction to Computing Activities

Basically, a computer is made up of thousands of high-speed, on-off switches that are connected in an organized manner so that something approaching English language statements can be used to record first a program of instructions and then the data necessary to accomplish a wide variety of mathematical and logical symbol manipulation activities.

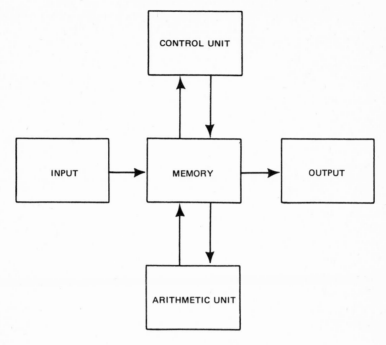

FIG. 1. Simplified diagram of a computer

It is convenient to look at the functioning of a computer in terms of the simplified diagram in figure 1. The five functional components are:

1. One or more *input* devices for transforming symbolic information external to the machine into internally usable form. A punched card reader is an example of an input device,

2. One or more *output* devices for transforming the internal symbols back into external form. The computer's printer is an example of an output device.

3. One or more *memory* devices capable of storing symbols before, during, and after processing.

4. An *arithmetic unit* that adds, subtracts, multiplies, and divides numbers, and performs other kinds of operations on nonnumeric symbols (e.g., COMPARE).

5. The *control unit,* which is the executive of the computer. The control unit is wired to understand and obey a repertory of *instructions,* or commands, calling the other units into action when necessary. The individual instructions are generally simple processes such as to GET a symbol (or a file or a record) from a specified place

in memory, to PUT a symbol some place in memory, and to MOVE a symbol a certain number of places to the left or right in working storage.

The control unit usually resembles a typewriter with a bank of flashing lights above it; the memory and arithmetic units are enclosed boxes that elicit very little attention, and the input and output devices (sometimes called *peripheral* units) can be of many forms—magnetic tape drives, magnetic disk spindles, punched card readers, high-speed printers, and several other kinds of more specialized units.

Presenting data to the computer system is similar in many ways to communicating with another person by letter. The intelligence to be conveyed must be reduced to a set of symbols. In the English language these are the familiar letters of the alphabet, numbers, and punctuation, arranged into words and, according to a prescribed syntax, into phrases and sentences meaningful to another person who reads and interprets them. Similarly, communication with the computer system requires that information be reduced to a set of symbols and that the symbols be combined according to a syntax that is understandable to the computer. The symbols used in presenting data to the computer are the same as those used in speaking English. However, the words and syntax differ from those commonly used by people because the information to be represented must conform to the design and operation of the machine. The important fact is that intelligence is conveyed from people to computers by means of languages somewhat the same as the English language.

Information to be used with the computer is first converted to machine-readable input on some device such as those discussed in chapter 5. The media may be punched cards, paper tape, magnetic tape or disk, magnetically encoded documents, or optically scannable documents. Data are represented on the punched card by the presence or absence of holes in specific locations. In a similar manner small holes along a paper tape represent data in a precise coded form. On magnetic tape or disk the symbols are small magnetized areas, called *spots* or *bits,* arranged in a regular pattern that is understandable to the computer. When magnetic ink characters are printed on paper documents, the shape of the characters and the magnetic properties of the ink permit the printed data to be read by both man and machine. The shape of the characters, in contrast with the background paper, permits optical characters to be read by both man and machine.

An input device of the computer system (figure 1) is a machine designed to read information from one of these input media. In the reading process, recorded data are converted to or symbolized in electronic form. The data can then be used by the machine to perform data processing operations. An output device is a machine that receives information from the computer system and records the information on punched cards, paper tape, magnetic tape or disk, or printed forms.

It is not surprising that the user of computing services often becomes thoroughly confused in the process of selecting the best computer and computer system for his needs. The names of some of the better-known general-purpose computers—IBM, UNIVAC, NCR, Control Data, Burroughs, Honeywell—are common enough. However, these companies do not all sell the same products, so that it is impossible just to compare on price, quality, and service as one might do with other things sold by nationally known manufacturers. One computer salesman, for example, may suggest using magnetic tapes for storage of data, another may say disks are best, a third may recommend punched cards or some other form of storage as being the most economical—*and* the differences between these approaches mean entirely different computer systems. If one adds to this the variation in the sizes of different computers—everything from self-contained desk-top units to those requiring separate buildings to house them—and some esoteric terminology like *service bureau, time sharing, remote terminal, in house,* it becomes very difficult for even the well-trained computer scientist to keep it all straight.

Part of this confusion can be dispelled by discussing the real differences between some of these key terms.

Stored program computers. In one sense, any mechanical or electromechanical machine capable of performing either mathematical or logical word manipulation functions can be defined as a computer. However, the concept of a stored program eliminates adding machines and a large majority of the small calculating devices. Stored program computers are those that permit one first to read into the machine a series of instructions that are to be performed sequentially (a program) and then to read into the machine the data with which to execute the program. Stored program computers may be broadly classified on the basis of size, cost, and capability into three groups:

1. Desk-top computers—usually self-contained units that will in fact rest on a desk and still leave room for a person to work. These units may be purchased for under $10,000. However, the number of program steps is limited, and the amount of data that may be stored at any one time is quite small. In practice these units are most valuable for performing mathematical operations that require fair

amounts of calculating power applied to small quantities of numeric data (e.g., for computing square roots, variances, standard deviations).

2. Small-scale computers—consisting of from three to as many as five or six separate hardware units, which often can be housed in a space no larger than about 100 square feet. Examples are the IBM System/3, the Burroughs 1700, the Honeywell Model 58, and the NCR Century 50. These computers usually consist of a card reader, a combined memory-control-arithmetic device, and a printer, and they rent for $1,500 to $2,000 per month. Small-scale computers were designed specifically to tap the market for data processing in small businesses. They can be used to perform some of the applications in museums, but the limited storage capacity (even though some employ magnetic tape and/or magnetic disk storage) limits their effectiveness for museum cataloging.

3. Large-scale computers—the behemoths occupying their own buildings or at the very least separate sections of a building, often with raised floors and special air-conditioning equipment. Some of the familiar models are the IBM 360 (Model 40 and larger), the IBM 370 (Model 135 and up), the CDC 6600, and the UNIVAC 1108. The cost of these complex systems is commensurate with their capacity and processing capability. Rental alone may run to tens of thousands of dollars per month. However, when the performance is compared with small-scale computers, it is equally astounding. These machines are capable of performing the most complex types of calculations at electronic speeds; they can store millions of characters of data for rapid access; and they can perform a large number of different operations at the same time—for example, while the output from one program is being printed (at 1,000 or more lines of print per minute), output from another program may be temporarily queued up on a disk waiting to be printed, yet another may be in the computer with the program steps being completed sequentially, and a fourth may be in the process of being entered by means of the card reader.

In-house computers. Any computer that is either owned or leased by its principal user is considered to be "in house." There are, of course, many advantages to this arrangement. By far the most important is the fact that it gives the user absolute control over when and how his computer is used. He also determines what projects have first priority and so on. The disadvantages, however, are also significant: the cost of the computer (whether on lease or purchased), the space given over to it, the staff required to operate it, etc., are all fixed costs that go on whether or not the computer is operating.

Most medium- and large-size business firms have their own in-house computers, and the fixed costs can be justified by the increased information the computer provides in many areas of the business enterprise—that is, the computer is usually kept busy at least eight hours per day and often longer. With some of the small-scale computers now available, even relatively small businesses frequently have found that an in-house computer more than pays its own way. However, there are few museums for which an in-house computer can be justified.

Service bureaus. Some businesses, most scientific research organizations, and virtually all museums are in the difficult position of needing large-scale computers to perform the kinds of operations of greatest benefit to them, but the amount of time such a computer would be used does not justify the rental cost, the space requirements, and the manpower requirements imposed by such a system. In order to fill this need, a type of business enterprise has been developed in the United States in which large-scale computer time is sold to numerous clients when and as it is needed. Most service bureaus provide for special messengers to pick up, at the customer's place of business, either punched cards or documents from which service bureau personnel prepare the computer input. Processing is then done on a large-scale computer, and the messengers deliver the output from the high-speed printer back to the customer's place of business. Charges are made only for services actually performed and for computer time actually used in doing the work for that customer. The fixed costs of renting the computer and maintaining a professional staff are borne by the service bureau and prorated, together with a margin of profit, to the numerous service bureau customers. Service bureaus are an important part of the American computer industry, and computerized museum catalogs can usually be maintained by service bureaus more economically than by in-house computers. However, the selection of a service bureau can be every bit as important as the employment of a major executive, and it should be considered with equal care. Here are a few suggestions on what to do and what not to do.

1. Do not take the salesman's word for anything. If the company he represents is sound, he will want to show you their plant and have you meet those who actually do the work. He will also welcome your conversations with satisfied customers.

2. If you are planning to use standard program packages (i.e., sets of programs developed previously and used by several customers),

look at the output from each of the programs carefully to be sure that it will satisfy your needs.

3. Talk to customers; talk to computer salesmen; talk to anyone you may know who is involved with the computer industry locally. You will not, of course, receive universally favorable reactions, but if you talk to enough people, you will get a pretty good idea of the reliability and stability of the service bureau you are considering using.

Time sharing. The preceding description of service bureaus assumed that data would be transmitted to and from the service bureau office by special messengers and processed for the customer a *batch* at a time. This type of processing logically is called *batch processing* in order to distinguish it from *real-time processing*. Real-time processing is normally carried on over telephone lines connecting teletype terminals in the customer's place of business with the large-scale computer in the service bureau so that each statement entered through the terminal is processed (translated, verified, and if desired, executed) immediately. In real-time processing, information previously stored on the service bureau's computer is available at any hour of the day previously agreed upon by the two parties. Usually the customer must pay some kind of fixed charge in exchange for having his data always "at the ready," but this is minimal compared to the cost of maintaining his own computer system, and it does give him the right to do processing whenever he wants (for example, the right to query his catalog at any time during the hours when his museum is open) rather than having to enter a request for the retrieval of data and then wait several hours or days for the service bureau to perform the search and print. Both batch processing and real-time processing can, of course, be carried on with in-house computers as well as they can with service bureau computers. However, the idea of time sharing is usually thought of as the sharing of service bureau computer time through real-time processing, with customers entering requests for data and the service bureau displaying the requested data on teletype terminals remote from the computer.

Flow Charts

In order to process data, a computer needs explicit instructions that are understandable in a context of information that has previously been fed into it and stored there. Regardless of how complex an operation may be, the repertory of instructions available to the programmer, that is, the different operations he can tell the computer to perform with the data it encounters, are few in number. To get the desired results, he must tell the computer to execute sequentially each of the instructions that is appropriate; he must also tell it the location in the computer system where it can expect to find the data with which to carry out each job step. These instructions are usually written out on special forms, and each line on every form is key-punched into a single card. The deck of punched cards then becomes the instructional input to the computer telling it what to do when data cards (or data from tapes, disks, etc.) are received as input.

Before the program sheets can be written out, however, it is necessary to think through the logic that will be written into the step-by-step instructions for the computer. The best way to record this logic is by means of a *flow chart*. There are other ways of performing this function (e.g., decision tables), but anyone who understands what is involved in flow charting can pick up other techniques of recording program logic when necessary.

A flow chart is a diagram that visually displays the sequence in which the operations are to be performed in an information processing system. Because uniform flow chart symbols are used by computer personnel everywhere (figures 2A and 2B), it is possible for one person to design the logic of a system, to describe this in flow chart form, and then to pass the flow chart on to a programmer for preparation of the actual machine instructions.[11]

Flow charts will be used extensively later in this book. As an illustration of how they should be interpreted, note the differences between figures 3 and 4. Figure 3 is a schematic representation of an overall project (not related in any way to museum cataloging) with each rectangular box signifying a series of computer program steps, each of which might be set up as a separate program or as a subroutine within a larger program. Such a flow chart is created so that everyone involved can reach agreement as to what will be done on the computer. Sometimes this type of chart is called a *system flow chart*. Working from a chart such as this, a system analyst will prepare a more detailed flow chart (a *programming flow chart* or *block diagram* such as that illustrated in figure 4) for each major segment or box on the system flow chart. The programming flow charts then become the detailed instructions from which the computer programmers write the step-by-step instructions that eventually become sequential commands to the computer.

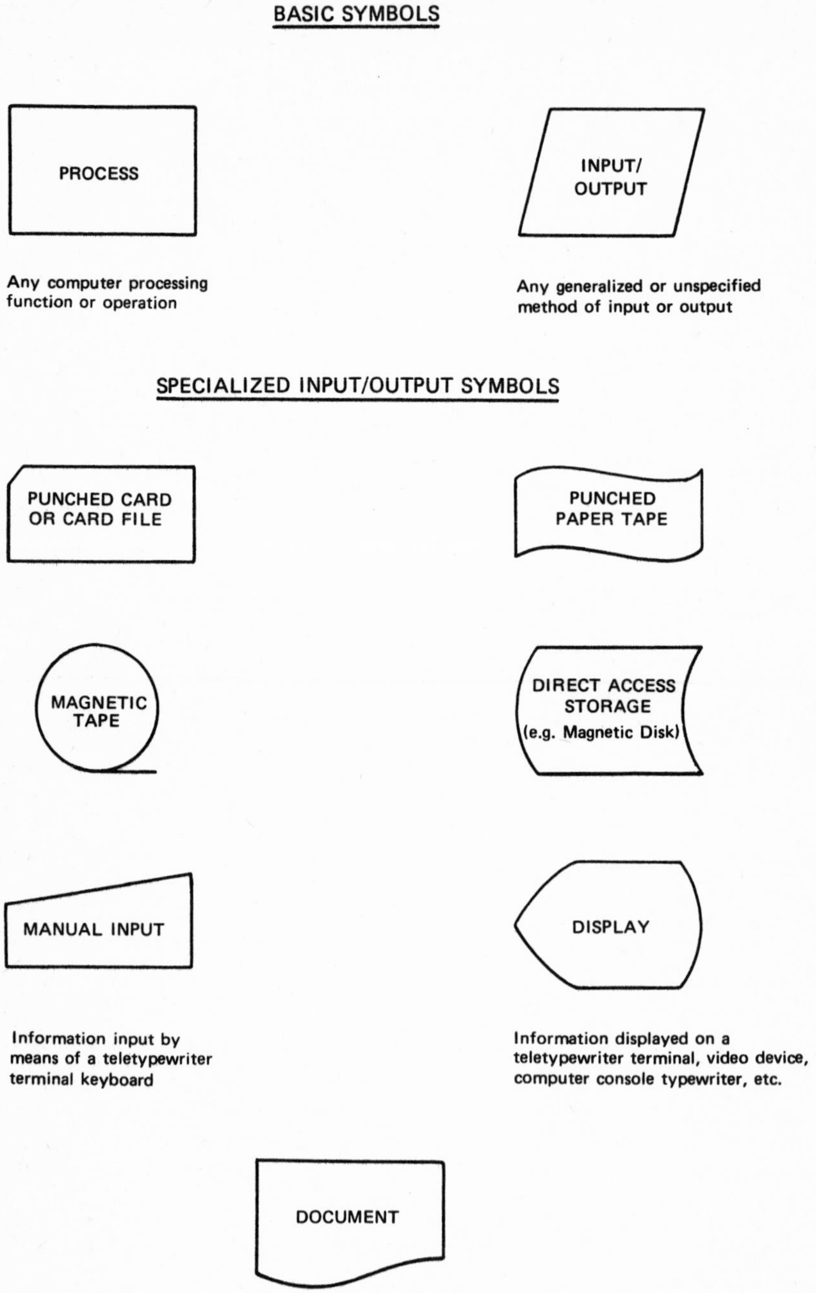

BASIC SYMBOLS

PROCESS

INPUT/
OUTPUT

Any computer processing
function or operation

Any generalized or unspecified
method of input or output

SPECIALIZED INPUT/OUTPUT SYMBOLS

PUNCHED CARD
OR CARD FILE

PUNCHED
PAPER TAPE

MAGNETIC
TAPE

DIRECT ACCESS
STORAGE
(e.g. Magnetic Disk)

MANUAL INPUT

DISPLAY

Information input by
means of a teletypewriter
terminal keyboard

Information displayed on a
teletypewriter terminal, video device,
computer console typewriter, etc.

DOCUMENT

FIG. 2A. Explanation of flow chart symbols

SPECIALIZED PROCESSING SYMBOLS

KEYING

Any operation performed on a
key-driven device such as a
card punch, a card verifier
or a typewriter

MANUAL
OPERATION

Any operation performed without
mechanical aid...
i.e., "at human speed"

CONNECTIVE SYMBOLS

A flow line to show the
sequence of operations
and data flow direction

Data flow from one location
to another via telecommunication

Exit to or entry from a
flow chart on the same page

Exit to or entry from a
flow chart on another page

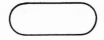

A terminal point in a flow chart ...
i.e., START, STOP, INTERRUPT, etc.

FIG. 2B. Explanation of flow chart symbols

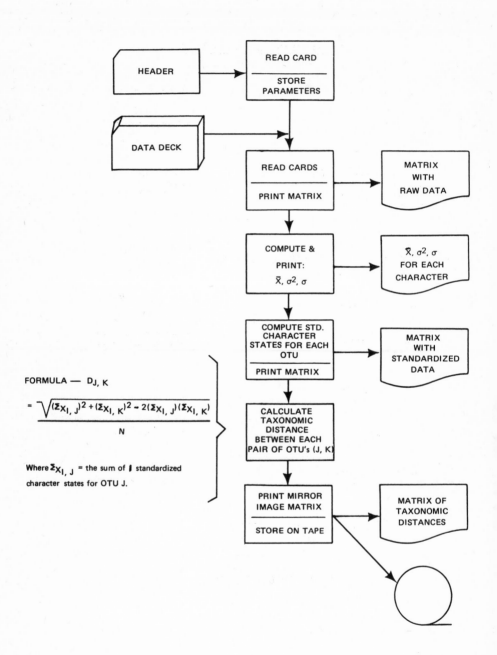

FIG. 3. System flow chart for MRTXRGC. (Reprinted from *Computers in Anthropology and Archaeology* [White Plains, N.Y.: IBM, 1971]).

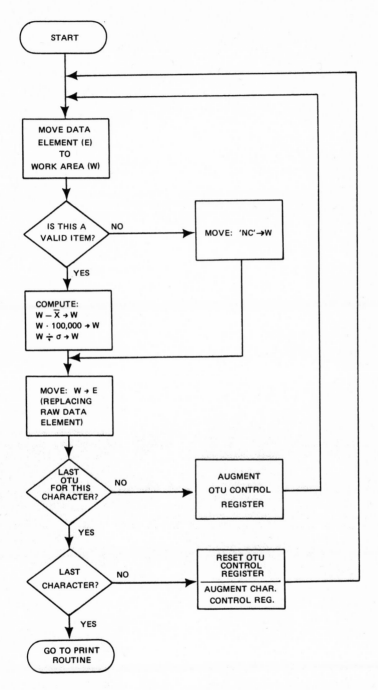

FIG. 4. Program flow chart for a portion of MRTXRGC. (Reprinted from *Computers in Anthropology and Archaeology* [White Plains, N.Y.: IBM, 1971]).

Potential Uses of Computers in Museums

In the early days of the computer era the applications that most quickly demonstrated their economic utility were in the fields of accounting, engineering, and science—that is, in fields where there had previously been a severe limitation either in the techniques of accumulating large quantities of numeric data rapidly or in the techniques of performing massive calculations rapidly. It has only been in the last eight or ten years, at most, that scientists from other disciplines have begun to fully appreciate the capacity that computers have to perform word manipulation functions. Numeric activities, though, continue to be the first thing most people think of as the computer applications with the greatest potential in any institution.

There are several numeric activities in a museum:

1. Payroll processing. Payroll processing has become such a commonplace computer application that almost all service bureaus and many banks and other organizations with excess computer capacity will now process payrolls of almost any size for a price that often is worth investigating. For the public or quasi-public museum it is even sometimes possible to arrange for excess computer time to be donated to the museum for this purpose.

2. Budgetary control. Standard packages to perform accounting functions other than payroll are almost as common as payroll packages. The entire accounting operation, for example, up to and including the preparation of monthly statements that compare budgeted and actual income and expenditures can sometimes be handled by an outside service bureau on a large computer more efficiently than it can be done by clerical personnel within the museum. Another alternative, of course, is to install what has been defined here as a small-scale computer to perform the payroll function and other accounting functions. This may be a feasible alternative for some of the larger museums, but it must be recognized that the size of computer required to handle these functions usually is not adequate for computerized museum cataloging.

3. Attendance figures. A third area of numeric activity within museums is the use of the computer to accumulate and analyze attendance figures. Most service bureaus do not have package programs to accomplish this function. However, the required programming is relatively simple, and it may be worth the one-time cost to have a service bureau write programs for this purpose. Since the programming is relatively simple, attendance figures can also be

maintained on desk-top computers or small-scale computers.

With all three of these activities the initial computerization decision usually is a choice between installing a small-scale computer in house and going to a service bureau of some kind. If the president of the local bank (where there happens to be excess computer time available) is also a member of the museum's board, it may be relatively easy to decide not to install an in-house computer. Even if the museum is required to pay full commercial service bureau rates, there are two other reasons for favoring this alternative.

1. The several numeric activities in a museum are not complex computer applications. Most service bureaus now have package programs that can be adapted to the needs of each institution with only minor modification. They do this work on large, very fast computers. Because of this, they can give the customer attractice rates if their operations are at all efficient.

2. Small-scale computers (the size and type that most museums would lease to perform their numeric activities) usually are not adequate to handle the word manipulation functions described below, and it is these applications that ultimately will have the greatest payoff for museums. Unless the numeric activities themselves require a large-scale computer, it is usually best to begin with a service bureau.

The word manipulation capability of computers offers to museums a group of potential applications that are a little more unusual than the numeric applications, not as well known, not as well understood, and certainly not as commonly provided for in the standard program packages of the service bureaus. On the other hand, in contrast to numeric applications, this type of computer activity usually requires the use of a large-scale computer (there are some exceptions to this that are noted in chapter 6) and relatively complex programming. Word manipulation applications present lots of problems—some of them only partially solved today—but they also offer the museums the opportunity to use modern computing facilities to provide information that either is not presently available or is available only by spending a good deal of time and effort.

The word manipulation activities in a museum are as follows:

1. Collection catalogs. The subject matter of this book, including accessioning, object registration, and object indexing.

2. Membership lists. The clerical effort expended by many museums in order to be (reasonably?) sure that a wealthy benefactor does not receive a dun notice for annual dues is staggering. One museum,

for example, that has a membership of just under 10,000 employs three persons full time just to maintain the membership card files and send out annual dues notices.

3. Development lists. Another activity closely related to membership is the fund-raising function. This function has many facets to it and is unique in every museum, but there is a common denominator in the lists of names and addresses and other selected information that enables the director or other responsible official to contact the "right" individuals, either with mailings or with personal appeals.

4. Library catalogs. Many museums have extensive library holdings. The cataloging of books, manuscripts, photos, films, slides, maps, and other ephemera in museums should follow the same classificatory schemes that are used for the collection catalogs. These classificatory schemes are not always the same as the Library of Congress and Dewey systems employed by the library profession.

The word manipulation activities listed here are all closely related in one very important way: *the computing facilities and the computer programs required to prepare and maintain a computerized museum catalog can, in most cases, be utilized without change to do all of the membership list processing, development list processing, and library cataloging.* The implications of this fact are seldom fully appreciated by museum personnel when evaluating possible computer applications. However, from the discussion of computerized museum catalogs in the next section it will become apparent that these are all examples of applications requiring the use of generalized information systems.

An *information system* may be thought of as a set of computer programs designed to accomplish a number of integrated and related word manipulation activities. Commands such as STORE, SELECT, SORT, MERGE, INDEX, COUNT, and LIST do, in fact, instruct the computer to accomplish functions approximating those indicated by the command terms. Depending upon the complexity of the operation, these commands may be thought of as complete and relatively independent programs, or they may be only some designated large or small part of programs. Each time one or another of the programs is needed, it must be called forth specifically and given the information necessary for it to STORE data, SELECT data, SORT, MERGE, or LIST data. The information necessary for the computer to carry out (to *execute*) these programs includes: the location of the data that is to be used (on a magnetic tape, on punch cards, etc.), the format of the data that is to be used, the location where the operator wants the results placed (again, on a magnetic tape, on punch cards, or perhaps, on a high-speed printer), and the form or format of the output. Sometimes an information system will have all of these instructions or program parameters built into the fixed program package. However, when the information necessary to execute each program in the package can be specified each time some of the programs are run, the system can be used with a wide variety of data and is considered to be a *generalized information system*. Most of the systems discussed in this book are generalized information systems. Thus, they can be used to process a wide variety of symbolic, language-type data.

There are many other potential applications of computers in museum work. Ultimately, perhaps, the most significant have not even been listed here: the more or less esoteric research projects such as the use of a computer by Carl Dauterman to coordinate, control, and analyze the makers' marks on Sèvres porcelain; [12] the use of the computer for statistical analyses such as the work of David Wolf on human skeletons described in chapter 2; the use of the computer at several stages in the preparation of manuscripts for publication; the use of the computer to control bookstore and other inventories. Finally, we should never forget that the computer is the most efficient tool available for pulling together intermuseum comparative figures (e.g., those required by the American Association of Museums in order to prepare the *1971 Financial and Salary Survey*). All these activities, however, require specialized programming and organization of data. They do not have the general applicability of the seven numeric and logical word manipulation functions listed previously.

Computerized Museum Catalogs

The general idea of a computerized museum catalog can be expressed rather simply: All the catalog data on each object in the collection is recorded one time only in the form of input to a generalized information system; the records are then sorted as needed and (usually) printed on the high-speed printer to produce as many different catalogs as the different information needs of the museum may require. All simplified statements, of course, have the advantage of being understandable and the disadvantage of never being quite adequate to really express what it is all about. This general picture of a computerized museum catalog is no exception.

There are five different types of activity or phases involved in the total operation of a computerized catalog (see table 2). Manual

Table 2
The Structure of Computerized Catalog Systems

Phases	Functions	Key Decisions
I Data identification	Object selection	Collection, processing, and sorting of specimens
	Data determination	Attribute identification Classification Coding
II Data documentation	Forms design	Format
	Recording for entry	Punch cards, terminal keyboard, paper tape, magnetic tape, magnetic cards, optical character scanner
III Data entry	Input to computer	Batch processing, real-time processing
	Verification	Automatic (with machine checks for terminology and syntax), manual (off-line) Hard copy or display format
IV File maintenance	Error correction	
	Sorting Merging Indexing Storing	
V File inquiry (data analysis).	File search (retrieval) Sorting Summarizing	Research design criteria (search and sort parameters)
	Calculations	Statistical tests
	Report generation	Format

Adapted from "Computer-Aided Decision-Making Procedures for Archaeological Field Problems" (Sylvia W. Gaines, Ph.D. diss., Arizona State University, 1972).

cataloging systems must also accomplish these same activities in one way or another, although the order in which the functions are performed may be quite different. The first phase—data identification—is the extremely important matter of deciding what should be contained in the catalog. The content of museum catalogs is the subject matter of the next chapter. Data documentation (phase II) is concerned with the forms to use in recording the documentation that becomes input to a computerized catalog and alternate ways of converting the data on these forms into machine-readable language. A detailed discussion of these problems is contained in chapter 5. Finally, there is the information system necessary to create and maintain a computerized museum catalog (phases III, IV and V in table 2). Data entry, file maintenance, and file inquiry are interrelated activities that can only be evaluated within the context of particular information systems. It is possible, however, to present a generalized picture that will indicate some of the possible alternatives and the way that the several programs in such a system produce computerized museum catalogs.

First, four more terms must be defined:

1. A *record* is all the documentation about an object that is stored in the computer system—on magnetic tape, a magnetic disk, or somewhere else. (Computer scientists will find this and perhaps the following definitions completely inadequate. The definition of a record given here is, in fact, a specific instance of a logical record, not a physical record, and the concept is very difficult to define except in terms of a related file or fields.)

2. A *file* (or a *master file*) consists of all the records that are stored in a defined (and labeled) section of a particular magnetic tape or disk.

3. A *field* is that portion of a record containing one specific observation (one category of data) about an object.

4. A *tag* is a specific identifier or label (a number, a set of letters, or a distinctive symbol) by which the computer recognizes a record, a file, or a field. A tag for a field indicates content (the category of data); therefore, it may be repeated in as many records as necessary. A record tag or a file tag is a unique identification device used to distinguish one record from another and one file from another.

Each information system is programmed on the assumption that records and fields will be formatted in a dependable manner. In some systems records and fields are said to be "tightly structured" (i.e., each field is alloted a certain number of character positions in the record and the category of data is indicated by the position of the field in relation to other fields). Other systems are more nearly free form. In some the fields can be of any length and in any position relative to each other, for the category of data contained in the field is indicated by a numeric tag at the beginning or the end of each "string" of characters. In yet other systems the only categories of data placed in separate fields are the object registration number and a list of key words to be indexed. (In some even the registration number is simply another "key word.") The "text" of the record in these systems is a completely unstructured free-form paragraph.

There are advantages and disadvantages to each of these approaches to the structuring of the records. Generally speaking, it is much simpler and quicker to record data in an unstructured system than it is to have to carefully examine every character to be sure that it appears in exactly the right location and in precisely the right (perhaps coded) form. However, free-form record structures require more complex (and expensive) programs for the data to be processed correctly; free-form record structures usually require more storage space for a comparable quantity of data, which in turn means more computer time to retrieve, select, sort, and process; and free-form record structures are not the most efficient for recording any data that are to be further processed statistically. With records that are to be regularly used for research purposes as well as for the production of a catalog some structuring of the record formats is usually desirable. At least one of the systems that will be described in chapter 6 provides for the recording of data in either a structured or a partially unstructured form.

As with the structuring of records, it is possible to approach the functions of data entry, file maintenance, and file inquiry in several ways; and what is best for a particular museum will depend upon the information needs at that institution. The flow charts in figures 5 through 9 will suggest some of the alternatives that are available using different information systems. The symbols used in these flow charts are explained in figures 2A and 2B. For convenience, punched cards are shown as the usual input medium. There are, of course, several alternatives to this.

Data entry. Regardless of whether the records are structured or unstructured, the data entry process is usually one of those shown in figure 5. There is no significant advantage or disadvantage to any of these systems of entry. It takes longer to sort new records into registration number sequence and then merge them with the prior

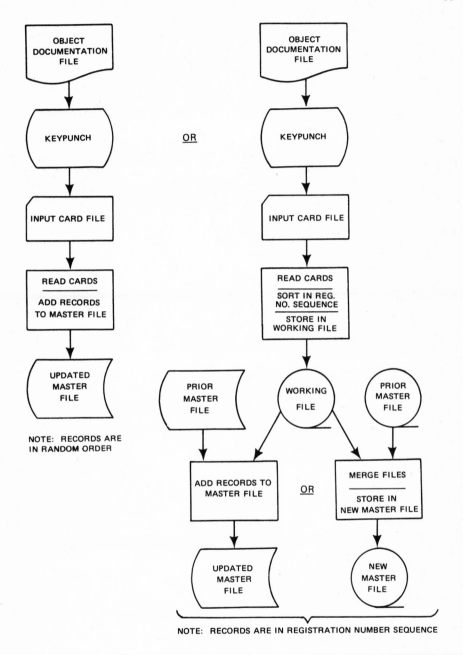

FIG. 5. Alternate methods of data entry

master file than it does to simply store new records on the end of the prior file. However, with records in random order the user must refer back to a computer listing by registration number in order to locate a particular record in the computer file for updating or correction.

File maintenance. All information systems include one or more programs to correct or otherwise change records that have been recorded previously. These and other file maintenance functions that are system specific will not be diagrammed here. However, if the system includes provisions for the building of a computerized index or indexes (not all systems have this), this can be done in at least two different ways, as shown in figure 6. (In figure 6 and later illustrations in this chapter all storage files are shown as magnetic tapes. In most instances the symbol for a magnetic disk would be equally appropriate.)

It is more efficient, especially with large data files, to index only the new or incoming data and then to merge the index to new data with a prior index file than it is to reindex the entire master file each time new data is entered. However, with some information systems the way the data are structured precludes the more efficient approach to indexing. Either of the indexing procedures can be used to create a single index of all key words included in the catalog or to create a number of indexes—one for each category of data selected for indexing.

File Inquiry. The options chosen by a computer scientist for entering data into an information system have a direct relationship to the way he envisions the system being used—that is, to the system of file inquiry that he creates as the normal or usual method of retrieving data. There are three basic approaches (figures 7, 8, 9), and it is well to consider very carefully which of these most closely approaches the way you will probably want to handle the normal request for information from the catalog. Some of the information systems do provide options, such as going either to prepared lists for answers to the routine questions (figure 7) or to special computer search routines for answers to nonroutine questions (figure 8). All information systems, though, are designed to work most efficiently in only one mode of file inquiry.

Many individuals have an aversion to using books of computer print-out as a regular source of reference. They are bulky, hard to handle because of their size, and they very quickly become dog-eared with use. However, book type listings of the collections, prepared

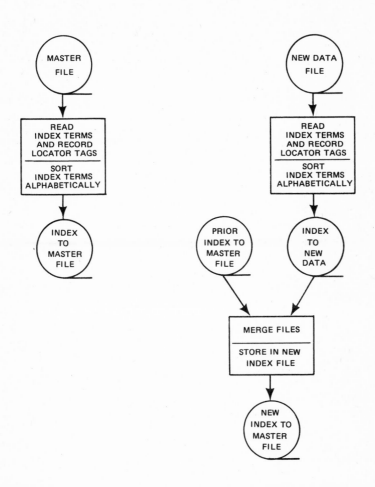

FIG. 6. Alternate methods of indexing

42

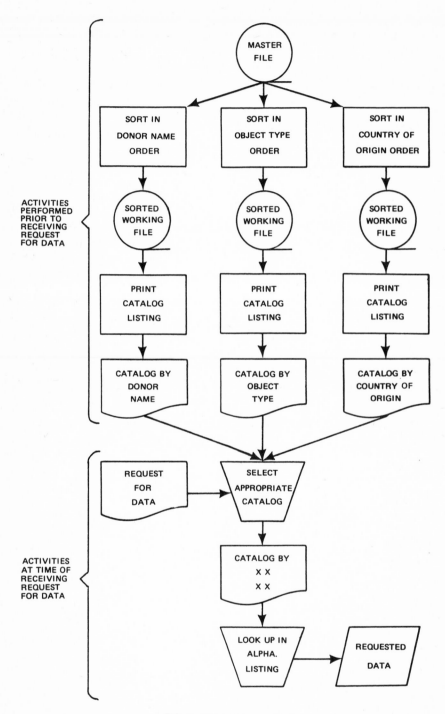

FIG. 7. File inquiry mode 1

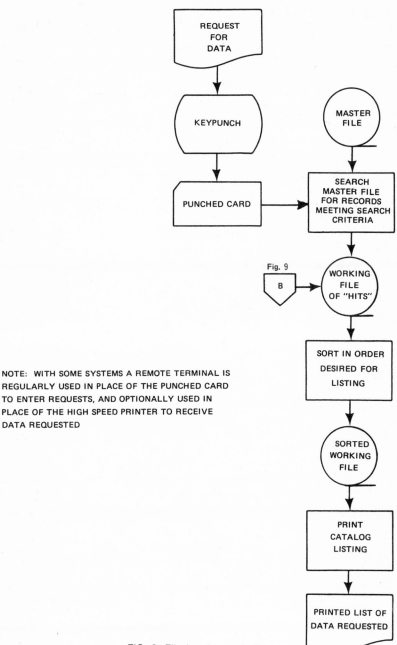

REQUEST FOR DATA

KEYPUNCH

MASTER FILE

PUNCHED CARD

SEARCH MASTER FILE FOR RECORDS MEETING SEARCH CRITERIA

Fig. 9

B

WORKING FILE OF "HITS"

NOTE: WITH SOME SYSTEMS A REMOTE TERMINAL IS REGULARLY USED IN PLACE OF THE PUNCHED CARD TO ENTER REQUESTS, AND OPTIONALLY USED IN PLACE OF THE HIGH SPEED PRINTER TO RECEIVE DATA REQUESTED

SORT IN ORDER DESIRED FOR LISTING

SORTED WORKING FILE

PRINT CATALOG LISTING

PRINTED LIST OF DATA REQUESTED

FIG. 8. File inquiry mode 2

44

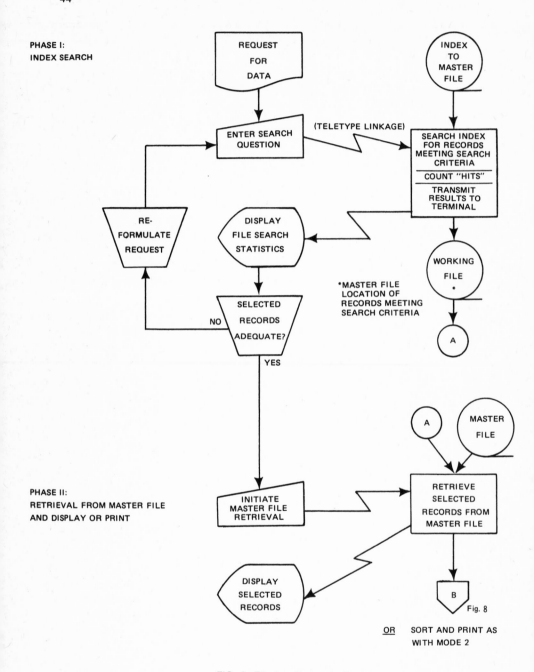

FIG. 9. File inquiry mode 3

occasionally (perhaps once each year with supplementary lists for new accessions) and distributed as needed throughout the museum, are by far the least expensive of the three modes of file inquiry. This is so because such listings require a computer for retrieval purposes only occasionally, whereas the other modes require that a computer be available to search the master file whenever a request for data is processed (mode 2) or that a computer be available at all times, either in house or through a time-sharing operation (mode 3).

The listings indicated as a basis for the mode 1 method of answering requests for data do not have to be in the form of the usual computer print-out. At the Museum of Modern Art, for example, catalogs are prepared in this way with the output in the form of cards that are subsequently filed in the sequences of the most common catalog inquiries (see figure 50, page 146).

As indicated previously, an information system consists of a group of individual computer programs designed to work together, with output from one program formatted so that it can be used as input to the next, etc. Each individual program is made up of a series of instructional steps that the computer carries out dependably and in sequential order. The languages in which the individual programs are written are called, appropriately, *programming languages.* Examples include such familiar languages as FORTRAN, COBOL, ALGOL, SNOBOL, and PL/I. Some of these programming languages (e.g., FORTRAN, COBOL) can be used on many different brands of computer equipment; others are more limited. However, even when an information system has been written in a widely used language such as COBOL, moving from one brand of hardware to another always requires some modification of the programs to adapt them to the new equipment. The extent of this will vary considerably from one situation to another, but it can run into several man-months of programming time.

Information systems may consist of anywhere from a dozen or so programs to as many as fifty or sixty programs. A recent study identified more than 150 information systems available for all brands of computer equipment as of May, 1972, enough for the authors of the study to conclude that "a sufficient number of systems are available having a wide range of abilities and relatively low cost [so] that one cannot afford not to consider using an available system." [13] Probably no more than a dozen of these systems have been used for museum cataloging, and the problems of data compatibility discussed in the next chapter and in chapter 8 suggest strongly that this number

should not be expanded. Quite aside from the matter of data compatibility, however, the element of cost is a strong deterrent against hiring
programmers to come in and design an individualized system for any
museum.

Computer programming is expensive! The developer of one of the
information systems described in chapter 6 has estimated the total
cost of development at approximately $250,000. This is a complex
system, and that experience is not necessarily typical. However, even
the simplest of information systems is sufficiently complex so that
is is worth the effort to examine existing systems used by museums
and, if necessary, to adapt an existing system to an available brand
of computer hardware or to the specialized needs of your museum
rather than to start over again to reinvent the wheel.

There are several reasons for the development of such a large
number of information systems. One of these is the old story of
simultaneous invention by two or more persons in different locations
with each thinking he has created the ultimate system. Another is
that different systems have been created to accomplish approximately
the same thing on different brands of computers. In addition, there
are honest differences of opinion on what constitutes the best kind
of system, and these differences of opinion are expressed in the programming philosophy of the developers. Most of these differences—
those that have found their way into museum catalogs—will be apparent from the comparative descriptions in chapter 6.

4

What to Record:
The Content of Museum Catalogs

IN THIS chapter we return to consider in greater detail the content of catalogs. In terms of the structure of computerized catalog systems (table 2), this is part of phase I, data identification. Object selection is beyond the scope of this book, but the function of data determination is an essential part of it.

I indicated in chapter 2 that a catalog should contain whatever information seems to be desirable in terms of the data needs of each museum and the practical realities of economics. This general statement is still valid. However, one of the main objectives of the Museum Data Bank Coordinating Committee has been

to coordinate the data categories and recording conventions used in computerized museum catalogs so that any museum, large or small, can catalog its collections for eventual computer entry and be confident that the work will not have to be redone at a later date.

This objective has been interpreted to mean the writing of a statement of data standards, which includes data category definitions, recording conventions, and dictionaries of terms as appropriate and necessary (1) to guide museums in the development of catalogs for different kinds of collections and (2) to serve as a common basis for the eventual sharing of catalog data among museums, perhaps by means of networks as discussed in chapter 8.

This chapter may be considered as a tentative statement of data standards as set forth by the Museum Data Bank Coordinating Committee.

Data Determination: Objects, Attributes, and Classification

As a point of beginning, let us assume that the usual or normal or "most common" museum catalog consists of a collection of recorded

47

observations about physical objects in which (1) each *record* comprises the recorded observations about one object and (2) each *observation* expresses a classification of the object according to an attribute or dimension that is distinct from all other attributes or dimensions. Attributes or dimensions may be thought of as standardized frames within which different kinds of observations are expressed. In this discussion such standardized frames are called *data categories,* and the largest part of this statement of data standards consists of a series of numbered paragraphs, each of which contains the definition of a single data category.

If the preceding paragraph were a complete presentation of the problem, cataloging would not be too difficult. However, there are several variations on this generalized statement that must also be considered:

1. It is not valid to assume that one record always comprises the recorded observations about one object. Often it is necessary, either temporarily or permanently, to think of one record as the observations about one lot of objects. If a record is created for each lot of objects accessioned (to identify each purchase, each bequest, etc.), and it is the intent to eventually catalog each object individually, this does not present a major problem, for as the individual objects are described in detail they can be assigned record numbers that are subdivisions of the original lot number and the status of one record equals one object is eventually reached. With some kinds of collections it is not economically feasible to ever plan on creating a record for each object. With the artifacts that are collected from an archaeological excavation, for example, it may not be feasible to create a *catalog* record (i.e., as permanent museum documentation) that is any more refined than one record per site per excavation season or collection. In such cases one record will always be the equivalent of one lot of materials, and the only way the items can be separated within the single catalog record is by adding additional data categories for "number of ceramic sherds," "number of lithic fragments," "number of bone fragments," etc.

2. One record may sometimes comprise the recorded observations on more than one object, but the reverse can also occur: all the recorded observations that are pertinent about one object may not be contained in a single record. It is not economically feasible, for example, for an art museum to place in the record of every painting by a given artist all the known biographical material about that artist. In some of the information systems described in chapter 6,

it is possible to "link" records automatically so that a basic object record can call forth any pertinent person, place, or document information that is referenced in the object record. Biographical details, thus, can be recorded a single time and still be retrieved as if they were a part of each record in which the individual's name appears. Even when this automatic linking is not possible, however, any catalog should always provide data categories for recording the locations of "additional data."

3. No one list of data categories can ever be developed that will be appropriate, necessary, and desirable for the recording of all museum collections. The variation in the kinds of observations that are made as a basis for classifying different kinds of collections (and even the same kind of collection in different museums) is so great that each data category must be looked at in terms of its utility for classifying a particular kind of museum specimen under a given set of circumstances. For example, a record number, an owner's name, a donor's name, the date acquired, and condition of an object are all data categories that might be meaningful regardless of the kind of collection with which one is dealing. However, most of the observations that are made about museum specimens are relevant only to the viewpoints of curators who deal with certain classes of objects. Function, for instance, is an essential observation for a historical collection, and it is an optional observation, sometimes inferred from tenuous evidence, for an archaeological collection. Function may be meaningful in classifying a natural science collection, but there the concept is something different from a consideration of the function of a man-made object. Conversely, the Linnaean system of classification is basic to the biological sciences, but it is seldom used and then only in a peripheral manner in the classification of a historical collection.

4. Even though each observation expresses a classification of an object according to a distinctive attribute or dimension (a definable data category), the method of scaling used in the classification of one kind of collection may be different from that used with another kind of collection—that is, the same data category may be used in a somewhat different manner from one collection to another. Perhaps the best example of this is the observations that are made concerning the spatial origins of an object. For the curator of an art collection there are usually two data categories required to express geographic/political provenance: the country of origin (nationality or birthplace of the artist, national school or style, site of discovery,

or any other connection) and a specific place of origin (city, state, city and state, etc.). However, a geologist requires separate data categories for state (country is usually omitted), county, city or town, and—if he is a vertebrate paleontologist—the specific site name; an archaeologist, normally working within a single state, records only the county, a specific locality description (i.e., how to find the site again), and a site number; and a biological scientist will usually use a complete hierarchy of locality terms starting (at the broadest level) with continent, ocean, or biogeographic region. These several methods of recording spatial origins amount to different systems of classification that are regularly used within a single observational class or data category. In such cases subcategories that are appropriate only for particular disciplines must be set up as guides for the development (and searching) of catalogs.

All these variations and special situations are taken into consideration in the data category definitions that are presented here.

Most of the time we are not conscious of the process we go through in classifying physical objects. Subconsciously we *always* do a preliminary mental sort by asking, "What is it?" It is only after we have satisfied ourselves that "this is an item of the general class *x*" (bird's egg, stone, fossilized fish skeleton, chair, clock, gun, pottery, basket, etc.), that we are able to make the further statement, "All items of class *x* are usually described using attributes 1, 4, 5, and 14; therefore, these attributes should be included as a part of the observation and recording of this object." To place an object in class *x* is to state a preliminary point of view from which the object is to be described, or in other words, to state a set of data categories that are appropriate for the documentation of objects of that type. A data strategy statement, therefore, must include, in addition to data category definitions, a guide to the data categories most commonly used to document different classes of objects. It is only in the smallest of museums, where a single computer file may contain the records on several kinds of objects, that this preliminary classification is likely to be incorporated into the computerized catalog (see page 70). In most instances it is simply a guide to the appropriate data categories for different kinds of objects. It is the independent variable that determines the dependent variable, data categories.

A classification of the kinds of objects recorded in museum catalogs can be approached in several ways. In gross terms all perceivable physical objects were originally (1) animate, (2) inanimate but natural, or (3) man-made. From another point of view, museum objects can be classified in terms of scholastic disciplines and the kinds of objects with which each discipline is concerned. Neither of these is adequate to bring together in a single classificatory taxon those objects that are usually described with a particular set of observations or data categories. Table 3 is a preliminary object classification developed for this purpose. It is a broad and at times cross-disciplinary

Table 3
Preliminary Object Classes

Archaeological materials	
Prehistoric artifacts	AART
Floral and faunal remains	AFFR
Human remains	AHUR
sites	ASIT
Art objects	ART
Biological specimens	
Botanical specimens	BOT
Fossils	FOS
Zoological specimens (nonhuman, alive or not)	ZOO
Ethnographic, historic, or modern man-made objects	
Artifacts	HART
Historic sites	HSIT
Physical science specimens	
Geological specimens	GEO
Library items	
Books, manuscripts	BOOK
Maps, photographs, ephemera	MAPE
Motion pictures	MPIC

grouping of types of collections that may be used as a guide for either establishing or searching particular collections. The acronyms in table 3 are the same as the column headings in table 4. The latter table in turn directs one to the most commonly used data categories for each preliminary object class. Definitions and recording conventions to be used with each data category begin on page 57.

Data Category Definitions

Once it has been determined that an object is of a general class x out of a possible range of $x, y,$ and $z,$ it is then possible to make some statement as to the second level detailed observations or classifications that *may* be meaningful for that object.[14] The word *may* is emphasized here, for the observations that *are* meaningful can only be determined by the purposes of each museum's catalog.

The observations that *can* be made about perceivable objects can be extended almost indefinitely—certainly into a list of observational categories that is too long for the human mind to readily grasp. However, the observations about museum specimens that are most often used for collections management purposes seem to fall into one or another of several generic groups:

1. Object identification, location, and other bookkeeping type data
2. History of the object as a specimen, artifact, or record
3. Origins of the object: cultural and temporal
4. Origins of the object: spatial
5. Description of the object: physical characteristics
6. Description of the object: content or decoration.
7. Classification of the object: typological and functional.

In the paragraphs that follow, the most common observational categories within each of these generic groups are defined and discussed. Each data category is assigned a consecutive paragraph number in order to identify that data category as distinct from any other data category. When used in a particular information system, these numbers would be the equivalent of and perhaps converted into tag numbers that identify data fields within the computer records. The terms *annotator* and *annotation class number* have sometimes been used to identify numeric tags that are used to identify data categories or *annotation classes*.

The list of observational categories presented here should be considered tentative. Undoubtedly, it will be changed as different museums and different classes of objects dictate the need for additions, deletions, and more precise definitions. For the present, anyone setting up a new catalog should both select from and add to this list as the needs of the particular museum require.

In summary, these data category definitions and the cross-reference table (table 4) are intended as a "short form" list of observational categories that (1) will serve as a guide to any museum in the creation of its own cataloging system, (2) will serve as a guide to any individual desiring to search the catalog of some museum other than his own, and (3) eventually will serve as a basis for the exchange or summarization of data contained in the catalogs of many museums.

Object Identification, Location, and Other Bookkeeping Data

An essential attribute of any cataloging system is the provision for a positive identification of the specimen, artifact, or record in a manner that is distinct from every other possible specimen, artifact, or record. In a manual cataloging system this is accomplished by assigning a distinctive registration number or catalog number (or both) to each object. In a computer cataloging system at least two data classes must be used for this purpose, and others may be desirable with some kinds of objects.

The two absolute minimal classes that *must be completed for every computer record* are:

1. Record number. Each computer record must have a distinctive number assigned to it for identification purposes. This may be the unique accession number, registration number, or site number used to identify a lot or an object, or it may be a separately assigned catalog number. It does not matter what numbering system is used as long as each record is identified with a distinct set of alphanumeric characters. If numbers are assigned by lots when objects are first accessioned, the record number can be the lot number (see paragraph 6 below), with additional subnumbers and records created as individual items are cataloged. If the objects themselves have numbers affixed to them for identification, it is usually desirable to have that same number entered as the record number.

2. Recording institution. With computer catalogs that may someday be partially or fully merged with other similar catalogs, it is possible to have less than positive object identification from record numbers alone. In addition it is essential that every record contain an acronym or an abbreviation identifying the recording institution. Normally, though not necessarily, this will be the institution that owns and/or controls the object.

Additional data classes that are useful as identification or location devices with some types of museum objects are:

3. Other record numbers. In addition to the number that is used as the distinctive record number, man-made objects often have affixed to them other sets of numbers or numbers and letters. Often these are the catalog numbers of present or former owners. If they assist in the positive identification of the object, they should be recorded.

4. Photograph negative numbers. In some museums photographs are artifacts that must be described with a complete set of data classes. Often, however, artifacts are regularly photographed, partly as a means of identification in case of loss or theft and partly for study, publication, or publicity purposes. When this is done, a record of the negative numbers (or slide numbers) should always be recorded in the catalog under the record number(s) of the artifact(s) appearing in the photograph.

Table 4

Data Categories Commonly Used to Catalog Different Object Classes

Par. No.	Description	AART	AFFR	AHUR	ASIT	ART	BOT	FOS	ZOO	HART	HSIT	GEO	BOOK	MAPE	MPIC
	Bookkeeping Type Data														
1	Record number	X	X	X	X	X	X	X	X	X	X	X	X	X	X
2	Recording institution	X	X	X	X	X	X	X	X	X	X	X	X	X	X
3	Other record numbers	X			X	X				X	X		X	X	X
4	Photograph negative numbers														
5	Additional data	X	X	X	X	X	X	X	X	X	X	X			X
6	Number of items	X	X	X	X	X		X	X	X	X	X			
7	Storage location	X	X	X		X	X	X	X	X		X	X	X	X
8	Present value	X	X	X	X	X	X	X	X	X		X	X	X	X
	History of the Object														
9	Collector	X	X	X	X		X	X	X			X			
10	Date collected	X	X	X	X		X	X	X			X			
11	Expedition	X	X	X	X		X	X	X			X			
12	Recorder	X	X	X	X	X	X	X	X	X	X	X	X	X	X
13	Date recorded	X	X	X	X	X	X	X	X	X	X	X	X	X	X
14	Method of acquisition	X	X	X		X		X	X	X		X	X	X	X
15	Date of acquisition	X	X	X		X		X	X	X		X	X	X	X
16	Donor	X	X	X		X		X	X	X		X	X	X	X
17	Owner	X	X	X	X	X	X	X	X	X	X	X	X	X	X
18	Possessor	X	X	X	X	X	X	X	X	X	X	X	X	X	X
19	History of ownership					X		X					X	X	X
20	References	X	X	X	X	X	X	X	X	X	X	X	X	X	X
	Cultural and Temporal Origins														
21	Manufacturer, printer									X			X	X	X
22	Artist, photographer					X				X			X	X	X
23	Technician, artisan, lithographer					X				X				X	X
24	Author												X	X	X

Table 4 (continued)

Par. No.	Description	AART	AFFR	AHUR	ASIT	ART	BOT	FOS	ZOO	HART	HSIT	GEO	BOOK	MAPE	MPIC
25	Date for display	X				X				X			X	X	X
26	Earliest possible date	X	X	X	X	X				X	X		X	X	
27	Latest possible date	X	X	X	X	X				X	X		X	X	
28	System							X				X			
29	Series							X				X			
30	Stage							X				X			
31	Cultural period	X			X	X				X	X		X	X	X
32	Developmental stage, style	X				X				X					
33	Cultural classification	X			X					X					
Spatial Origins															
34	Place of discovery	X	X	X		X	X	X	X	X		X			
34a	Continent, ocean, biogeographical region						X	X	X						
34b	County					X	X	X	X	X	X	X	X	X	X
34c	State or province					X	X	X	X	X	X	X	X	X	X
34d	County				X						X	X			
34e	City or town						X	X	X	X	X	X			
34f	Site name				X		X	X			X	X			
34g	Specific address				X		X		X		X	X			
35	Place of origin	X													
36	Locality or site number	X	X	X				X							
37	Intrasite provenience	X	X	X											
38	Township/range/section				X										
39	Latitude/longitude				X		X	X	X		X				
40	Other expressions of locality				X		X	X	X		X	X			
41	Altitude				X		X	X	X						

Table 4 (continued)

Par. No.	Description	AART	AFFR	AHUR	ASIT	ART	BOT	FOS	ZOO	HART	HSIT	GEO	BOOK	MAPE	MPIC
42	Depth						X		X						
43	Group							X				X			
44	Formation							X				X			
45	Member							X				X			
	Physical Description														
46	Condition	X	X	X	X	X	X	X	X	X	X	X	X	X	X
47	Material	X				X				X		X		X	X
48	Technique	X				X				X					
49	Medium					X									X
50	Color	X				X				X		X			
51	Form (shape)	X				X				X		X			
52	Dimensions, weight	X			X	X				X	X		X	X	
53	Features, attached parts	X			X	X				X	X				
54	Number of parts	X				X				X					
55	General description	X	X	X	X	X				X	X		X	X	
	Content or Decoration														
56	Title				X	X					X		X	X	X
57	Language												X	X	
58	Specific subject(s)					X				X			X	X	X
59	General subject					X				X			X	X	X
60	Inscriptions, markings					X				X			X	X	
61	Decorative motif	X				X				X			X	X	
	Typological Classification														
62	Artifact types	X													
63	Phylum (division)		X				X	X	X						
64	Subphylum (subdivision)	X	X					X	X						
65	Superclass	X	X					X	X						

Table 4 (continued)

Par. No.	Description	AART	AFFR	AHUR	ASIT	ART	BOT	FOS	ZOO	HART	HSIT	GEO	BOOK	MAPE	MPIC
66	Class		X					X	X						
67	Subclass		X					X	X						
68	Infraclass		X					X	X						
69	Cohort		X					X	X						
70	Superorder		X					X	X						
71	Order		X					X	X						
72	Suborder		X					X	X						
73	Infraorder		X					X	X						
74	Superfamily		X					X	X						
75	Family		X				X	X	X						
76	Subfamily		X					X	X						
77	Tribe		X					X	X						
78	Subtribe		X	X				X	X						
79	Genus		X	X			X	X	X						
80	Subgenus		X	X				X	X						
81	Species		X	X			X	X	X						
82	Infraspecific rank		X	X			X	X	X						
83	Infraspecific name		X	X			X	X	X						
84	Author of taxon	X	X	X			X	X	X	X					
85	Year of publication	X	X	X			X	X	X	X					
86	Identifier	X	X	X			X	X	X	X					
87	Date identified	X	X	X			X	X	X	X					
88	Preliminary object class	X	X	X	X	X	X	X	X	X	X	X	X	X	X
89	Broad informal class	X	X	X	X	X	X	X	X	X	X	X	X	X	X
90	Specific informal class	X	X	X	X	X	X	X	X	X	X	X	X	X	X

5. Additional data. For reasons of economy, detailed research on particular specimens may be recorded someplace other than in the main computer catalog. This may be a separate computer file or it may be an unpublished file of data that is not recorded in any computer record. The main catalog, however, should contain a reference to such additional data. The entry may contain either the name of the file or simply a yes-no statement that additional data is available at the recording institution.

6. Number of items. If a single record number is assigned to a lot, the number of items included in that lot should be recorded on the catalog regardless of whether they are physically homogeneous specimens. If desired, several data categories may be used to record the numbers of items of different kinds included in the lot—that is, with each category expressing "number of x items," "number of y items," etc.

7. Storage location. The location (room number, bin number, drawer number, etc.) where an object is normally stored can be an extremely useful piece of information for inventory control purposes. In an active computer file regular entries can be made so that this data category can be used as a basis for actual physical control—for example, by changing the storage location to read ON LOAN TO ——— MUSEUM, or ——— EXHIBIT, CASE ———. However, even if movements are controlled by some other means, it is still worthwhile to have a catalog record of the permanent storage locations.

8. Present value. Some museum specimens have sufficient intrinsic value to be regularly appraised for insurance purposes. When values are recorded, they should be included as a part of the catalog. (In most computer systems this category is "protected information," which is not retrievable through any network operation.) Care should be exercised to always record present value in a consistent format, so that summaries and across-the-board (%) changes can be made by the computer. For example, if amounts are recorded on one record in whole dollars, without commas and dollar signs, they should be recorded this way on all records.

An appraisal is meaningless unless one knows when it was made. Because the computer record may eventually contain multiple valuations, made at different times, the valuation date should be recorded as a part of the valuation entry—perhaps separated from the dollar amount by a space-hyphen-space (e.g., 2850ɓ-ɓ711015) [15] or by some other combination of symbols.

History of the Object as a Specimen, Artifact, or Record

The circumstances concerning collection, discovery, or acquisition of an object are an important part of any catalog. The specific data categories required to record this will vary considerably from one discipline to another, but the following twelve categories appear to be regularly used:

9. Collector. The name of the individual who recovered the object from its natural surroundings and identified it as a scientific/cultural specimen/artifact, or the name of the director of the expedition or excavation.

10. Date collected. The date the object was collected or excavated.[15]

11. Expedition. The title of the expedition during which the collection or excavation was conducted.

12. Recorder. The name of the individual who prepared the catalog record for computer entry, and who should know the source of any information appearing in the record.

13. Date recorded. The date the entry was completed.[15]

14. Method of acquisition. With many museum artifacts it is important to know how the object was acquired by the present owner: gift, bequest, purchase, loan, etc. If the date of acquisition (paragraph 15) and the method of acquisition are known, additional details can be obtained from accounting records if needed. (However, see also paragraph 16.)

15. Date of acquisition. The date acquired by the present owner.

16. Donor. The one exception to the statement in paragraph 14 concerning the use of accounting records for details regarding acquisitions is the names of donors. An important by-product of a computerized catalog is the ability to maintain current lists of all objects given to the museum by different individuals. Any artifact received as a gift or bequest should always have the donor's name as a separate sortable category on the catalog record. As with other categories in which sorting of the files is important, it is essential that one recording format (e.g., last name first) be consistently followed. (In most computer systems this category is "protected information," which is not retrievable through any network operation.)

17. Owner (if other than the recording institution). In some instances it may be desirable to catalog objects that are not owned by the recording institution. If an object is acquired on loan (see paragraph 14), other than as part of a temporary exhibit, it is essential

that the owner's name appear on the catalog record. The owner's name should also appear when items are cataloged, perhaps for research purposes, that are not in the physical possession of the recording institution. In the recording of archaeological or historic sites the owner will likewise be someone other than the recording institution. As with donor names, consistency of format is essential.

18. Possessor (if other than the recording institution). Objects on permanent loan sometimes present special problems that necessitate recording both the owner (paragraph 17) and the present possessor or custodian separate from the recording institution.

19. History of ownership. Remarks about the known or conjectural sequence of ownership, changes of location, dates and circumstances of transfer, etc. In small museums, where an attempt is made to keep the computerized catalog information to a minimum, this type of data may be maintained in a manual file and noted as "additional data" (see paragraph 5).

20. References. Documentary sources referring to or illustrating the object. Entries in this category may take any form. However, some information systems provide the possibility of searching and sorting documentary references either by (a) suggesting a fixed format for all entries or (b) subdividing author, year, title, journal, and so on into separate data categories.

Origins of the Object: Cultural and Temporal

All objects of interest to museums have a spatial provenance; most objects have a temporal placement of some kind; and man-made artifacts can all be characterized according to their cultural origins. Because of the close (often overlapping) relationship between the terms used to designate time periods and cultural periods, it has been found convenient to place cultural and temporal origins together. Spatial provenance (geographical or political origins) are grouped separately.

With man-made artifacts, especially specialized collections such as motion pictures, it is possible to provide a lengthy list of categories for all the persons who have in some way been associated with creating the production. In the list that follows, provision has been made for only four groups of individuals. The persons responsible for the creation of *most* types of artifacts can be cataloged adequately within these classes.

21. Manufacturer, printer. The name of the firm (or occasionally the individual) that manufactured the object on a production basis,

printed a work of art, manuscript, book, map, photograph, or other ephemera or produced a motion picture.

22. Artist, photographer. The name of the creative individual, workshop, or school to which the object is currently attributed. For different kinds of objects this may be an artist, maker, designer, photographer, or motion-picture director. If multiple entries are made in this data category, the names of secondary artists or secondary (alternate) attributions will be sorted and listed as the equivalent of primary artists. Separate data categories may be added to provide for these.

23. Technician, artisan, lithographer. The name of the individual who contributed to the making of the object as a technician, stone carver, caster, or lithographer.

24. Author. The name of the author of a play, a motion picture, a book, or other written documents.

Temporal provenance may require, for different kinds of objects, as many as seven different data categories (paragraphs 25 to 31).

25. Date for display. A standard *number* or *numeric phrase* attached to the object by its possessor for use on labels to indicate the time of origin of the object (see also paragraph 31 below). This may be a probable date, a probable range of dates, or an approximation of the most probable date (e.g., c. 1750).

26. Earliest possible date. The earliest year to which the object can be attributed. This represents a limiting date only and need not approximate the actual date of origin. This data category is intended to be usable for searching and sorting purposes. Therefore, dates should be represented in a standard format consisting of an Arabic numeral preceded by a minus sign (for B.C.) or a plus sign (for A.D.). Known modern fakes should be given a modern date, not the date of the imitated style.

27. Latest possible date. See paragraph 26.

28. System.

29. Series.

30. Stage.

Geological and paleontological specimens are normally dated in a hierarchy of system, series, and stage rather than by reference to the Christian calendar. It is recommended that the terminology of the *Lexicon of Geological Names of the United States* be followed.

31. Cultural period. The *name* assigned to a particular time period (horizon or epoch) during which cultural traits and assemblages remained relatively stable within definable geographic or political areas. (Note: this class should be contrasted carefully with Develop-

mental stage or style, paragraph 32, and with Cultural classification, paragraph 33; see also paragraph 25.)

32. Developmental stage, style. The name assigned to a particular technological stage or style of construction, painting, decorating, etc. This is a formal or content unit, primarily, rather than either a spatially or temporally limiting dimension. Styles may be repeated by different cultural groups at different times and places. Developmental stage may also be used with natural science specimens to indicate immature forms, etc. Unless stated, adult maturity is assumed.

33. Cultural classification. In archaeological research a name is often assigned to objects with the explicit intention of placing them in a particular time-space-formal content context. The names used for these classificatory units may be broad or narrow in regard to any one of the three dimensions, but the emphasis is on the composite of the three dimensions rather than a temporal period (paragraph 31) or style of construction (paragraph 32).

Origins of the Object: Spatial

All museum specimens were either discovered or created at a particular place. With some classes of objects spatial provenance is normally described in terms of political units (countries, states, or provinces, and specific localities). With others, precise geographical placement is also significant, and with yet other classes, provision must be made for the geological structure. Each of these methods of designating spatial origins creates special kinds of problems with some collections.

Political provenance. Political provenance designations involve the specimen's description in terms of political units.

34. Place of discovery. Record the name of the place from which the object came or where it was discovered or created. This may be an undifferentiated statement of locality (i.e., paragraph 34 alone), or it may require a series of data categories (paragraphs 34a through 34g) in which are recorded hierarchically related political place names that can be searched, sorted, and listed either as individual data categories or sequentially from the largest through the smallest. As long as the largest data category in the hierarchy is used as defined, any subdivisions may be user defined for a particular collection (i.e., it is not necessary to use the entire hierarchy.) For example, in art museums it may be desirable to use only the Country of origin

(paragraph 34*b*) and one other data category as an undifferentiated statement of specific locality (say 34*c*).

34*a*.Continent	or	Ocean	or	Biogeographical region
34*b*.Country		Subarea (NE, SW, etc.)	)))	
34*c*.State or province		Island group	))	Entirely
34*d*.County		Island	))	user
34*e*.City or town		City or town	))	defined
34*f*. Site name		Site name	))	
34*g*.Specific address; directions to a site		Specific address;) directions to a) site)		

35. Place of origin (if different from place of discovery). Occasionally an artifact is discovered in a context that allows it to be placed spatially, temporally, and culturally somewhere other than where it originated in nature, as evidenced by its identifiable chemical and physical properties. An example might be copper *found* in a context of the Ohio Hopewell which *originated* in Upper Michigan and was probably carried into the Ohio region by prehistoric man. In such cases the place of origin should be recorded in a data category separate from the place of discovery. The subparagraphs described in paragraph 34 may also be used here if desired, but this will seldom, if ever, be necessary.

Geographical and geological provenance. In addition to or in place of political provenance designations, up to seven possible data categories may be required to record provenance in precise geographical terms and three to record geological provenance.

36. Locality or site number. In the natural sciences, including archaeology, sites where an object was collected or excavated are frequently given specific numbers in order to identify them precisely on maps and to summarize all data from that site. Consistency of format is essential for retrieval purposes.

37. Intrasite provenience.[16] In archaeology, data are frequently summarized by levels, squares, or other designations *within* a given site. In order to make such summaries possible, it is essential that

the record on every object contain a precise designation of exactly where it was found and that such data be recorded in a consistent manner for retrieval and sorting.

38. Township/range/section. When the township and range method of designating a specific locality is employed, the data should consistently be entered in a way that will facilitate the summarization of information by largest units and within this by smaller units. This is not possible with the normal engineering method of recording. However, one format that has been used successfully is shown in the following example: T23N, R15W, NW, NE, NE. The letters "T" and "R" (for township and range) are essential, and the numerals must have leading zeros (e.g., T03N will sort ahead of T23N, but T3N will not). The designations NW, NE, NE refer to ¼section, ¼¼section and ¼¼¼section.

39. Latitude/longitude. As with township/range/section designations, the data should be entered to facilitate summarization by largest units and within this by smaller units. This may be done either by always recording a composite entry with longitude first (e.g., 72°09′22″N, 108°27′02″E) or by prefacing each part of the entry with appropriate symbols (e.g., L072°09′22″N and LA108°27′02″E).

40. Other expressions of locality. Any method used for the precise designation of locality other than those described in paragraphs 38 and 39 (e.g., Marsden Squares, Global Reference Code) should be recorded so as to provide the same summarization possibilities discussed in paragraphs 38 and 39.

41. Altitude.

42. Depth.

In the natural sciences the precise altitude (or depth beneath the ocean or ground surface) where the specimen was collected is an important part of placing it in the proper environmental habitat. As a standard format it is suggested that there be a space between the data and the unit of measure, that there be no punctuation used, and that abbreviations be FT (for feet), MS (for meters), and FM (for fathoms).

43. Group.

44. Formation.

45. Member.

Geological and paleontological specimens are normally located in a hierarchy of geological units that name the layers or strata in accordance with standardized terminology in each region of the earth.

Description of the Object: Physical Characteristics

The physical and genetic attributes of biological specimens are, by definition, sufficiently dependable to be summarized in a recognized typological classification. In such cases the condition of the specimen (see paragraph 46) usually is the only physical characteristic that needs to be recorded. Man-made artifacts, however, are extremely variable—so much so that typological classification is often of little value. In searching, sorting, or summarizing artifacts, those that "belong together" frequently can be determined only by grouping objects of the same material, form, color, or size. In order to accomplish this, provision must be made to record these physical characteristics in separate, sortable categories.

46. Condition. The words used to record the condition of a specimen will vary considerably from one class of objects to another. Each curator should try to develop brief expressions (one or two words each) to express condition, and then use them in a consistent manner.

47. Material. The name of any material or materials that make up the object (e.g., a geological specimen) or out of which the object is constructed (e.g., a man-made artifact).

48. Technique. A brief statement of the methods that were used to create an artifact. In some cases standard phrases for describing techniques include references to the instruments or tools used as well as materials. However, a phrase such as PEN & INK is, in fact, an expression of technique. The terminology and phraseology commonly used in any particular discipline should be the guide to follow.

49. Medium. A standard word or phrase attached by the possessor to the object in order to describe the physical features adequately for use in labels, catalog entries, reproduction captions, etc. This entry may be the same as that for describing technique (paragraph 48).

50. Color. The colors used in an oil painting are usually so varied and difficult to describe that there is no reason to include them in a catalog record. However, color terms are searchable cataloging devices for objects such as American Indian pottery.

51. Form (shape). Form, like color, is a searchable cataloging device for ceramic vessels, textiles, basketry, many other classes of ethnographic and historic artifacts, and some biological specimens.

52. Dimensions, weight. In research projects in which dimensions or weight are to be summarized or otherwise manipulated for statistical purposes, separate data categories should be established for each measurement. However, a *descriptive* category may also be provided

so as to include in the catalog a general indication of the physical size of artifacts. Entries may be in any form desired (e.g., 16″ x 20″; 318 mmH, 216 mmW; etc.) since this class of data is not ordinarily used for computer sorting.

53. Features, attached parts. With some artifacts it is helpful to have a separate category for the description of attached parts or associated features without having to describe these parts or features as separate catalog items. A few brief words, for example, are often adequate to describe the frame of an oil painting, the handle of a ceramic vessel, the beaded overlay on a textile, or a bird's egg or nest.

54. Number of parts. Some artifacts (e.g., a tea set, a smoking kit, a miniature diorama) consist of several physically distinct objects thought of as a unit and cataloged as one record. For control purposes it is desirable to include in the catalog the number of separate objects that make up the single catalog record, even though the objects may not be individually described.

55. General description. It is not possible in a limited list of data categories to provide places for the recording of every physical attribute of every kind of object. Any significant remarks about additional physical characteristics (those *not* covered in paragraphs 46 through 54) should be recorded in this general category. Care should be exercised, however, to limit general remarks to brief and significant statements, and not to duplicate information recorded elsewhere.

Description of the Object: Content or Decoration

With art objects, photographs, books, maps, etc., the physical characteristics of an object may be of minor importance compared to what is portrayed in or on the object (i.e., its content). Somewhat related to content (in the sense of being separable from other physical characteristics) are the classes of data required to describe the decoration and inscriptions on artifacts.

56. Title. The title used by the possessor in his most recent catalog and/or his current files. Titles may be recorded in any language using the Latin alphabet (most computer systems do not make provision for others).

57. Language. The name of the language used in a book, manuscript, map, album, portfolio, motion picture, etc.

58. Specific subject(s). The specific subject(s) class should contain only the sortable and indexable key words for the subject matter

portrayed or discussed in the artifact being cataloged (see also paragraph 59). The terms used may be the names of real persons, fictional characters, mythological beings, deities, ships, events, or places (i.e., proper nouns), or they may be generic nouns.

59. General subject. A general description of the subject matter or scene represented or the decorative patterns employed, if these are not adequately conveyed by the terms used to record specific subjects (paragraph 58) and motifs (paragraph 61).

60. Inscriptions, markings. Marks, transcriptions, translations, transliterations, descriptions, or mention of major inscriptions or marks, usually those attributed to the artist, designer, artisan, or maker of the object, including but not limited to signature, date, dedication, inscribed title, and impression or cast number.

61. Decorative motif. The name only of a recognized, typical motif used to decorate the object. As with specific subjects (paragraph 58), this data class should contain only the sortable and indexable key words for the motifs with which the object is decorated.

Classification of the Object: Typological and Functional

The assignment of a type name to a specimen or artifact is the experts' way of using a single word or phrase to imply the composite of a rather precise physical description and genetic or phylogenetic relationship. It is a shorthand means of abbreviating a lengthy series of descriptive characteristics. The Linnaean system of classifying biological specimens is sufficiently well established in the biological sciences so that further description of a specimen's physical characteristics is considered unnecessary. With man-made objects the type concept is also used (e.g., in archaeology), but all artifacts do not fall as readily into established taxonomies as do their genetically related counterparts in the biological sciences.

62. Artifact types. Type names should not be used for artifacts unless the authority for the designation is shown (see paragraph 84). If both type and variety names are used, the precise authoritative type designation should appear first, followed by the abbreviation VAR (variety) and the variety name.

In the Linnaean system of classification an established hierarchy of taxa are recognized, and provision should be made for data categories corresponding to each level in this hierarchy.[17]

63. Phylum (division).

64. Subphylum (subdivision).

65. Superclass.
66. Class.
67. Subclass.
68. Infraclass.
69. Cohort.
70. Superorder.
71. Order.
72. Suborder.
73. Infraorder.
74. Superfamily.
75. Family.
76. Subfamily.
77. Tribe.
78. Subtribe.
79. Genus.
80. Subgenus.
81. Species.

At the infraspecific level numerous terms are used (at times inconsistently), and it usually is best to provide only two additional categories, one each for

82. Infraspecific rank.
83. Infraspecific name.

In the classification of specimens some disciplines (e.g., ornithology) employ almost the entire Linnaean hierarchy on a regular basis; others (e.g., botany) use only selected levels in the hierarchy; and yet others (e.g., conchology) vary the categories that are used so as to record specimens at the lowest level at which the specimen can be identified. This variability poses no major problems if there is a consistency in the pattern of recording individual specimens. Family, for example, should be recorded for *all* specimens, including those for which genus and species are known, if on *some* specimens family is the lowest identifiable taxonomic level.

The authority for a type designation, either in the Linnaean system or in a taxonomy of man-made artifacts, can usually be recorded using four data categories (see also footnote 15).

84. Author of taxon. The name(s) of the individual(s), recorded in standard bibliographic fashion for the appropriate discipline, who are credited with the type name or taxon of which the subject specimen or artifact is an example.

85. Year of publication. Year of publication for the document where the taxon is first identified.

86. Identifier. The name of the person who assigned the taxon or type name to this specimen.

87. Date identified. (See footnote 15 for techniques of recording dates.)

88. Preliminary object class. If it is considered to be either necessary or desirable to include the preliminary object classification in the recorded documentation on each object (see the following section, "Naming the Collections and/or Files"), a separate data category should be provided for this purpose. The acronyms for this entry are given in Table 3.

Informal typological and functional names are often given to museum specimens either in addition to or in place of the formal designations (paragraphs 62 through 87). The common name for a stuffed bird or animal, for example, may be recorded because the Latin name for the specimen has not been determined, or it may be used as an additional means of identification (e.g., to be used on display labels).

Two levels of classification are suggested for common names:

89. Broad informal class. The name of a broad functional, morphological or other class of objects of which the specimen or artifact is a member. Functional classifications should always be made according to some authoritative reference such as the *Outline of Cultural Materials.*[18]

90. Specific informal class. Any subdivision of the classification described in paragraph 89 that is found to be a logical way of properly identifying or naming the object in the catalog.

The common names given to natural science specimens are based upon many different kinds of characteristics. Consider, for example, the etymology of names such as MOCKINGBIRD, CATBIRD, or SCISSOR-TAILED FLYCATCHER. With man-made objects, the contents of paragraphs 89 and 90 should be considered as the classification and naming of objects on the basis of most obvious, original intended function or use. In a generalized historical museum, for example, one might start by classifying every object within one of the following twelve broad functional classes:

1. Personal artifacts
2. Household furnishings and equipment
3. Tools and equipment of crafts, trades, and professions (individualized activities other than household)
4. Buildings and building hardware
5. Art objects
6. Recreational objects
7. Religious objects
8. Military objects
9. Industrial objects (i.e., the artifacts of mass production, includ-

ing associated activities such as advertising, marketing, finance, and general office operation)

    10. Transportation devices

    11. Communication devices

    12. Records and documents

Art objects (number 5 above) might be further defined as those artifacts of man which were created originally for purely esthetic purposes (as opposed to applied or decorative art, in which the function of the object is primarily something other than esthetic, even though it is used as a vehicle for artistic expression). The classification and naming of art objects might then be organized as follows:

(paragraph 89)	*(paragraph 90)*	
Painting (or drawing; any two-dimensional original)	Oil	
	Water color	
	Pen and ink	
	Charcoal	
	. . . (etc., many more)	
Print (any two-dimensional reproduction)	Block print	
	Engraving	
	Etching	
	Lithograph	
	Photograph	
	Serigraph	
Sculpture (three-dimensional art)	Bronze (see note)	
	Ivory	
	Porcelain	
	Wood	
Minor arts	Crochet	Needlework
	Embroidery	Sailor's valentine
	Lace	Sampler
	Leatherwork	Scrimshaw
	Macrame	Tapestry
	Needlepoint	

(Note: Sculpture is assumed to be in the round unless the object name is followed by the further term BAS-RELIEF or HIGH-RELIEF.)

The names given to individual objets d'art in this organizational framework are based upon medium rather than function. The reason for this is that these are the names that artists and art historians (the specialists in this area) customarily give to the objects with which they work. However, in the total system, function is implied by the fact that these are all considered as "art objects" in the hierarchical structure, even though that term does not appear on the catalog sheet for any individual object.

Naming the Collections and/or Files

In most museum catalogs some method of separating the records of the collections into major groups is usually found to be desirable, even if it is nothing more than a separation on the basis of curatorial responsibility. If searches of unknown collections are ever to be feasible, the searcher must know the categories of data probably used to catalog each class of objects, but first he must be able to locate the museums having collections of the kind he wants to search. Each computerized catalog file (though not necessarily each record), therefore, must be identified by some kind of file designator term(s) to indicate the kinds of records it contains.

It is suggested that computerized museum catalog files be formalized according to one of the following: (1) If the collections are general and mixed and the file contains records of objects from more than one preliminaty object class, then *each record* should contain an entry for the preliminary object classification—recorded with the acronyms on Table 3 (data category 88)—and the name assigned to the entire file should indicate the characteristics of the mixed collection (an example might be KENTUCKIANA). (2) If collections and files are organized by preliminary object classification, then the file name or designator should include the appropriate preliminary object class acronym (Table 3). (3) If the collections and files are large, the file names may be yet finer subdivisions (e.g., entire files on CIVIL WAR GUNS, MAMMALS, COLEOPTERA, 19TH CENTURY FRENCH PAINTINGS). These file names may or may not be included in each record in the file (normally they are not). Therefore, each museum producing computerized catalog files should maintain an index of file names or designator terms so that a query can be directed first to the appropriate file(s) and then to the appropriate record(s).

5

Creating the Records:
Forms, Punch Cards, and Related Matters

DATA DOCUMENTATION (phase II on table 2) includes all aspects of manually recording the observations that are made about objects, typing or retyping the permanent documentation from an initial rough draft, manually transcribing portions of this documentation onto forms for computer entry, and then, perhaps, performing yet another typing operation or its equivalent in order to prepare punched cards or some other form of computer input. In the aggregate these activities are usually the most expensive part of any cataloging system. Because they involve the human use of relatively simple tools, they are also the types of activities most subject to cost increases as a result of inflation. However, a great deal can be done to minimize this category of expense by employing appropriate electromechanical aids and by the careful systemization of each task. There is seldom much that can be done to lessen the expenditure of human energy in the functions of object selection and data determination (the other major classes of human activity involved in museum cataloging), but the astute systems analyst will almost always notice ways in which the data documentation tasks can be performed more efficiently.

If careful consideration is given to the interrelated nature of the several data documentation functions and a serious attempt is made to perform these functions efficiently, it is possible to obtain the input to a computerized catalog as a by-product of clerical operations that are being performed for other purposes anyway, and it is usually possible to provide computer input with an expenditure for manpower that is not substantially different from that required to produce an adequate manual catalog. This does *not* mean either (1) that there will not be an added expenditure if there is inadequate documentation to begin with, or (2) that the total cost of maintaining a computerized catalog including manpower and the rental of computer equipment, will be no greater than the total cost of maintaining a manual catalog. However, with well-planned data documentation (i.e., where a serious attempt is made to achieve some measure of efficiency), it is possible to prepare records for computer entry *and enter them in the computer* as cheaply as the same records can be typed and filed in a manual catalog file. Retrieval of data from a computer file is a separate type of cost that should be compared with the cost of obtaining the same information from a manual file, and the fixed costs of maintaining a computer system are yet a third element in the total cost comparison. Here we are comparing only the costs of data documentation—up to the point of having a usable catalog file available.

These statements regarding costs must be recognized for what they are, namely, generalized observations. In most museums the existing costs of object documentation and cataloging are not known, so that there is no basis for determining whether some other way of performing these functions would be more or less expensive. What usually happens is that a first look at data documentation from the standpoint of efficiency of the total system reveals many possibilities for improvement (i.e., either for better information availability or for reduction of the cost of obtaining information or both), whether or not a decision is eventually made to adopt a computerized system.

Forms Design

The first step toward achieving an efficient cataloging system is in the design of adequate forms. A number of things are involved in forms design, but at the outset one should recognize that good forms are almost always a trade off or compromise between the needs of the individual who will be completing the form initially and the person who will be utilizing the data on the form, perhaps for keypunching or some other form of computer input.

The general goals to keep in mind when designing a form should always be do not rewrite unless absolutely necessary, do not retype unless absolutely necessary. This can also be stated: write it once, type it once. Before any thought is given to the actual design of forms, it is best to carefully review the entire data flow, from the original scratch notes of the curator or curatorial assistant who identifies, classifies, and codes the object to the completed computer record and/or hard copy documentation. In this review every task should be considered in the light of the general goals expressed above.

Numerous ways by which critical (and expensive) skills can be used most efficiently and duplicate efforts avoided will become obvious. A few ideas that others have found worthwhile are:

1. Give each curator a portable dictating device with which to record his identification and classification of the specimens. Clerical time is less expensive than curatorial time.

2. If labels are to be prepared for all specimens (e.g., with a natural history collection), obtain a machine such as the Friden Flexowriter to type the labels so that a paper tape can be produced simultaneously for use as input to the computerized catalog.

3. If the cataloging and object registration are carried out as a part of one integrated process, a single copy form can be typed once for eventual filing in the permanent documentation file (in registration number sequence); if this typing is done using a special typewriter head, it is possible to capture selected data for cataloging purposes by means of an optical scanner, thus avoiding the duplicate operations of typing and keypunching the same data.

4. If the existing documentation is in good shape, consider editing the present records by lining out unnecessary data and adding tag numbers, perhaps in a different color pencil or ink, and keypunch directly from the existing records rather than transcribing the records to a new form and then keypunching the data.

5. If the typed documentation is to be used only occasionally, as backup to a computer catalog, consider keypunching from manually prepared records and not typing the original records at all. (Why should a record be typed and then immediately retyped as input to the computer?)

After the data flow has been agreed upon, consideration can be given to the forms that will be needed to record data most efficiently. Forms design at its best is truly a type of artistic expression, and most of us will never become artists. As with other art media, though, a little fundamental knowledge and a lot of concentrated effort are the first ingredients of success. Some suggestions that will improve the overall efficiency of any form are:

1. Consider the flow of data as it will be recorded on the form. As nearly as possible allow the person who will be preparing the form to start at the top and work down.

2. Group related categories of data together. For example, do not provide a space at the top of a form for the name of the recorder or cataloger and a space at the bottom for the date recorded or cataloged. Sometimes it is helpful in filling out forms to have related

categories enclosed in boxes, but the same effect can be obtained by varying sizes of spaces.

3. After the first or second rough draft has been prepared, try to estimate the actual space needs with each category of data. For example, even though there is space on the page for it, do not extend a full line for data that will never be more than six or eight characters in length.

4. Whether a form is to be prepared manually or typed or both, always provide spaces with a vertical spacing equivalent to a normal two-space typewriter platen movement. For manual use anything less than this means an unnaturally cramped style of writing for most people. For typing, a normal platen movement, of course, is easier than having to make special adjustments for each line, and single spacing requires special care in placing the form in the typewriter to begin with. Instructions and line headings can be single spaced, or if the form is printed, they can be done in smaller-than-typewriter type.

5. Preprint on the form not just category headings and blank spaces but also any fixed data that is to be keypunched or otherwise entered as a part of a computer record. For example, tag numbers and field separator symbols should be preprinted at the appropriate places ahead of or behind each space; the name or acronym for the name of the museum should always be preprinted; and sometimes, if forms are designed for specialized data, the content of certain data categories other than the name of the museum may also be preprinted.

6. Forms can be prepared quite easily on an offset master duplicating device. Do not try to design a single form to be used into perpetuity for the recording of all different types of collections. Rather, design new forms as needed for each special collection, eliminating unnecessary categories, adding new categories as needed, and perhaps preprinting data that is fixed for that particular collection.

7. As a guide to key-punch operators, carry lines that designate blank spaces out so as to include all preprinted information that is to be entered in the computer. For example, the lines should include tag numbers and field separator symbols so that instructions can be given to the keypunch operator to punch everything that is underlined.

8. If forms are to be retained in manual files, provide spaces for the categories of data to be used for filing in the most convenient corner of the form. For example, if the forms are to be filed in letter-size filing cabinets (not in file folders), orient the data so that

the form is eleven inches across and eight and a half inches high and provide for the registration number (or whatever other category of data may be used for filing) in either the upper left or the upper right corner.

9. If most or all of the entries are likely to be from a limited number of possibilities and you want to control terminology carefully, use a short checklist type of entry, perhaps with a blank for the unusual but possible exception.

Most of these suggestions are illustrated in one way or another in figures 10 through 14.

Forms should be considered as just the first step in the total data documentation operation. When it is possible to determine in advance the information system and the method of data entry that will ultimately be used, the forms that are used to record the documentation initially can be designed to provide for the most efficient possible data conversion. Some information systems, of course, place more stringent requirements on the recording of data than others. In general the more tightly structured the records are (see page 38), the less room there is for flexibility in design of the forms to be used as input.

The principles of forms design can best be illustrated by examining the forms in figures 10 through 14. These forms were all designed to be used for the recording of either input to computerized museum catalogs or (in one instance) as input to something resembling a membership list.

Figure 10 is a form used to record data in the SELGEM system. Note that this system (and, thus, the form) requires that the first 14 characters of each 80 column line be structured in a precise manner. Each character or digit *must* be entered into the computer record in a certain location, and the form is designed to make it as easy as possible to record the data initially in the right place.

The form used for inventorying the extensive historical collections at the Margaret Woodbury Strong Museum (figure 11) provides for data categories that are consistent with those recommended by the Museum Data Bank Coordinating Committee (chapter 4). At the time the inventory was begun, the Strong Museum did not know what computer system might eventually be used, but it was assumed that it would be one of the systems described in this book. A somewhat arbitrary decision was made to print on the form the tag numbers and the field separators (i.e., = =) employed by the GRIPHOS system (as used by the Museum Computer Network, Inc.). If a decision is

ENTRY NUMBER

TRANS CODE:
2 = DELETE
3 = CHANGE
4 = NEW RECORD

1 MUSEUM   8
NUMBER

9

[0][1][0] [0][1] ARTIST
10   13

15 16   79 80

[0][2][0] [0][1] TITLE
10   13

15 16   79 80

[0][2]
13

15 16   79 80

[0][3][0] [0][1] SUBJECT
10   13

15 16   47 48

[0][2]
13

15 16   47 48

[0][3]
13

15 16   47 48

[0][4]
13

15 16   47 48

[0][5]
13

15 16   47 48

[0][6]
13

15 16   47 48

[0][4][0] [0][1] DATE OF
10   13   EXECUT.

15 16   79 80

[0][5][0] [0][1] MEDIA
10   13

15 [ ] OIL   [ ] WATER COLOR   [ ] PASTEL   [ ]
                                                 80
    [ ] MIXED [ ] UNCERTAIN   [ ] FRESCO

[0][6][0] [0][1] DIMENSIONS
10   13

15 16   79 80

[0][2]
13

15 [ ] SIGHT   [ ] APPROX.   [ ]
                                 80

[0][7][0] [0][1] OWNER
10   13

15 16   79 80

[0][8][0] [0][1] STREET
10   13

15 16   79 80

[0][9][0] [0][1] CITY
10   13

15 16   79 80

[1][0][0] [0][1] STATE
10   13

15 16   79 80

[1][1][0] [0][1] ZIP
10   13

15 16   79 80

[1][2][0] [0][1] SOURCE
10   13

15 16   79 80

[0][2]
13

15 16   79 80

[1][3][0] [0][1]
10   13

15 [ ] REPRODUCTION   [ ]
                        26

[0][2]
13

15 16   79 80

[1][4][0] [0][1] B.BLIO.
10   13   CITATION

15 16   79 80

[0][2]
13

15 16   79 80

[1][5][0] [0][1] SEE FILE
10   13

15   16   17

SI-1740
REV. 5-24-71

FIG. 10. Data recording form, NCFA Bicentennial Inventory of American
Paintings, Smithsonian Institution

78

Classification _____ 36 = =   Accession No. _____ 6 = =
Object _____ 32 = =   Identification No. _____ 106 = =
Location _____ 62 = =
Jacket File _____ 91 = =   Quantity _____ 136 = =

Title _____ 30 = =

Subject Repr. _____
_____ 38 = =

Inscription _____
_____
_____ 55 = =

Artist/ Author _____ 70 = =
Maker.
Mfr./ Printer _____ 74 = =

Type _____ 68 = =   Color(s)
Style _____ 64 = =   _____ 45 = =
Material/ Media _____ 48 = =
Technique _____ 46 = =
Decorative Motif _____ 42 = =
Design Layout _____ 43 = =

Country of Origin _____ 76 = =   Period/ Culture _____ 80 = =
Place of Origin _____ 78 = =   Display Date _____ 83 = =
Provenance _____ 178 = =   Earliest Date _____ 82 = =
   Latest Date _____ 84 = =

Dim: cm/ (in) _____ 51 = =

Negative No. B/ W :B- _____ Color: C- _____ Slide: S- _____ 60 = =

Condition _____
_____ 63 = =

Ident. Sources _____
_____ 95 = =

Donor _____ 12 = =   Address _____
Owner/ Lender _____ 102 = =   _____
Vendor _____ 14 = =   _____ 101 = =

Credit Line _____ 5 = =
Restrictions _____ 7 = =

Acquisition Cost _____ 3 = =   Appraisal Value _____ 104 = =

Description _____
_____
_____
_____
_____
_____ 35 = =

Received   (yr/ mo/ day) _____   First Appraisal
Accessioned (yr/ mo/ day) _____   Eval. Date _____ By _____
Cataloged   (yr/ mo/ day) _____
   Disposition Date _____
Cataloger _____   Recipient _____

   Method _____
   Value Received _____

Form No. 18-4/ 73

FIG. 11. Object documentation form, Margaret Woodbury Strong Museum

ultimately made to utilize this system, the forms will be ready for keypunching as they stand, *without retyping;* if a decision is ultimately made to adopt some other information system, a simple conversion program will have to be written to translate each line of data into proper input format for the system selected. But the forms will still be usable *without retyping.*

Working with somewhat the same assumptions (i.e., not knowing what information system would finally be adopted), the Kentucky Library Museum (figures 12A and 12B) decided to simply use the paragraph numbers from the MDBCC data strategy statement *as if* they were the tags that eventually would identify the kinds of information recorded in each space on the form. A translation of these numbers will probably be necessary to make them intelligible within the information system that ultimately is adopted. However, the writing of a simple conversion program to accomplish this is far less time consuming than it would be to go back and manually enter the "correct" tag numbers on every form before it could be keypunched or otherwise converted to machine-readable form.

The form used by the Arkansas Archeological Survey to capture data on archaeological sites in the state (figure 13) is an example of a special purpose catalog form. The existing documentation file was built up over many years and includes information on individual sites that is extremely varied both as to quantity and quality. Prior to entering the data into the computerized catalog, the existing documentation on each site was reviewed, analyzed, and reformatted, using the form illustrated. The form, of course, was designed so that it would be prepared manually and in one typing operation (in this case on a Magnetic Card/Selectric Typewriter) entered into the computer file. The form illustrated is *not* an archaeological site survey form that is used in the field—there is another form that is used for that purpose. This one was designed specifically to capture, for computer entry, data on the 6,000+sites previously recorded in the State of Arkansas.

Figure 14 is included here, in part, to illustrate the multiple use that can be made of a generalized information system once it is set up and operating. The Museum Data Bank Coordinating Committee, as one of its several activities, is attempting to develop an inventory of all the computerized catalogs maintained by museums and related institutions. The GRIPHOS system was already established at the instutition where the executive office was located. Therefore, it was a simple matter to establish a special set of tag numbers (note the

80

KENTUCKY MUSEUM - WESTERN KENTUCKY UNIVERSITY

WKLM   GENERAL
BOWLING GREEN, KENTUCKY   2   WORKSHEET

Object Identification, Location, & Value:
Record # _____ 1 Addit. Data_____ 5 # Items_____ 6

Other Rec. #'s_____ _____ 3 Pres. Val./Date_____ 8

Negative: B/W B-_____ 4 Color C-_____ 4 Slide S-_____ 4

Location _____ 7 Rec. Stat. _____

History of Object as Specimen, Artifact, or Record:
Collector/Date _____ 9 Acquisition Meth./

Expedit./Date _____ 11 Date_____

Recorder/Date _____ 12 _____ 14

Donor _____ 16 Vendor_____

Lendor_____ 17 Ownership Hist._____

_____ 19

Document. Ref. _____ 20

Credit Line _____

Origin of Object, Cultural & Temporal:
Mfr./Prtr./Tech._____ 21

Artist/Photog./Auth._____ 22

Dates: Display _____ 25 Earliest_____ 26 Latest_____ 27

(GEO) System _____ 28 Series _____ 29 Stage _____ 30

Culture: Period_____ 31 Classif. _____ 33

Stage/Style _____ 32

Origin of Object, Spatial:
Country of Or. _____ 34b State of Orig._____ 34c

Town/Township _____ 34d Site_____ 35

Description of Object, Content/Decoration:
Title _____ 56

Language(s) _____ 57

Spec. Subj.(s) _____ 58

Gen. Subj. _____ 59

Inscript./Marks_____ 60

Dec. Motif _____ 61

FIG. 12A. Object documentation form, Kentucky Library Museum

Object's Physical Characteristics:
Condition _____ 46

Material _____ 47

Technique _____ 48

Color(s) _____ 50

Form (shape) _____ 51

Dim.:wt/size _____ 52

Features _____ 53

Parts _____ 54

Addit. Descrip. _____

_____ 55

Classification of Object, Typological & Functional:
Genus _____ 79 Species _____ 81

Taxon Auth./Date_____ 84

Identifier _____ 86 Date _____ 87

Prim. Class._____ 88 Broad Cl. _____ 89

Spec. Class._____ 90 Object _____ 91

INTRA-MUSEUM USE ONLY

Date & Initial:
Acknowledged _____   First Appraisal _____
Agreement Form _____   Eval. Date _____by_____
Registered _____   Disposition Date _____
Donor Card _____   Recipient _____
Catalogued _____   Method _____

MISC. NOTES _____
_____
_____
_____
_____

KMWS-1

FIG. 12B. Object documentation form, Kentucky Library Museum

SITE KEY-PUNCH FORM   State Survey No._____ 806

Site name_____ 830 Reporter's no._____ 906
Other name(s) or
Designations_____ 930

County_____ 808 Map ref._____ 809

Coordinates T_____, R_____, S_____, ¼_____, ¼¼_____, ¼¼¼_____ 812
Instructions to site_____

_____ 813

Site size_____ 833 Landform_____ 814

Water source_____ 831

Features_____

_____ 876

Material_____

_____ 875

Cult. class._____ 840

Cult. stage_____ 842

Site usage_____ 838

Present condition_____

_____ 863

Coll./excav._____

_____ 839

Remarks_____

_____ 835

Pubs./ms./papers_____

_____ 920

Reporter_____ 816 Date_____ 820

Address_____ 817

Owner_____ 902 Tenant_____ 904

Address_____ 903 Address_____ 905

Accession nos._____

_____ 870

Photo neg. nos_____

_____ 860

Date Survey Visit_____ 828 Date Rcpt._____ 832

Elevation_____ 824 Exposure_____ 822 Depth deposit_____ 837

Nature of deposit_____ 336

FIG. 13. Site documentation form, Arkansas Archaeological Survey

MDBCC 2==   M20==

_____   STATE, REGION, OR NATION

_____ 1005==   PROJECT NAME   M4==

DBA ___   CONTACT NAME   M24==
DBP ___   TITLE   M25==
DBS ___   INSTITUTION   M26==
ADM ___ M6==   ADDRESS   M27==
PR ___   CITY,STATE,ZIP   M28==
CML ___   SECONDARY CONTACT   M29==

CORRESPONDENCE _____

_____   M40==

==

/NATURE OF ORGANIZATION/   IF a Museum:

| MUSEUM ___   GENERAL DISCIPLINE M10==   SOURCE OF SUPPORT   M16==
| MUSEUM CONSORTIUM ___   ART ___   PRIVATE ___
| COMMERCIAL ___   HISTORY ___   CITY ___
| GOVT. AGENCY   SCIENCE ___   COUNTY ___
| Local ___   M8==   ART/HIST ___   STATE ___
| State ___   ART/SCI ___   NATIONAL ___
| National ___   HIST/SCI ___   COLLEGE/UNIV. ___
|_____ __   ART/HIST/SCI ___   _____ ___

SPECIFIC DISCIPLINE   FUNCTIONS/SERVICES   M18==
                                                          EXHIBIT ___
_____   EXHIB/RESEARCH ___
_____   M12==   EXHIB/EDUCATION ___
                                                          EXHIB/RESEARCH/EDUC ___
ORIENTATION OF MUSEUM   M14==   _____ ___
CHILDREN ___   GENERAL PUBLIC ___
UNIV. COMMUNITY ___   _____ ___

==

/SUBJECT OF COMPUTER FILES/
GENERAL, SPECIFIC AND NUMBER OF RECORDS

_____   M32==
_____   M32==
_____   M32==
_____   M32==
_____   M32==

COMPUTER SYSTEM _____   M30==

STATUS _____   M35==
REFERENCES _____

_____
_____   M42==

FIG. 14. Data Bank Inventory form,
Museum Data Bank Coordinating Committee

letter M preceding numbers) to indicate the categories of data that were to be recorded. With the first communication, the information at the top of the form is completed, and if it is a museum, the institution is classified according to the data categories in the second part of the form. Finally, the kinds of data and the number of records are recorded in the lower portion. Needless to say there are many institutions that are, at this writing, only in the first stages of developing a computerized catalog. Entries are made under STATUS (category M35 = =) from the time of INITIAL INQUIRY until the system is OPERATIONAL.

Creating Computer Input

In order to create a *computer* record it is necessary to have a form that is suitable for entry and then to convert information on that form into one or another of the several input media that are understandable to the computer: oblong holes on cardboard cards, round holes in paper tape, magnetic spots on lucite tape, etc. In the introduction to computing activities these media were discussed as either input to or output from the computer. However, for the computer to operate at all, it is essential that some intervening machine be employed to create the *input* initially. There is a wide variation in the different machines that are available to accomplish this function, and most of them are made by at least two or more manufacturers.

On the following pages some of the types of equipment that are best suited to the creation of museum catalog input are discussed.

Card punches. By far the most common means of converting data to machine-readable form is through the use of machines such as the IBM 29 card punch, which is used to punch the familiar 80-column cards. Card punches are manufactured by other companies as well as IBM, but the 80-column card, originated in its present form by IBM, has been the standard form of data entry for so long that some information systems structure their internal computer records to conform to the 80-character format. One of the major advantages of punched cards is the ready availability in most communities of card punch machines on college campuses and elsewhere. Because of this availability, the use of a card punch as an input device is probably the most convenient method and hence the least costly for computer programs that utilize only moderate amounts of input data. The two major drawbacks of using card punches to create catalog input are: (1) the psychological impact of perpetuating dependence upon 80-character records or multiples thereof—with present equipment this is no longer necessary and it is a deterrent to most efficient record structuring and (2) the problem of keeping punched cards in their proper sequence. With lengthy or unstructured records (i.e., records that are *not* 80 characters long) it is essential that punched cards be maintained in the same sequence from the time they are punched until they are processed as input to the computer files. There are ways in which this sequence can be controlled and checked when the cards are processed as computer input, but checks of this kind are unnecessary when the data are initially recorded on some input medium that makes it impossible for the serial order of entry to be changed (e.g., magnetic tapes, paper tapes).

Magnetic tape and card inscribers. Instead of keypunching cards it is possible to record data directly onto magnetic tape. There are several companies now manufacturing magnetic data inscribers. These data devices are very similar to card punches except that the output is a roll of magnetic tape with the encoded data recorded upon it. When the tape is used as input to the computer file, it is simply mounted on a tape drive and read in sequentially in the same manner that the punched cards would be read in sequentially on a card reader. The advantage of direct key-to-tape inscribers is that the data are maintained in serial form. The principal disadvantage is that there is no opportunity to scan the data visually for the purpose of correcting obvious errors before it has been entered as computer input.

Two machines, both manufactured exclusively by IBM, are modifications of the concept of direct entry of data onto computer-readable magnetic tape. As with any other input device, these machines have certain additional advantages and disadvantages. One of them, the IBM Magnetic Tape/Selectric Typewriter (MT/ST), was designed initially to be used in the preparation of manuscripts. Anything that is typed on this device can simultaneously be recorded on a small magnetic tape cassette and played back letter by letter, line by line, or in total at typewriter speeds while corrections are made manually at the appropriate places and the corrected manuscript is rerecorded on another tape. The tape cassettes, though, can also be used as input to a computer file if they are first run through a special machine that transfers the data from the cassette to a magnetic tape of the proper size and density to be used as computer input. In practice the conversion devices are relatively expensive, so that unless such a device is readily available, the MT/ST is not recommended as a device for the regular input of catalog data. The other machine, known as the IBM Magnetic Card/Selectric Typewriter (MC/ST), is similar to the MT/ST except that in place of the magnetic tape cartridge the typed data is simultaneously recorded on 3½-inch-by-8-inch magnetic cards. The cards are formatted to contain up to 50 lines of typed data with each line approximately 100 characters long. The MC/ST has one distinct advantage over the MT/ST: one model (known as the *Communicating* MC/ST) can be operated as a remote terminal (see next paragraph). Once the data has been recorded and perhaps corrected on the magnetic cards, a telephone alongside the machine is used to dial the computer center wherever it may be located, and the magnetic cards are read as input to the computer from the remote terminal location. The MC/ST is the normal means of data entry employed by the Arkansas Archeological Survey. At the University of Arkansas computer center, data entered from the terminal are converted for processing as input to the GRIPHOS information system.

Remote on-line terminals. The MC/ST when used with the terminal attachment is a specific example of a general class of input devices called remote on-line terminals. These terminals look like electric typewriters with a few extra switches, and they are in fact not much more difficult to use than an electric typewriter. The only difference is that the terminal's keyboard is connected, either permanently or through telephone lines when the circuits are open, to a central computer located elsewhere. The terminals may be no further removed from the computer than in separate buildings on a university campus, or the terminals and the computer may be thousands of miles apart. In either case the procedures are similar. The terminal operator types a code word to identify himself. The computer responds by typing on the remote terminal typewriter in front of the user a signal showing that the lines are open and that the operator can proceed. The operator then enters the data directly into the computer. When he gives the computer an "end" signal, it prints out on the remote terminal typewriter what has been recorded at the computer center on either magnetic type or a magnetic disk. Remote on-line terminals are manufactured by a number of different companies, and they may be used either as a typewriter with terminal attachment or in a number of other different ways with special attachments such as a paper tape punch (see next paragraph), the magnetic card device described in the preceding paragraph, or with a cathode ray tube display in place of having the computer type hard copy on the terminal typewriter. Each of these has certain advantages and disadvantages. However, the one general characteristic of remote on-line terminals that is particularly desirable for museum applications is the fact that they make it possible to do all the computing operations in a time-sharing mode (see page 26). The fixed costs of maintaining a computer system are substantial enough so that a near-full-time operation is essential. With most museums this means some form of cooperative effort or time sharing. Remote on-line terminals, operated as part of a time-sharing system, give one the illusion of having his own computer without having to pay for it on a full-time basis. This will be discussed in greater detail when we consider catalogs of the future (chapter 8).

Paper tape punches. The range of possible input devices that are available begins to be apparent when one examines paper tape punches. At the National Museum of Natural History, for example, electric typewriters with paper tape attachments are now regularly used to type the labels that are attached to specimens. The punched paper tapes that are automatically produced as the labels are typed serve as input to the various catalogs produced using the SELGEM information system (figure 22, page 106). Similarly, if a catalog system for a library or museum is card oriented, it may be desirable to have two or three 3-by-5-inch cards prepared for each entry as soon as a book or other object is acquired, and it is imperative that these cards be prepared correctly. The input data may be typed as for any other form of conversion to produce a punched paper tape. The tape is then rewound and used to control preparation of the additional cards on the typewriter immediately after each entry has been typed. The correctness of each entry can be verified visually before the operator goes on to the next entry. The roll of punched paper tape, of course, can be delivered to the computing center for input processing whenever convenient.

A remote on-line terminal with a paper tape attachment presents yet another completely different dimension of catalog input. An example of this method of input is provided by the work of Dr. Sylvia Gaines at Arizona State University. A remote terminal typewriter with paper tape attachment was taken to an archaeological site some 400 miles distant from the computer center used to process the data. Data was entered off-line (i.e., with the terminal not connected to the computer), producing both a hard copy for visual inspection and a simultaneous paper tape. At certain hours of the day telephone lines were used to connect the terminal to the computing center, and the paper tapes were then "read" into the computer files at the maximum physical speed of the remote terminal typewriter. The remote terminal typewriter was also used, of course, to correct data previously recorded and to retrieve data appropriate to carrying on the archaeological excavation. The paper tape attachment was used only as an adjunct to putting accurate data into the computer files.

Magnetic ink/optical mark readers. Two methods of data input that may offer the best solutions to specific problems are the magnetic ink character recognition (MICR) and optical mark reading devices. The former was designed for banks and is still used primarily by them. Before issuing checks to a depositor, the bank prints its identification number and the depositor's account number on each one. The characters are printed with ink that contains iron oxide in a visually readable type font. After a customer writes a check, the first bank handling it imprints the amount of the check in a similar way. The inks can then be read magnetically by machines as well as visually by people, and the data can be converted to computer input without any clerical intervention.

Optical mark reading devices are more readily available to most persons than MICR readers and do not require the special equipment to imprint the records initially that is required for these. In marking, a small line is drawn on an input document (card or paper) with a pencil. The locations where lines are drawn on any document are read by an optical reader, either on-line (data are read directly into the computer) or off-line (data are punched into cards). Input documents may be specially designed punched cards marked with pencil in the appropriate data fields or they may be special paper forms of other sizes. Most persons associated with teaching have probably used optical mark reading devices to grade papers at one time or another. Standardized programs available on many college campuses offer such test-grading services to faculty members. The only requirements are that the test scores be recorded with suitable pencils on the standard multiple-choice forms that are provided and that a key be sent to the computer center so that the right and wrong answers may be accumulated and grade curves calculated accurately. Optical mark readers are designed to be efficient input devices with multiple-choice type data. Some of the entries in a museum catalog may be structured in the form of multiple-choice questions. However, most catalog entries are in the form of words or short phrases. Because of this, optical mark readers probably have limited use in museums, although this method of accumulating data should not be ignored.

Optical character readers. Magnetic ink or optical mark readers are sometimes called *optical scanning devices* because of their ability to scan and interpret significant patterns of ink or pencil markings in the same manner that the human eye scans and interprets these patterns. Some of these devices are not truly optical in nature, ᵣor they can comprehend only magnetic patterns. However, there is a similar category of input devices, called *optical character readers,* that are capable of scanning documents printed with any legible ink and interpreting the ink patterns that correspond to letters, numerals, and other special characters. Optical character readers normally require that input documents be typed with a special type font. One types out the documentation on a typewriter such as an IBM Selectric (with 10-character-to-the-inch spacing and a carbon ribbon), using a typewriter head having characters of a style that is perhaps a little unusual but certainly readable. The typed pages are then placed in a special optical reader that converts the data to a magnetic tape or disk usable as computer input. Experiments with optical character readers that have been conducted by the Information Systems Division of the Smithsonian Institution indicate that this is the least expensive technique available for the conversion of mass quantities of data from typewritten form to computer input. The conversion of typewritten documentation about individual museum specimens into suitable form for input to a computerized catalog is one of the major costs in any computerized museum cataloging system, and anyone designing a new catalog system should give serious consideration to this form of data input. Beyond a doubt optical character readers will become much more readily available within the next few years than they are today.

6

Computer Systems to Do the Work

IN AN earlier chapter (pages 34–35) information systems were defined as computer program packages that are designed to accomplish a number of logically integrated and related word manipulation activities; and it was pointed out (page 43) that there are between 150 and 200 information systems in use today. Many of these, of course, are specialized systems that would not be particularly useful in a museum environment. However, even when the specialized information systems are eliminated, there is still a large number of generalized information systems that potentially could be used for museum cataloging work.

In this chapter, seven information systems will be described in some detail. It would be possible, of course, to include cursory descriptions of numerous computer program packages that might be used to prepare museum catalogs, but this would amount to little more than a catalog listing itself. We have chosen instead to provide a small number of more detailed descriptions. It is hoped that enough information is included to enable the potential user to ask the right kinds of questions about any other system he might encounter.

Four criteria have been employed to determine which information system descriptions to include:

1. First consideration has been given to the description of systems presently being widely used for museum cataloging purposes. Beyond a doubt SELGEM and GRIPHOS are used by more different museums for this purpose than any of the other information systems. Since the characteristics of these two systems are quite different in certain respects, it was essential that first priority (including the most detailed descriptive accounts) should be given to them. The

other systems described here have not been as widely used for museum cataloging purposes as SELGEM and GRIPHOS, but in most cases they have been used in applications at more than one museum.

2. A few of the systems are included in order to exemplify particular operating characteristics that may be important in certain kinds of situations. For example, GIS is important because it has a rather sophisticated capability for the hierarchical structuring of records. This is a desirable attribute whenever there is any substantial data redundancy from one record to another. ELMS is described, even though its present use is limited to library cataloging, because it exemplifies the idea of both entry and retrieval of data through cathode-ray tube terminals. The unnamed system at the W. H. Over Museum is included as an example of what can be done with special programs written for a relatively small computer. GIPSY and TAXIR have some elements of both demonstrated utility for museum cataloging and special attributes that could be significant.

3. With the exception of the system written for the W. H. Over Museum, the information systems described here are all available for installation at museums other than where they are presently operating. The costs vary considerably from one to another, and the extent to which they are supported (i.e., by institutions rather than individuals, by active development of new or improved capabilities, by continued improvement of documentation, by having individuals available to handle problems) also varies considerably from one to another of the systems. However, they are in one way or another available for use elsewhere.

4. Finally, the systems described here are limited to those presently operating within the United States of America. Dr. John L. Cutbill has developed a program package called CGDS, which is being used by several museums in England and as a basis for experimental work for IRGMA (the Information Retrieval Group of the Museums Association in Great Britain) and the ICOM Committee on Documentation. Another system, entirely compatible with the principles expressed in this book, is being developed for the Canadian Inventory of Cultural Materials, and comparable systems are in various stages of development by museum groups in Germany, France, Switzerland, and elsewhere. The reasons for not including descriptions of these systems are several. The most important, though, is the fact that our objective here is to exemplify the principles of computerized museum cataloging using information systems that museums in North America might employ for this purpose.

A sincere attempt has been made in the preparation of these information system descriptions to be as objective as possible. Each of the systems has characteristics that make it usable in certain kinds of situations, but none of the systems described here is perfect enough to be *the* recommended system for all museums to adopt. Neither the Museum Data Bank Coordinating Committee nor I recommend any of these systems as being "the only way to go."

In preparing these descriptions, I first sent out a detailed questionnaire to the developers of the systems selected for inclusion in order to obtain as much information as possible in a comparable form. The firm of Ernst & Ernst was then employed to review the questionnaires, to review all published data on these systems, to visit with the developers of as many as possible, and to write the initial reports upon which this chapter is based. It was not my objective or the objective of Ernst & Ernst to evaluate the design of any of these systems or to compare the capabilities of any one of them with any of the others. Rather, the objective was to describe each of the systems in sufficient detail to enable the reader to decide for himself whether that system was suitable to meet his needs, after considering its operating capabilities, probable costs, and the support he could expect to receive from the developers.

The cost of utilizing the different systems has been a special area of frustration throughout this study. Estimates of start-up costs (those elements of cost necessary to acquire a program package and make it operational at a new location) are included with most of the package descriptions. However, operational costs (the recurring day-to-day costs of computer processing in order to build and update collection master files, perform information inquiries on data in these files, and retrieve the data for collection documentation needs) are not available at most locations, and when they are available, they are the result of such divergent internal pricing policies (i.e., policies regarding the rates charged for computer time and the ways these rates are applied) that they would not be usable as guides to a museum considering adoption of a particular system at some other location.

For example, a comparative study of the *same information system* (GRIPHOS) at two different locations, one where it is run on an IBM 370/155 with model 3330 disks and one where it is run on an IBM 360/50 with model 2314 disks, revealed (not surprisingly) that the time required to perform a certain function on the 360 was approximately twice the time required to do the job on the 370.

However, to further compound the problem, the charge to the museum for use of the 360 was $200 per machine hour, whereas the charge for the 370 at the other institution was only $100 per machine hour. The net cost of doing the work on the slower and smaller computer, thus, was actually four times as great as the cost to do the same work on the larger computer at another installation.

The Museum Data Bank Coordinating Committee files contain operational cost data on some of the information systems described here, and this information will be made available to anyone who may need it. However, the variables are so numerous that it is impossible to generalize about the costs of operating under any particular system without knowing how the system will be used and how charges for computer usage will be determined.

SELGEM
Package Description

Background

SELGEM, an acronym for SELf-GEnerating Master, is a package of generalized computer programs developed for use by museums for general information processing, including collection documentation, and for related research-oriented projects. It is designed to develop and maintain master files containing categorized data on collection objects, and to provide the capability to retrieve the information from the master files for the collection documentation needs of a museum.

SELGEM is described as a generalized type system because of its flexibility to be adapted to an individual museum's processing and documentation needs. It consists of approximately twenty-five basic programs (see table 5), designed to perform such functions as data input, file updating, editing, report writing, retrieval and miscellaneous utility functions. Each program consists of a set of parameters designating the manner in which the programs can be tailored to produce specific results. For example, in one instance the parameters of a report writing program may be set up to produce a catalog index from data retrieved from a collection master file. In a different situation a new set of parameters could be developed for the same report writing program to produce specimen labels from selected data retrieved from the collection master file.

SELGEM is a product of the Information Systems Division of the Smithsonian Institution, whose director is Mr. Stanley Kovy.

Table 5
List of Basic SELGEM Programs

Input programs	S E L 1 1 Ø —Paper tape record formatter
	R E A D P A —Generalized paper tape conversion
	S E L O C R —Optical character recognition conversion
	*S E L F C P —Punch card formatter program
Update and file maintenance program	S E L U P D —Master file update program
Editing programs	S E L E P T —Category and data frequency report
	S E L E X R —Sort program; category and data frequency report
	S E L C S H —Missing category search program
	S E L P A T —SELGEM format editing program
Utility programs	S E L M R G —Master file merge program
	S E L C O L —Master file collate program
	S E L K E Y —File sort key generator program
	S E L K E S —Generated key sort program
	S E L I B R —Library maintenance program
	S E L D R P —Data reconfiguration program
	S E L U B K —Master file to fixed length output program
Report writing programs	S E L L S T —Master file list program
	S E L R P V —Report writer–variable format program
	S E L T O T —Tabulator and statistical interface program
Query and retrieval programs	S E L E X T —Master file query and retrieve program
	*S E L L Q P —Latitude/longitude coordinate retrieve program
	*S E L I F S —Inverted file search program
Indexing programs	S E L K W X —Key word index build program
	S E L K W P —Key word print master index program
	S E L K F P —Key file print program

*Optional SELGEM programs

Its codevelopers are Mr. Reginald A. Creighton, Manager—Information Retrieval and Indexing Group, and Mr. James J. Crockett, Manager—Software Systems and Program Maintenance. In 1970 the development of SELGEM was accelerated through support by the National Museum of Natural History and the Information Systems Division of the Smithsonian Institution. It originated out of an earlier system called SIIR (Smithsonian Institution Information Retrieval) that had been previously used for information processing in the Institution.

Within the Smithsonian organization, eight affiliates use SELGEM on the computer located at the Information Systems Division. The National Museum of Natural History is the predominant user within this group. Outside of the Smithsonian Institution, SELGEM is offered without charge to any interested, noncommercial institution. Several university-operated museums and governmental agencies make up the independent group using SELGEM on their own computers.

SELGEM is being used to maintain the collection documentation on several kinds of curatorial, bibliographic, archival, and registration data, including:

1. Specimen slides.
2. Lecture notes.
3. Correspondence.
4. Phenomenon event records.
5. Interest profiles for data dissemination.
6. Catalogs, type registers, and checklists for collections.
7. Registry of tumors in lower animals.
8. Photograph dissemination.
9. Political slogans, mottos, and banners.
10. Dental paleopathology.

The most common approach taken in the use of SELGEM has been to develop formal data recording procedures and use the SELGEM programs to convert the data into computer master files by types of collections. SELGEM programs are used to retrieve, classify, and produce printed documentation output from the master files.

The SELGEM programs are designed for individual job (batch) processing, which requires the data to be manually conveyed to the computer for processing. At the Smithsonian Institution the system does not utilize data communications and teleprocessing equipment for transmitting data to the computer or for processing data files in a real-time manner.

SELGEM programs were developed on the Honeywell computer equipment at the Smithsonian Institution. The equipment on which SELGEM currently operates is described as Model H 2015, 96K memory, 6 tape drives (7-track, 800 bits per inch) and 3 disk drives (not required by SELGEM). The computer system requires a card reader and a card punch device. The software requirements for SEL-GEM include a COBOL compiler and sort program. Most of the SELGEM programs can operate within a 64K computer memory. File manipulation utility programs are provided as part of the SEL-GEM program options.

SELGEM, when used outside the Smithsonian Institution, has been adapted in several instances to computers other than Honeywell. These include Control Data 6400 and 3100; IBM 360 (Models 30 and 40); Univac 1106 and 1110; and GE 625. The capability to readily convert SELGEM to non-Honeywell equipment by the outside users has been attributed to the SELGEM programs being available in the COBOL language.

System Description

The system description of SELGEM will include the several elements that make up the processing system: the file design and data structure, the information processing flow and the functions of the related computer programs, and data indexing functions.

File design and data structuring. SELGEM data files are processed and maintained on magnetic tape, and the records are organized for sequential processing. There are three types of files used in SELGEM:

1. External media file. Typically prepared by a user's own program and not as a result of SELGEM program procedure. In the SELGEM information processing flow that follows, three types of external media files are illustrated: punched cards, paper tape, and optical character reading equipment output files.

2. Transaction file. Prepared by a SELGEM program from one of the three types of external media files. The function of the SEL-GEM programs is to take the different external media forms, strip off extraneous coding and characters that are peculiar to it, arrange the data in a standard format, and write the data on the transaction file.

The transaction file record contains seven fields and is formatted as an 80-column card (figure 15). The transaction codes used in field 2 of the transaction card instruct the SELGEM programs as to how the data in the transaction card is to be placed in the master file. These codes are shown in table 6. The purpose of the transaction file record is to furnish data to create or change a master file record. Each transaction card creates one line within a master file record.

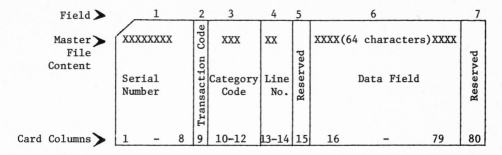

FIG. 15. SELGEM transaction card format

3. Master file. Used for the permanent data base, whose records are continually updated by a transaction file. Query and retrievals are usually performed using this type file.

The data structure of the SELGEM master file resembles closely the format of the transaction file, the only difference being fields 2, 5, and 7 are omitted in the master file record.

Table 6
Master File Update Transaction Codes

Transaction Code	Meaning	Performance
4	ADD	Enters data into the file from columns 16–79 of the transaction record, creating a line in the master file
3	CHANGE	Places the data bracketed by cent (¢) signs on the card into the corresponding positions of a line in the master file, replacing the previous contents of those character positions
2	DELETE	Removes from the masterfile the record reference by the serial number contained on the transaction. All the data lines in the record are deleted
1	PUNCH	Causes a transaction card to be punched for each line of the record referenced by the serial number
5	PUNCH AND DELETE	Performs the same function as transaction 1 "PUNCH" except that the data punched is deleted from the master file
6	REPLACE STRING	For the serial number and category code indicated, this function places the data bracketed by cent (¢) signs into the data string at the location indicated by the argument string

The following fields make up each line of the master file record:
1. Serial number (8 digits), record identification.

2. Category code (3 digits), field identifictation—a number to identify a data category.

3. Line number (2 digits), sequential number to control the number of lines of data used within a record.

4. Data field (64 characters), the data content for the particular category code and line number.

In terms of size, a unit record may contain up to 999 categories of data, and each data category may contain up to 99 lines of 64 data characters each.

The content of the data field may be a free-form text or a fixed-format of uniform size. Although there are no subdivisions within the 64-character field, the SELGEM programs that read the master file record are capable of interrogating the entire 64-character field or subdivisions within it.

At the beginning of the master file is a directory record that may be created at the option of the SELGEM user. This record defines the data categories that comprise the records stored in that particular file. Table 7 illustrates a typical directory record. The category codes are numbers assigned to the data categories.

The hierarchical structuring of master file records is available at the user's option. Hierarchical structuring in the SELGEM system is accomplished by a sequential relationship of the serial number and category code number. The manner in which the user assigns these numbers to the fields within a record determines the structuring effect to be achieved when the records are retrieved from the master file. Three rules apply to hierarchical structuring:

1. Records at lower echelons in the hierarchy must contain category code identifications numerically greater than records at higher echelons in the hierarchy.

2. Category codes that identify the first item of data of each echelon must be available in each record at that level.

3. Sets of data at each echelon in the hierarchy must be identified by unique serial numbers.

Figure 16 illustrates a portion of a hierarchical master file record in SELGEM applying the above rules. The tree-structuring effect that would be achieved when this record is retrieved is illustrated by the tree-structure schematic in figure 17.

The alternative to hierarchical master file structuring available to the SELGEM user is the unit record method of structuring. This method uses the full card approach illustrated in the transaction and master file data structuring discussed previously. Unit record

Table 7
Example of a Master File Directory Record

SERIAL	CATEG	LINE	DATA
00000000	005	01	ACCESSION NUMBER
		02	REMARKS
	006	01	ARTIST
		02	REMARKS
	010	01	ARTIST'S LIFE DATES
		02	REMARKS
	015	01	ARTIST'S NATIONALITY
		02	REMARKS
	020	01	TITLE
		02	REMARKS
		03	REMARKS
	025	01	DATE OF EXECUTION
		02	REMARKS
	030	01	MEDIUM
		02	REMARKS
	035	01	SUPPORT
		02	REMARKS
	040	01	DIMENSIONS
		02	REMARKS
	045	01	SIGNATURE
		02	REMARKS
	046	01	PRIMARY INSCRIPTIONS
		02	REMARKS
	050	01	ACQUIRED
		02	REMARKS
	051	01	ACQUISITION DATE
	052	01	PREVIOUS OWNER
	055	01	SUBJECT MATTER
	060	01	LOCATION
		02	REMARKS

versus hierarchical record structuring can be illustrated by comparing the file records illustrated in figures 18 and 19. In figure 18, an example of a unit record approach in SELGEM, 48 items of data must be carried for the employee "Jones." In figure 19, however, an example of carrying the same employee data record in a hierarchical structure, economies due to reduced file size may be achieved because only 23 items of data would have to be carried for employee "Jones."

Information processing flow. The computer programs that make up the basic SELGEM system are of seven types (figure 20):

1. Input programs.
2. Update and file maintenance programs.
3. Report writing programs.

4. Query and retrieval programs.
5. Indexing programs.
6. Data editing programs.
7. Utility programs.

Several optional programs have been included within the scope of the SELGEM processing capability described here. Their availability, however, requires a special request to the Smithsonian Information Systems Division. These optional programs will be noted as such in the descriptions that follow.

The system description of SELGEM is presented in a data flow sequence to illustrate the manner in which the computer programs interrelate as a functional system to provide the planned information needs of a museum. The narrative that follows describes the steps of a system approach using SELGEM. The list of programs in table 5 may be helpful as an occasional reference to understand the function of a program when referred to by its SELGEM name.

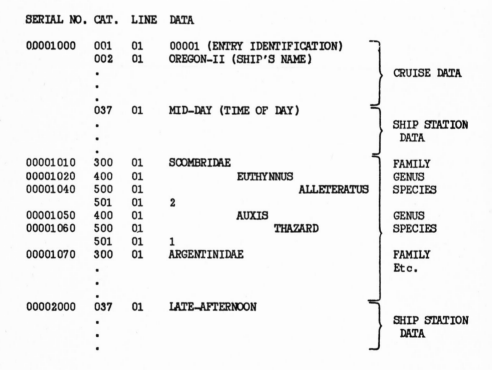

FIG. 16. Sample hierarchical record in SELGEM

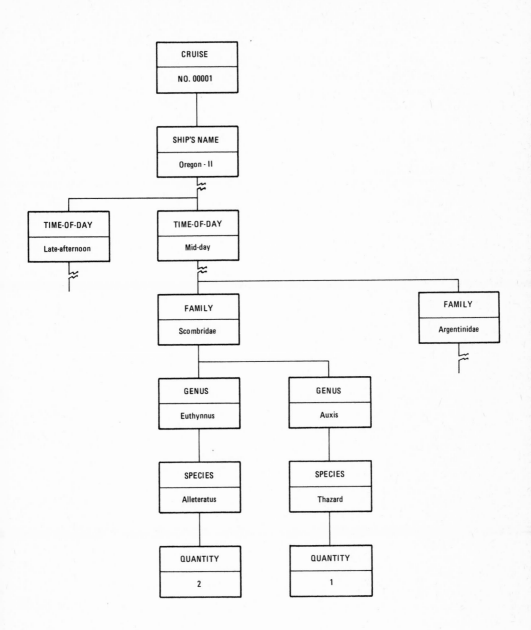

FIG. 17. Tree-structure schematic (relating to figure 16)

(Category 001 contains Employee Name, 002 contains Employer, 003 contains Positions, and 004 contains Wages)

Serial No.	Category No.	Data
00000001	001	JONES
00000001	002	ABC CO.
00000001	003	CARPENTER
00000001	004	$2.19
00000002	001	JONES
00000002	002	ABC CO.
00000002	003	CARPENTER
00000002	004	$2.48
00000003	001	JONES
00000003	002	ABC CO.
00000003	003	CHIEF CARPENTER
00000003	004	$2.80
00000004	001	JONES
00000004	002	ABC CO.
00000004	003	CABINET MAKER
00000004	004	$3.15
00000005	001	JONES
00000005	002	ABC CO.
00000005	003	CABINET MAKER
00000005	004	$3.52
00000006	001	JONES
00000006	002	ACME CO.
00000006	003	TRAINEE REFRIG. TECH.
00000006	004	$3.92
00000007	001	JONES
00000007	002	ACME CO.
00000007	003	REFRIG. TECH.
00000007	004	$4.32
00000008	001	JONES
00000008	002	ACME CO.
00000008	003	REFRIG. TECH.
00000008	004	$4.81
00000009	001	JONES
00000009	002	ACME CO.
00000009	003	REFRIG. TECH.
00000009	004	$5.31
00000010	001	JONES
00000010	002	COOL-IT INC.
00000010	003	AIR COND. TECH.
00000010	004	$5.84
00000011	001	JONES
00000011	002	COOL-IT INC.
00000011	003	SUPV. AIR COND.
00000011	004	$6.40
00000012	001	JONES
00000012	002	COOL-IT INC.
00000012	003	SUPV. AIR COND.
00000012	004	$7.63

(48 items of data carried)

FIG. 18. Unit record structure in SELGEM

(Category 001 contains Employee Names, 002 contains Employer, 003 Positions,

and 004 Wages)

Serial	Category	Data
00000001	001	JONES
00000002	002	ABC CO.
00000003	003	CARPENTER
00000004	004	$2.19
00000005	004	$2.48
00000006	003	CHIEF-CARPENTER
00000007	004	$2.80
00000008	003	CABINET MAKER
00000009	004	$3.15
00000010	004	$3.52
00000011	002	ACME CO.
00000012	003	TRAINEE REFRIG. TECH.
00000013	004	$3.92
00000014	003	REFRIG. TECH.
00000015	004	$4.32
00000016	004	$4.81
00000017	004	$5.31
00000018	002	COOL-IT INC.
00000019	003	AIR COND. TECH.
00000020	004	$5.84
00000021	003	SUPV. AIR COND.
00000022	004	$6.40
00000023	004	$7.63
	001	SMITH

(23 items of data carried)

FIG. 19. Hierarchical record structure in SELGEM

Input preparation. Three methods are provided by SELGEM for the conversion of information on object documentation files into machine-readable records for processing by SELGEM computer programs. Figure 21 illustrates the use of an object documentation file form for a SELGEM application. The three methods of input preparation as illustrated in the flow chart in figure 22 are:

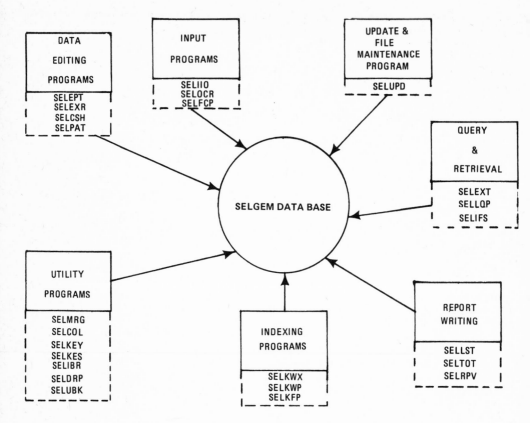

FIG. 20. SELGEM system overview

1. Key-punch equipment—used for the preparation of punched cards when this form of input to SELGEM programs is used. The optional SELGEM program SELFCP may be used when the punched card format needs to be changed to the SELGEM transaction card format (see figure 15).

2. Typewriter equipment with punched paper tape auxiliary output would be processed by the SELGEM program called SEL11Ø and subprogram READPA (Paper Tape Conversion and Formatter Programs).

3. Optical character recognition—data gathering forms prepared on a typewriter using an OCR print font can be sent to a service bureau with OCR equipment for conversion of the information to machine-readable form. This data would be processed by SELGEM program named SELOCR (Optical Character Recognition Program).

NATIONAL COLLECTION OF FINE ARTS
DATA COLLECTION FORM

REGISTRAR CATEGORY CODES
AND REGISTRAR CATEGORIES

1 = PAINTING   5 = DRAWING
2 = SCULPTURE   6 = WATERCOLOR
3 = MINIATURE   7 = FURNITURE
4 = PRINT   8 = OTHER DECORATIVE ART

SERIAL NUMBER

☐ ☐☐☐☐☐ ☐☐
1   2   6 7 8

TRANSACTION CODE:
2 = DELETE
☐ 3 = CHANGE
4 = NEW RECORD

CAT.	LINE			

001 01 ARTIST: ☐ 15   BOHM, MAX _____ 79 ☐ 80

02 ☐ 15   16 _____ 79 ☐ 80

002 01 ARTIST LIFE DATES: (STANDARD) ☐ 15   1868 - 1923 ☐
16 19 20 21 24   25

02 (FREE FORM) ☐ 15   16 _____ 79 ☐ 80

003 01 TITLE OR FUNCTIONAL TYPE: ☐ 15   INCIDENT IN THE ENGLISH CHANNEL, AN _____ 79 ☐ 80

02 ☐ 15   16 _____ 79 ☐ 80

004 01 SUBJECT MATTER: ☐ 15   ☐ PORTRAIT [X] LANDSCAPE ☐ HISTORY AND ALLEGORY ☐ NONREPRESENTATIONAL ☐ 80

☐ GENRE ☐ STILL LIFE ☐ DECORATIVE ART ☐ FIGURE STUDY

02 REMARKS ☐ 15   MARINE _____ 79 ☐ 80

005 01 DATE OF EXECUTION: (STANDARD) ☐ 15   1919 ___ ___ ☐
16 19 20 21 24   25

02 (FREE FORM) ☐ 15   16 _____ 79 ☐ 80

006 01 SIGNATURE: ☐ 15   SIGNED UPPER LEFT: MAX BOHM/1919 _____ 79 ☐ 80

007 01 ACCESSION NUMBER: ☐ 15   1929.6.6 _____ 79 ☐ 80

008 01 OBJECT CLASS AND MEDIA: ☐ 15   [X] PAINTING ☐ PRINT ☐ WATERCOLOR ☐ FURNITURE ☐ 80

☐ SCULPTURE ☐ DRAWING ☐ MINIATURE ☐ OTHER DEC. ART

02 REMARKS: ☐ 15   OIL ON CANVAS _____ 79 ☐ 80

009 01 DIMENSIONS: ☐ 15   35 X 30 IN. _____ 79 ☐ 80

02 ☐ 15   16 _____ 79 ☐ 80

010 01 SOURCE: ☐ 15   ☐ MUSEUM PURCHASE [X] GIFT OF ☐ LONGTERM LOAN BY ☐ TRANSFER FROM ☐ 80

02 REMARKS: ☐ 15   GELLATLY, JOHN _____ 79 ☐ 80

011 01 DEPARTMENT: ☐ 15   [X] 18-19TH CENTURY PAINTING AND SCULPTURE ☐ DECORATIVE ART ☐ 80

☐ CONTEMPORARY PAINTING AND SCULPTURE ☐ BARNEY COLLECTION

☐ PRINTS, DRAWINGS, AND WATERCOLORS

012 01 GEOGRAPHIC ORIGIN: ☐ 15   ☐ FOREIGN ☐ 23

FIG. 21. Sample of object documentation file form

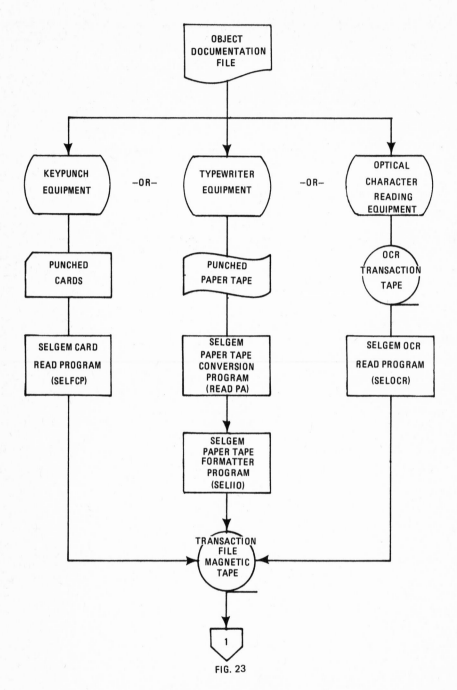

FIG. 22. SELGEM input preparation flow chart

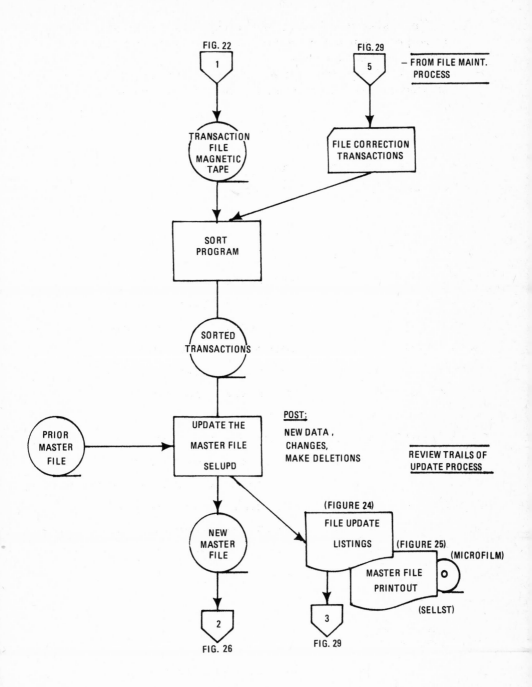

FIG. 23. Master file update flow chart

The transaction file on magnetic tape, prepared from one of the three procession options above, would go to the next step in the system, master file update.

Master file update. Each of the aforementioned input preparation alternatives result in a magnetic tape in transaction format whose

UPDATE REPORT
02/23/73

SERIAL	CATEG	LINE	TRN	DATA	COMMENTS
00470220	050	01	4	TEST/ADD	
00470225	031	01	4	TEST/ADD	
00470225	040	01	4	TEST/ADD	
00470225	050	01	4	TEST/ADD	
00470560	081	01	3	¢TEST/CHANGE¢	CHANGE INSERTED
00470560	081	01	3	¢TEST-CHANGE¢	SEQUENCE ERROR--TRANS REJECTED
00470560	082	01	3	¢TEST-CHANGE¢	NO MATCH ON MASTER—TRANS REJECTED
00470560	083	01	3	¢TEST-CHANGE¢	CHANGE INSERTED
00470562	086	01	3	¢FAIL/CHANGE¢	NO MATCH ON MASTER--TRANS REJECTED
00470564	081	01	3	¢TEST/CHANGE¢	CHANGE INSERTED
00470564	082	01	3	¢TEST/CHANGE¢	CHANGE INSERTED
00470564	083	01	3	¢TEST/CHANGE¢	CHANGE INSERTED
00470565	081	01	3	¢TEST/CHANGE¢	CHANGE INSERTED
00470566	080	01	3	¢FAIL/CHANGE¢	NO MATCH ON MASTER--TRANS REJECTED
00470567	081	01	3	¢TEST/CHANGE¢	CHANGE INSERTED
00470567	081	01	3	¢TEST/CHANGE¢	SEQUENCE ERROR--TRANS REJECTED
00470567	¢82	01	3	¢≠3RMT ERROR¢	FORMAT ERROR--TRANS REJECTED
00470571	271	01	6	H¢XX¢	

CATEG = Category Code
TRN = Transaction Code

FIG. 24. Example of master file update report

contents first must be sorted to the same sequence as the records to be updated in the museum's master file.

The actual updating in which records from the transaction file are placed in the master file is performed by the program named SELUPD (figure 23). The transaction code in the transaction file (table 6) determines the functions of adding new records to the master file, revising or adding to existing records in the master file, or deleting records from the master file. As the master file is updated, a master file update report (Figure 24) is prepared as a record of the update processing. In the illustration, "TRN" code 3 made changes to file records, and "TRN" code 4 added new data to the master file. As file updating is completed, the option is available of printing a file master list (figure 25) of the entire contents of the updated master file using program SELLST. The listing of the entire master record illustrated in figure 25 shows the data as it is stored line by line in the master file. In the example, record number 10000170, in a unit record structure, contains 12 categories of one line each, except for category number 025, which contains two lines. The listing then continues with the printing of the next record in the master file, number 10000200.

Data editing. The SELGEM user is provided with the capability of reviewing the accuracy and consistency of the data that has been added or changed in the master file. Two editing methods are available (figure 26). SELGEM program SELEPT prepares a category and data frequency report to identify data inconsistencies in the master file. In figure 27, for example, the user requested that category "040" be printed in order to check the recording of a person's name in a selected number of records in the collection master file. The following observations may be noted from the results.

1. The first item, AMMOBACULITES, does not appear to be a person's name. The number beneath the data name is the serial number of the file record where the correction should be directed. This would be used when initiating a file correction transaction, as illustrated by the flow chart in figure 29.

2. The several columns of serial numbers in item 5 indicate the frequency of MD.GEOL.SURVEY in the contents of category 040.

3. Items 7 and 8 illustrate an inconsistency in spelling a person's name.

Program SELPAT, a preprocessor for the category and data frequency report, provides a means of validating the format of records to insure that the proper type of data is being entered into data categories within master file records.

HIRSHHORN MASTER FILE
                                                                MASTER LIST

SERIAL	CATEG	LINE	CAT-DEFINITION	DATA
				1111222222222233333333334444444444555555555566
				6789012345678901234567890123456789012345678901
10000160	005	01	ACCESSION NUMBER:	JH 67.42
	006	01	ARTIST:	NANKIVELL, FRANK ARTHUR
	010	01	ARTIST'S LIFE DATES:	1869 - 1959
	015	01	ARTIST'S NATIONALITY:	AUSTRALIAN
	020	01	TITLE:	CHILDREN ON ROCKS BY SEA
	030	01	MEDIUM:	OIL
	035	01	SUPPORT:	CANVAS
	040	01	DIMENSIONS:	17 1/2 X 25 1/2 INCHES
	050	01	ACQUIRED:	IRA SPANIERMAN, NEW YORK
	051	01	ACQUISITION DATE:	1967
	052	01	PREVIOUS OWNER:	MITCHELL WORK, NEW JERSEY
10000170	005	01	ACCESSION NUMBER:	JH 734
	006	01	ARTIST:	NAY, ERNST WILHELM
	010	01	ARTIST'S LIFE DATES:	1902 - 1968
	015	01	ARTIST'S NATIONALITY:	GERMAN
	020	01	TITLE:	UNTITLED
	025	01	DATE OF EXECUTION:	1954 -
		02	REMARKS:	54 - LOWER RIGHT
	030	01	MEDIUM:	OIL
	035	01	SUPPORT:	CANVAS
	040	01	DIMENSIONS:	22 7/8 X 31 INCHES
	045	01	SIGNATURE:	NAY - LOWER RIGHT
	050	01	ACQUIRED:	KLEEMAN GALLERIES, NEW YORK
	051	01	ACQUISITION DATE:	1954
10000200	005	01	ACCESSION NUMBER:	JH 69.26
	006	01	ARTIST:	NEWMAN, BARNETT
	010	01	ARTIST'S LIFE DATES:	1905 - 1970
	015	01	ARTIST'S NATIONALITY:	AMERICAN
	020	01	TITLE:	COVENANT
	025	01	DATE OF EXECUTION:	1949 -
	030	01	MEDIUM:	OIL
	035	01	SUPPORT:	CANVAS
	040	01	DIMENSIONS:	48 X 60 INCHES
	050	01	ACQUIRED:	HAROLD DIAMOND, NEW YORK
	051	01	ACQUISITION DATE:	1968
	052	01	PREVIOUS OWNER:	MR. + MRS. JOSEPH SLIFKA, NEW YORK
10000220	005	01	ACCESSION NUMBER:	JH 67.41
	006	01	ARTIST:	NICHOLSON, BEN

FIG. 25. Example of a partial master file listing

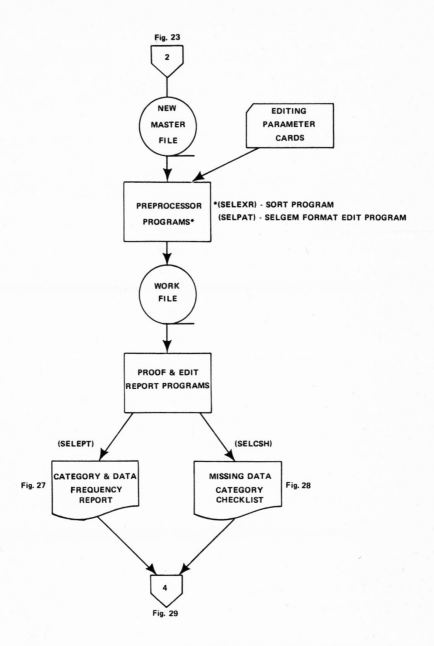

FIG. 26. Data editing flow chart

SELGEM CATEGORY AND DATA FREQUENCY REPORT

CAT LINE....................................CATEGORY CONTENTS......................(FOLLOWED BY SERIAL NUMBER LIST)

(1) 040 01   AMMOBACULITES
               00290216
     * CATEGORY, LINE, AND DATA TOTAL   1

(2) 040 01   ARNOLD, 1904
               00651361
     * CATEGORY, LINE, AND DATA TOTAL   1

(3) 040 01   BARR
               00170359   00170360   00170361
     * CATEGORY, LINE, AND DATA TOTAL   3

(4) 040 01   BELLEROPHON
               00210512
     * CATEGORY, LINE, AND DATA TOTAL   1

(5) 040 01   MD.GEOL.SURVEY
               00166884   00166885   00166886   00166887   00166888   00166889   00166890   00166891   00166892   00166893
               00166894   00166895   00166896   00166897   00166898   00166899   00166900   00166901   00166902   00166903
               00166904   00166905   00166906   00166907   00166908   00166909   00166910   00166911   00166912   00166913
               00166914   00166915   00166916   00166917   00166918   00166919   00166920   00166921   00166922   00166923
               00166924   00166925   00166926   00166927   00166928   00166929   00166930   00166931   00166932   00166933
               00166934   00166935   00166936   00166937   00166938   00166939   00166940   00166941   00166942   00166943
               00166944   00166945   00166946   00166947   00166948   00166949   00166950   00166951   00166952   00166953
               00166954   00166955   00166956   00166957   00166958   00166959   00166960   00166961   00166962   00166963
               00166964   00166965   00166966   00166967   00166968   00166969   00166970   00166971   00166972   00166973
               00166974   00166975   00166976   00166977   00166978   00166979   00166980   00166981   00166982   00166983
               00166984   00166985   00166986   00166987   00166988   00166989   00166990   00166991   00166992   00166993
               00166994   00166995   00166996   00166997   00166998
     * CATEGORY, LINE, AND DATA TOTAL 115

(6) 040 01   MILLER, D. J.
               00131347   00131398   00131399   00131410
     * CATEGORY, LINE, AND DATA TOTAL   4

(7) 040 01   MOFFITT, F. H.
               00131442
     * CATEGORY, LINE, AND DATA TOTAL   1

(8) 040 01   MOFFIT, F. H.
               00131361
     * CATEGORY, LINE, AND DATA TOTAL   1

(9) 040 01   MULLER-IMLAY ET AL.

FIG. 27. Example of SELGEM category and data frequency report

Another data editing method is the missing data category checklist, figure 28. This report permits the user to request a check of specific serial number records in the master file and print a list of those categories with missing data.

File maintenance process. As the flow chart in figure 29 illustrates, several reports provide suitable references for performing file maintenance: file update listings (figures 24 and 25), category and data frequency reports (figure 27) and the missing data categories checklist (figure 28). The update report in figure 24, an example of data from an actual computer printout, illustrates data errors that can occur

SELGEM CATEGORY CODE CHECKLISTING

SERIAL NUMBER	....MISSING CATEGORY CODES...				
00477931	084	240	280		
00477932	083	084	190	240	280
00477933	084	240	280		
00477934	084	240	280		
00477935	084	240	280		
00477936	071	084	190	240	280
00477937	084	240	280		
00477938	084	240	280		
00477939	084	240	280		
00477940	084	240	280		
00477941	084	240	280		
00477942	084	240	280		
00477943	084	240	280		
00477944	084	240	280		
00477945	084	240	280		
00477946	240	280			

FIG. 28. Example of missing data categories checklist

with the updating of a master file. (These are errors that require correction through subsequent file maintenance processing.)

During the file maintenance review function, errors found may be corrected by preparing file maintenance transactions to change, add, or delete the erroneous data from the master file. The file corrections are prepared for keypunching and used to update the master file (see master file update flow chart, figure 23).

Data retrieval. This phase of the SELGEM system relates to what is usually the major objective for undertaking the development of a collection master file: to produce catalogs, collection records, accession log books, specimen labels, etc. Several alternatives and options

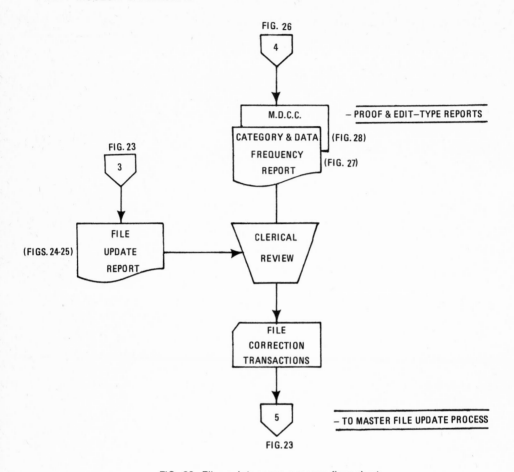

FIG. 29. File maintenance process flow chart

are made available for retrieval of information stored in the collection master files during the course of their updating.

The SELGEM data retrieval function, as illustrated in the flow chart in figure 30, entails four levels of processing.

A. Request. Submitting and preparing requests for information to be searched for and retrieved from the master file. Information requests may include retrieval for study projects, management information requests, etc.

B. Retrieve. Options are available to the SELGEM user as to the manner of retrieval that would best suit the output information desired.

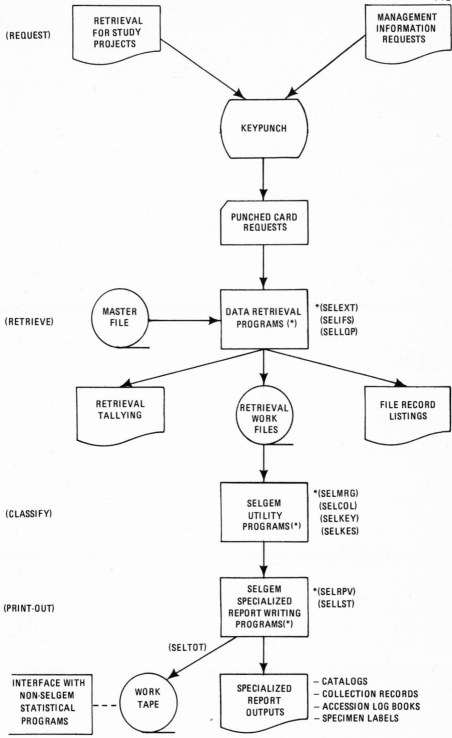

FIG. 30. Data retrieval process flow chart

The SELGEM program SELEXT is the master file query and retrieval program generally used when a search is performed directly to the data file. In SELEXT, two types of compare parameters are defined for the query and retrieval program:

1. Data evaluation for defining the search parameter values. Data in the master file may be compared with search parameter terms on the basis of "equal to," "greater than," or "less than," or on the basis of the corresponding negative operators (e.g., "not equal to"). If multiple variables are included in the search parameters, the Boolean logic terms "and" or "or" may be used in conjunction with the comparative terms.

2. Action evaluation or defining what should be done by the program when the desired record information is located. There are several options available. For example: *(a)* Output option—the selected output may be put on a high-speed printer or written on a magnetic tape file for further program processing; *(b)* Tally output option—a series of counters may be activated and their totals printed out at the termination of processing; *(c)* Replace option—data in the master file record, located by specified search parameters, can be deleted or replaced with other specified data on a conditional basis.

Other specialized forms of data retrieval programs are available to the SELGEM user. For example, the program SELIFS (an optional program), uses an indexed file for faster retrieval when very large master files must be searched. Also, the program SELLQP (an optional program) retrieves records by geographic localities of the users choice. Use of this retrieval capability is dependent upon the user putting latitude and longitude or global reference code data into the master file records during the building of the data base.

C. Classify. When parts of data records are retrieved from the master file, sorting or collating may be required prior to output report processing. Several programs are available for this purpose such as SELMRG (master file merge by serial number), SELCOL (file collate by data field), SELKEY and SELKES (specialized tagging and sorting programs).

D. Print-out. This, the last step of the data retrieval function, outputs the data selected from the data base in a prescribed report form. The SELGEM user has several options for standard output listings depending upon the system functions performed.

1. SELRPV (Report writer program) permits the user to customize the output data for special type reports. This program

has the flexibility to edit and format data for management-type reports, catalog file cards, collection indexes, specimen labels, etc.

2. SELTOT (Tabulator and statistical interface program) may be used to produce tabulations of quantitative data in the master file, and produce basic columnar listings of the results. This program can also produce a magnetic tape file for use with non-SELGEM statistical program packages.

3. SELLST (Master file list program) will produce a listing from a master file. The user may select an entire file print-out or select records within serial number ranges or individual categories.

Data indexing functions. As previously noted, SELGEM master files are organized sequentially on magnetic tape by the first thirteen characters of the record (serial, category, and line number). Normally, the use of SELGEM programs for data retrieval is through a sequential search of the master file records. However, indexing methods using optional SELGEM programs may be employed for retrieval or query on very large master files where the amount of change is small. SELGEM programs SELKWX, SELKWP, and SELKFP are key word indexing programs designed to produce temporary or permanent index masters in the standard SELGEM data format from any SELGEM unit record or hierarchically structured master file. The optional program SELIFS is the inverted file search program used to retrieve records from a master file.

SELGEM does not directly provide statistical type processing functions ordinarily required for research projects. However, SELGEM interface-type programs like SELTOT may be used to select and format records on the basis of desired variables, and then convert the data to fixed field and record lengths, and produce a magnetic tape work file for statistical processing by specialized programs such as SPSS (Statistical Package for the Social Sciences) or BMD (Bio-Medical Data). Other SELGEM programs used for data structuring and reconfiguration are SELDRP (Data Reconfiguration Program) and SELUBK (Fixed Length Record Formatting Program).

Implementation and Future Support

SELGEM is well documented as a system. Several general brochures describe the system capabilities, and additional system manuals that are in the preparation process will be helpful to users. The SELGEM user receives a copy of the COBOL programs source language listings and copies of the computer programs on magnetic tape. The characteristics of the program tape are as follows: unblocked records, card-image records, no header labels, BCD (binary coded decimal) mode and density of 556 or 800 BPI (bits per inch) on 7-track tape. A SELGEM program called SELIBR is available to the user for maintaining the programs on a tape file.

The SELGEM user receives a program manual (Basic Programmers Documentation) with detailed program descriptions to supplement the system brochures and to instruct the SELGEM users in setting up and operating the programs. This documentation and the program package is basically the extent of direct support that the Smithsonian Institution, Information Systems Division, is presently equipped to provide SELGEM users.

There are three aspects to the system support of SELGEM that prospective SELGEM users should understand:

1. Information Systems Division personnel provide users with as much assistance as they can by means of telephone and the mails. However, the user must provide his own programming personnel to adapt the system to the computer he intends to use and his own consulting personnel (as needed) to evaluate the information needs of his museum and the manner in which SELGEM can best meet those needs. A users' group called MESH (Museum Exchange for SELGEM Help) periodically prepares a newsletter as a vehicle for the interchange of system ideas, user problems, and computer programs, and the MESH members offer help to each other on the utilization of SELGEM. However, MESH is not organized to assist with a new installation.

2. Direction is not given to the SELGEM user regarding the modifications that may be required to implement SELGEM. The use of computer equipment other than Honeywell could require three to four months of skilled programming time. Smithsonian Information Systems Division is not currently maintaining or otherwise controlling the dissemination of alternative versions of SELGEM modified for use on other equipment. Users are given "updates" to SELGEM as improvements or extensions are incorporated, but these may be troublesome depending on the approach each user has taken to implement the SELGEM programs.

3. The assignment of data categories (annotation classes) is entirely a SELGEM user option. The Information Systems Division of Smithsonian Institution makes no attempt to set guidelines or standardize on the assignment of codes for commonly used categories to be followed by all users.

Plans by the Information Systems Division of the Smithsonian Institution relate principally to developing system improvements to SELGEM. Upgrading documentation and program transferability would also be part of future improvements. Plans do not include any major redesign or change to the basic systems approach of SELGEM. The improvements planned are to develop an integrated language to enable SELGEM users to establish parameters of SELGEM programs more easily. This improvement is in the nature of a command language of unified syntax and vocabulary that will be developed concurrent with the task of standardizing the present manner of specifying optional program parameters.

There are also plans to continue basic system enhancements requested by SELGEM users that would improve and extend the information processing capability of SELGEM.

Adaptability of the package to use standard data categories. SELGEM appears to be flexible enough to adapt to any manner of data category coding as long as the designated coding could be maintained in a sequential manner and is limited to three characters or less.

Adaptability of the package to interact with other packages. The straightforward design and the unit record approach of SELGEM make it a rather easy system to interface with. An interesting feature of each file is its directory record (table 7). This directory record identifies the data categories of the records in the file. This may be particularly important when hierarchical structuring is used.

Cost Considerations

There are two major aspects of cost that should be considered when evaluating the use of SELGEM.

Start-up costs. Start-up costs are principally nonrecurring costs associated with the procurement and implementation of the computer programs. The SELGEM package is made available by the Smithsonian Institution without charge. However, there is a cost to start up SELGEM if the user is planning to use computer equipment other than the type used by Smithsonian Institution. Determining the start-up cost a SELGEM installation may require is dependent upon the extent of system needs planned by the museum and the extent the SELGEM package must be adapted to meet these system needs.

The Information Systems Division indicates that the experience of implementing the basic SELGEM system may approximate $5,000 for planning, testing, and implementing the SELGEM programs. This cost could vary depending upon the number of programs the user elects to implement, the quality and experience of the data processing personnel available, and the amount of computer time required to test the programs. Since SELGEM has been adapted to several types of computers, the user of SELGEM is afforded the opportunity to investigate these sources (through MESH for example) as a means of minimizing start-up costs.

Operational costs. Operational costs are recurring costs of the day-to-day computer processing in order to build and update collection master files, perform information inquiries on data in these files, and retrieve the data for collection documentation needs. For a discussion of the problems of estimating operational costs see pages 92–93.

GRIPHOS
Package Description

Background

GRIPHOS, an acronym for General Retrieval and Information Processing for Humanities-Oriented Studies, is a generalized data base oriented computer system. The GRIPHOS package has principally been associated with the United Nations Library in New York; the Museum Computer Network, Inc., a nonprofit organization which markets and supports the operation of GRIPHOS; and the Department of Computer Science at the State University of New York at Stony Brook.

GRIPHOS, as a generalized type system, offers users the flexibility to perform the processing and documentation needs relating to a museum's collection. The GRIPHOS program library is quite extensive. In addition to programs regularly used by Museum Computer Network, Inc., members, it also contains programs for specialized user needs such as those at the United Nations. Those programs most commonly and widely used are included in this description of the GRIPHOS package. These number approximately 30 programs, and they are designed to perform functions such as file create, file update, maintenance, retrieval, report writing, and utility functions. Each program contains a set of parameters that permits the user to alter the functions of the programs as required. For example, a retrieval program can be directed to select certain data categories under various logical conditions for inclusion in a catalog report. In another situation, the same retrieval program might be modified by a different set of parameters to retrieve data and produce catalog cards.

The developer of GRIPHOS was Dr. Jack Heller, Professor of Computer Science at State University of New York at Stony Brook. The development and earliest use was at the United Nations, Indexing and Retrieval Division, for library bibliographic record keeping.

In 1968 the establishment of the Museum Computer Network (MCN) inaugurated the use of GRIPHOS by museums. Mr. David Vance is now president of Museum Computer Network, Inc., and directs its administrative and user group activities. Users are required to pay an annual fee for membership in MCN in order to obtain the GRIPHOS programs. The user is provided with a copy of the GRIPHOS program library in machine-level language (object programs). The user is not permitted to make modifications to the programs because it is the intention of MCN to maintain tight control over the uniformity of the GRIPHOS system for all its users.

In the museum field GRIPHOS has been most widely used by art museums for maintaining catalog files, biography files, and film library files. Since 1971 the use of GRIPHOS has expanded into the field of archaeology with universities and others maintaining files on site data and artifacts, principally for research purposes.

The GRIPHOS package requires a medium-to-large-scale IBM computer. The minimum usable hardware configuration is an IBM 360/40, 256K memory, one direct access device, and one tape drive. The GRIPHOS package has operated on the following IBM computers: 360/40, 360/50, 360/65, 360/67, 360/75, 370/145, and 370/155. GRIPHOS operates in a job-oriented (batch) mode, as there are no programs within the package enabling the use of data communications for on-line processing between a centrally located computer and remote terminal locations. However, several of the present GRIPHOS users have provided their own interface programs to permit remote job entry processing on GRIPHOS.

The operating system required to utilize GRIPHOS is OS/MFT. This is the IBM operating system using the multiprogramming feature that allows for a fixed number of tasks to operate in the computer simultaneously. GRIPHOS has also been run using MVT, the feature that allows a variable (rather than fixed) number of tasks to be controlled simultaneously by the operating system; and GRIPHOS has been run using V-OS, which is a "virtual memory" operating system feature.

The programming language that GRIPHOS is written in is called PL/I, a language used principally on IBM computers. The programs provided to the user have been compiled from the PL/I source language to machine language. When the user receives them, the programs are ready to be turned over to the computer facility for operation. The use of the PL/I program language, and the fact that GRIPHOS programs are compiled into machine language using the IBM OS/360 operating system, limit the operation of the GRIPHOS package to only IBM equipment at the present time.

System Description

The description of the GRIPHOS package will include several elements that make up the processing system: file types, data structure, the information processing flow and functions of the related computer programs, and the data indexing functions.

File types. GRIPHOS data files are organized and structured for processing on direct-access file storage devices. There are four types of files used in GRIPHOS:

1. Directory file. Contains the titles and record location addresses of all other files created for use in the GRIPHOS system. There should ordinarily be only one directory file for each GRIPHOS user.

2. Master files. Used for the permanent storage of data. The records are comprised of data input from the transaction files (see paragraph 4) and grouped into a logical record format.

3. Index files. Contain categories of data selected from master files for the purpose of facilitating retrieval of data records from master files. The records in this file are not ordinarily used for storage, but rather they contain key words and corresponding record addresses. Files may be constructed to contain single or multiple indexes.

4. Work files. Temporary storage-type files used in intermediate processing steps where data will no longer be needed after completion of a processing phase. A transaction file containing data for input processing to a master file is an example of a work file used in GRIPHOS.

All files used in GRIPHOS must be initialized by a file create master program prior to their first use in assigned data processing steps. The file create program assigns region numbers and areas on the direct access storage device where the data will subsequently be stored by an input pro. essing program. (This processing flow will be further illustrated in the section "Information processing flow.")

Region sizes assigned to master files are determined by the GRIPHOS user, based on the expected size of the data records. GRIPHOS permits variability of record sizes. When the actual record data stored in master files requires less space than the designated region size, the unfilled portion of the region remains unused. When the amount of data is greater than the region size, the GRIPHOS input processing program automatically assigns the balance of the record data to another region.

Data structuring. In GRIPHOS the data prepared for entry into a master file is first gathered and recorded in a transaction file. The structure of the transaction file record differs from the structure of data in the master file record.

1. Transaction data structure. The format for GRIPHOS transaction data is quite simple, as illustrated in figure 31.

1st Field				2nd Field			{ {		
DATA (a)	TAG NO. (b)	EOF	DATA		TAG NO.	EOF	{ {	EOR	
xx ⌣ xx ⌐b	xx ⌣ xx	==	xx ⌣ xx ⌐b	x ⌣ x	==	{ {	⌐b 0==		

FIG. 31. Transaction data structure

The basic structure of the transaction data consists of *(a)* data and *(b)* a tag number. The data field may contain up to 5,000 positions, and the tag number field may contain up to 7 positions. Separating the data and the tag number positions is a blank position (b̸), and following the tag number position is a double equal sign (= =) to identify the end of each data field (EOF). A series of data fields may be similarly constructed. Following the last field in each transaction record is an EOR, or End of Record Identifier (O = =). The transaction file can continue with another transaction record, which begins its first field immediately following the previous EOR indicator, or the EOR indicator can signal the last record of the transaction file.

The tag number field illustrated on figure 31 is used to record annotation class numbers that are assigned by the Museum Computer Network, Inc. A partial listing of the annotation class definitions established by the MCN is shown in figure 32.

The use of annotation classes by the GRIPHOS user is illustrated by an example of an object documentation file form in figure 33. This form, developed by a present GRIPHOS user, is used for the

14==   Vendor.
        Name only of the person or organization that sold the object to the possessor.
        Note: Include the city if necessary for identification.
        Example: Richard_Feigen Gallery, Chicago.
114==   Anonymous vendor.
        Note: This information will be coded as classes 9 and 112 above.
15==   Remarks about the vendor.
16==   Expedition.
        Unique designation of the expedition that excavated or collected the object.
        Note: Include the year if necessary for identification.
17==   Remarks about the expedition.
18==   Excavator or collector.
        Name only of the person who excavated or collected the object.
* 118== Recorder.
        Designation of the person who recorded the object.
19==   Remarks about the excavator or collector.
* 119== Date of catalog record.
* 20== Season.
        The year in which the object was collected or excavated.
        Note: Use four digits.
22==   Year of acquisition.
        The year in which the object was acquired by the possessor.
        Note: Use four digits. If only the decade is known, use asterisk in place of final digit.
24==   Purchaser.
        Name only of the person or organization to which the deaccessioned object was sold, given or traded.
25==   Remarks about the purchaser.
26==   Old loan number.
        The number under which the possessor formerly cataloged the object as a loan.
27==   Remarks about cancellation, deaccession or return to lender.
        Note: If confidential this information may be placed in class 9.
66==   The Museum of Modern Art accession number.
        Note: For use only at The Museum of Modern Art.
86==   The Metropolitan Museum of Art accession number.

Section II – Description

30==   Title.
        The title used by the possessor in his most recent catalog and/or his current files. The title may be in any
        language using the Latin alphabet.
        Examples: – Balzac: Le chef d'oeuvre inconnue.
                   – The _Body Lay There, in the Doorway of the Church the People had Built.
                   – Les _Demoiselles d'Avignon.
                   – The _Gramineous Bicycle Garnished with Bells and Dappled Fire Damps and Echinoderms Bending
                     the Spine to Look for Caresses.
                   – Study for "_Nuit de Noël".
                   – Row House: View from Living Room.
                   – Seated Nude.
                   – Untitled.
                   – ˙(untitled).
                   – YX=K Green and Red.
                   – FN/GD.
                   – (Woman's head.)
31==   (number formerly used for title, not currently in use.)

*Annotation Classes noted on Figure 33.

FIG. 32. Partial list of Museum Computer Network annotation classes

Arkansas Archeological Survey

Record No.
72-629- _8/4 34 2_ _____ 1005==

Owner or Possessor
MAI ____ 102==

Owner's Cat. No.
_8/4342_ _____ 106==

Collected by (Organ. or Indiv.)
HARRINGTON, M. R. ____ 16==

Year Collected
_1916 - 1917_ _____ 20==

Place of Origin
AR, HEMPSTEAD, WASH, HARRINGTON'S SITE I 78==

Site No.
_3HE35_ _____ 176==

Intra-site Provenience
_____ 178==

Description:
Object Category
JAR, COLLARED ( ) (?) ( ) _____ 32==

Type
CROCKETT CURVILINEAR INCISED ( ) (WEBER) ( ) 68==

Authority for Type NAme
SUHM & JELKS, 1962 _____ 69==

Rim Shape
RIM _TAPERED_ _____ 142==

Lip Shape
LIP _FLAT_ _____ 142==

Base
BASE _CONVEX_ _____ 142==

Handle Type
HANDLE _____ 142==

Height	Max. Diam.	Wall Thick.	Orifice
_160_ 152==	_145_ 154==	_5_ 150==	_128_ 156==

Materials
POT # _SLIP, BLACK_
_____ 48==

Techniques
INCISION, PLASTIC PASTE
_____ 46==

Design Layout
COLLAR, ANNULAR
_____ 43==

Design Motifs
INTERLOCKING SCROLL BAND
_____ 42==

Condition
COMPLETE _____ 63==

Photo Nos.
_____ 60==

General Description and Remarks _COLLAR WITH ANNULAR INCISED LINES.
SUSPENSION HOLES AT 0° AND 180°. BODY HAS CENTRAL ELEMENTS
AT 0°, 60°, 120°, 180°, 240° AND 300°_

_____ 35==

Recorder
WEBER, J.C. ____ 118==

Date Recorded
_730130_ _____ 119==

FIG. 33. Example of GRIPHOS object documentation file form

ANNOTATION ▸	RECORD NO.			OWNER OR POSSESSOR			OWNER'S CAT. NO.		
	DATA	TAG	EOF	DATA	TAG	EOF	DATA	TAG	EOF
DATA ▸	72-629-8/4342	ƀ	1005	==	MAI	ƀ	102	==	8/4342	ƀ	106	==

ANNOTATION▸	COLLECTED BY (ORG. ORIND.)			YEAR C⟨	⟩TE RECORDED			
	DATA	TAG	EOF	DATA ⟩	⟨ DATA	TAG	EOF	EOR
DATA ▸	HARRINGTON, M.R.	ƀ	16	==	1916–⟩	⟨0130	ƀ	119	==	0==

F   FIG. 34. Example of transaction data structure using data in figure 33

gathering of data on pottery objects. Comparison of figure 32 with figure 33 will illustrate the use of several MCN annotation classes.

The creation of a transaction data record from the data gathered on a GRIPHOS object documentation record as shown in figure 33 is illustrated by a partial transaction data record shown in figure 34.

2. Master file data structure. Input processing, in which new records are added to the master file, is performed by GRIPHOS program MCNINO1 (Input Processing Program). The processing performed by this program will be discussed in the section "input preparation." Figure 35 illustrates the master file record format into which the input processing program converts the transaction data file. Note that (a) the region number is assigned by the GRIPHOS

← FIRST FIELD →				
REGION NUMBER	TAG NO. LENGTH	TAG NUMBER	DATA FIELD LENGTH	DATA FIELD
		1005		72-629-8/4342

← FOURTH FIELD →			
TAG NO. LENGTH	TAG NUMBER	DATA FIELD LENGTH	DATA FIELD
	16		Harrington, M.R.

FIG. 35. Illustration of GRIPHOS master file record format

file create program and *(b)* the data field is the data as it is received from the input transaction file. It is stored in the format as it would be displayed in output documentation when retrieved for reporting purposes. The GRIPHOS user may designate special annotations within a record to be used only for display purposes. In order for such special annotations not to affect the manner in which a record is sorted or indexed, a separate sort string is automatically generated by program MCNINO1 that omits the character string described within the delimiters ( )   ( ). The application of this technique is illustrated in figure 33. Lines 6 and 7 of the object documentation file form show comments that would be displayed in parentheses when the fields were retrieved and printed but would not otherwise be available for sorting and processing.

As the fields in the master file record are constructed by the GRIPHOS input processing program, two nontransaction data fields are always added to the record (tag number length and data field length), and when the user adds special annotations in the manner noted above, additional nondata fields are added (sort string length and sort string data). From the experience of GRIPHOS users, these nontransaction data fields add about a 20 to 30 percent overhead factor to the planning of GRIPHOS master file and record size requirements.

Hierarchical record structuring. GRIPHOS, using input processing program MCNINO1, allows for hierarchical structuring of record input to the collection master file. The arborescent (tree) structure of the data records is designated in the input transaction through the use of symbolic references to link the data fields together. For example, in figure 36 a tree structure is represented with symbolic references that allow the user to systematically arrange data fields into relational subrecords. The beginning or "Root" subrecord contains the information that would otherwide appear in each of the subrecords of a nonhierarchical structure. The input processing program MCNINO1 takes the symbolically referenced data and systematically constructs each subrecord in the hierarchy. Thus, each subrecord has an address and these addresses are used as "address pointers" in linking the subrecords together.

Each subrecord in the structure contains an "up" pointer to the subrecord in the level directly above it and "down" pointers to all of the subrecords in the level directly below it that are linked to it. In figure 36 the Root subrecord has no up pointer since it is at the top; but the Root subrecord has down pointers to subrecords

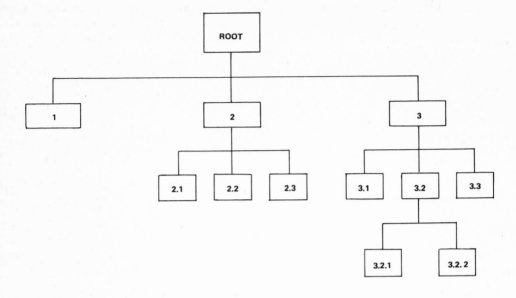

FIG. 36. Use of symbolic references to illustrate a GRIPHOS hierarchical record structure

1, 2, and 3. Subrecord 3 has an up pointer to the Root and down pointers to subrecords 3.1, 3.2, and 3.3. Subrecord 3.1 has only an up pointer to 3. Subrecord 3.2 has an up pointer to 3 and down pointers to 3.2.1 and 3.2.2. Thus the pointers serve to trace the tree structure from the root to the tip of each branch and back again.

Figure 37 illustrates an application of hierarchically structured data, using, as an example, artifacts from one grave lot of a hypothetical archaeological excavation. The GRIPHOS input transaction for purposes of adding the data to the records of the master file would be as follows:

3P039 176= = HAZEL SITE 168= = SCHOLTZ 16= = 1964
20= = + +1+ + STONE 48= = KNIFE 32= = !!2!! SHELL
48= = !!2!1!! BEAD 32= = !!2!2!! GORGET 32= = !!2!3!!
SPOON 32= = !!3!! POTTERY 48= = + +3!1+ + BOWL
32= = NEELEY'S FERRY PLAIN 68= = + +3!2+ + WATER
BOTTLE 32= = 2 136= = !!3!2!1!! NODENA RED AND
WHITE 68= = !!3!2!2!! CARSON RED ON BUFF 68= = !!3!3!!
PIPE 32= = 0= =

The transaction includes the structuring of data and annotation class numbers discussed earlier in "data structuring," and also the symbolic

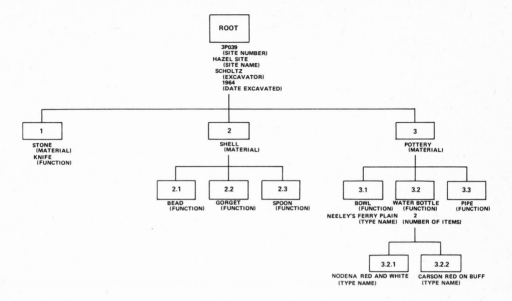

FIG. 37. The recording of artifacts from one grave lot in a GRIPHOS
hierarchical structure

references that identify the hierarchical structuring to the GRIPHOS input program MCNINO1. These symbolic references, which precede the subrecord data, are set off by the delimiters + + or !!. (The + + delimiter is used when more than one annotation class is included within a subrecord, and the !! delimiter when there is only one annotation class.)

The master file record that would be produced from the data in the preceding example is illustrated in figure 38.

A GRIPHOS program named JOIN permits the user to interconnect two records for which there is a common data field. Either hierarchically or unit structured records can be joined to allow the extension of records to include related fields of data recorded in other records. An example of the utility of this feature is the joining of records describing works of art with records that contain biographical information about the artists. Input parameters to the JOIN program specify the annotation class upon which to match records. in this example, the match would be made on the class that contains the name of the artist. An address pointer to the biographical record is added to the annotation class with the artist's name in the record that describes the art work. Thus, a data retrieval operation could gather simultaneously information about both works of art and the artists who produced them without having to duplicate the biographical data in the record of each work of art.

SUB-RECORD SYMBOLIC REFERENCES (AS IN INPUT TRANSACTION AND ON FIGURE 37)	INTERNAL COMPUTER SUB-RECORD ADDRESS	RECORD CONTENT (DATA FIELDS AND UP AND DOWN POINTERS)
ROOT	1234	3P039 176== HAZEL SITE 168== SCHOLTZ 16== 1964 20== D 1235 D 1236 D 1240
1	1235	STONE 48== KNIFE 32== U 1234
2	1236	SHELL 48== U 1234 D 1237 D 1238 D 1239
2.1	1237	BEAD 32== U 1236
2.2	1238	GORGET 32== U 1236
2.3	1239	SPOON 32== U 1236
3	1240	POTTERY 48== U 1234 D 1241 D 1242 D 1245
3.1	1241	BOWL 32== NEELEY'S FERRY PLAIN 68== U 1240
3.2	1242	WATER BOTTLE 32== 2 136== U 1240 D 1243 D 1244
3.2.1	1243	NODENA RED AND WHITE 68== U 1242
3.2.2	1244	CARSON RED ON BUFF 68== U 1242
3.3	1245	PIPE 32== U 1240

FIG. 38. Illustration of a GRIPHOS master file content

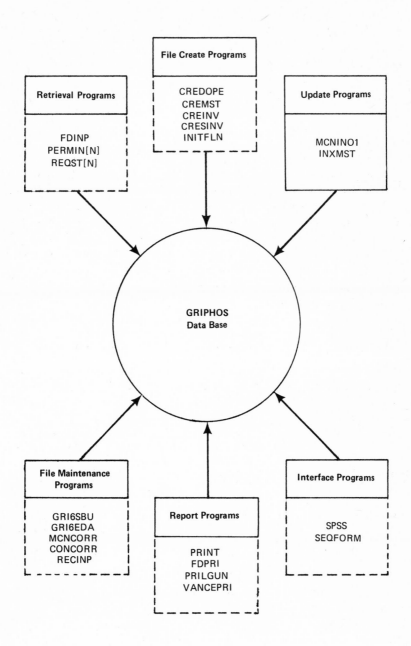

FIG. 39. GRIPHOS system overview

Information processing flow. A brief overview of the GRIPHOS system is illustrated by the chart in figure 39. The system consists of six types of programs:

1. File create programs.
2. File update programs.
3. Maintenance programs.
4. Retrieval programs.
5. Report programs.
6. Interface programs.

The system description of GRIPHOS is presented in the sequence of its information processing flow to illustrate the manner in which the computer programs interrelate as a functional system to provide the planned information needs of a museum. The narrative that follows describes the steps of a systems approach using GRIPHOS.

Create computer files. All direct access files used by the GRIPHOS package must be initialized before data can be put into the files. There is a GRIPHOS program for different types of files to be created, as illustrated in figure 40.

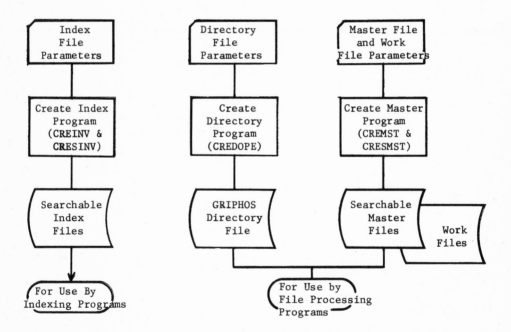

FIG. 40. Create GRIPHOS files flow chart

The directory file is created, usually only once, using GRIPHOS program CREDOPE. This file identifies and shows the current status of each of the other files created and used in the GRIPHOS system. It serves as a cross-check to be sure that records are entered in the right files.

Master files and work files are created by the GRIPHOS program called CREMST (create master file). This program defines and allocates regions of given sizes as determined by the user's parameters. Based on the user's information needs, he has the option of generating inverted files for file searching or indexing purposes using programs CREINV and CRESINV. The use of indexing programs will be discussed further in a subsequent section on "Data indexing functions."

Program INITFLN can be used to reinitialize master files and index files when their parameters (i.e., file name, file size, record size) are to remain as they were but the content of the file must be "erased" so that the file can be reused. INITFLN is normally used only with work files.

Input preparation. In the GRIPHOS information processing sequence, the conversion of information on the object documentation file form (figure 33) into a transaction data file for processing by GRIPHOS computer programs is illustrated by the flow chart in figure 41.

Keypunch equipment is shown here as the method of converting object documentation records into machine-readable computer input. However, the file update program (MCNINO1) accepts properly formatted data from magnetic tapes and disks as well. As with other information systems, when data is not captured initially by keyboarding into the same operating system used to control GRIPHOS (e.g., when data is entered through a remote terminal system or a paper tape system), user-supplied conversion programs may be required.

File updating process. The file updating process involves adding new records to a master file from input transaction data, as illustrated by the flow chart in figure 41. The updating of the collection file is performed by a program named MCNINO1. This program is used only to add new records to the data base. The program prints a record input directory, figure 42, which contains messages to identify the region addresses where each new record has been stored. These addresses remain permanently assigned to the records until they are deleted from the file. There are no options in this program to produce a complete listing of the data added to the master file (however,

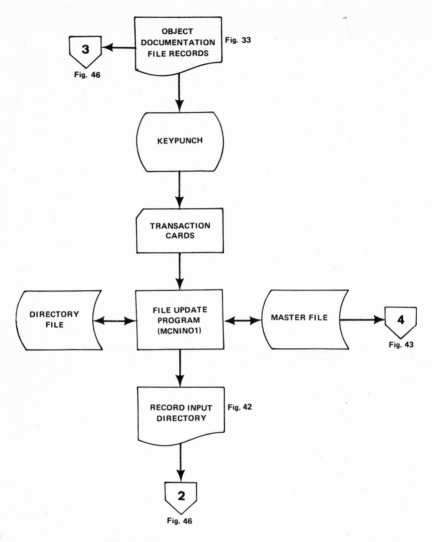

FIG. 41. Master file updating flow chart

see the discussion of program PRILGUN on page 136 for an alterna-tive print-out approach).

Editing process. The editing process is an option the user elects in order to review the accuracy of data added to the master file, by requesting the printing of certain reports that display the contents of master file records. This step is illustrated by the flow chart in

```
MCNDOPE AASA1 1005        07/01/72 07:53.27

71-519-26-3
RECORD ENTERED INTO REGION      855
71-519-26-4
RECORD ENTERED INTO REGION      856
71-519-26-5
RECORD ENTERED INTO REGION      857
71-519-26-6
RECORD ENTERED INTO REGION      858
71-519-26-7
RECORD ENTERED INTO REGION      859
71-519-26-8
RECORD ENTERED INTO REGION      860
71-519-27-1
RECORD ENTERED INTO REGION      862
71-519-27-2
RECORD ENTERED INTO REGION      863
71-519-27-3
RECORD ENTERED INTO REGION      864
71-519-27-4
RECORD ENTERED INTO REGION      865
71-519-28-1
RECORD ENTERED INTO REGION      866
71-519-28-2
RECORD ENTERED INTO REGION      867
71-519-28-3
RECORD ENTERED INTO REGION      868
71-519-29-1
RECORD ENTERED INTO REGION      869
71-519-29-2
RECORD ENTERED INTO REGION      871
71-519-29-3
RECORD ENTERED INTO REGION      873
71-519-29-4
RECORD ENTERED INTO REGION      874
71-519-29-5
RECORD ENTERED INTO REGION      876
71-519-29-6
RECORD ENTERED INTO REGION      878
71-519-29-7
RECORD ENTERED INTO REGION      880
71-519-29-8

GB1004 MCNINO1 WARNING
THE TAG S)( )68 IS NOT NUMERIC
IT WAS FOUND IN THE STRING
GARY ( )(DAVIS
```

FIG. 42. Example of record input directory

figure 43. GRIPHOS programs provide types of reports that allow data in the master file to be manually checked for validity and consistency. The requestor of the proof and edit reports is required to provide the specific direct access file addresses for the records to be reviewed. The record input directory from the master file update process (figure 42) can be of value for reference to those records most recently added to a master file.

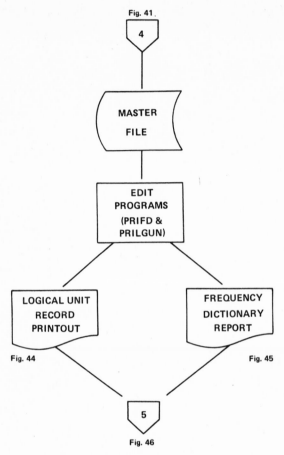

FIG. 43. Editing process flow chart

Two types of reports provided by GRIPHOS are useful for file data editing:

A. Logical unit record print-out (figure 44). This report, prepared by program PRILGUN, is an unformatted listing of all data fields in all records in the master file.

B. Frequency dictionary report (figure 45). This report, prepared by programs FDINP/SORT (an IBM utility program)/PRIFD, contains three columns of data:

1. Column 1 contains the number of entries, corresponding with the data content shown in column 2.

2. Column 2 contains the data as it is stored in the file.

```
    125
MUSEUM OF MODERN ART FILE002 FROM DATA TEXT 06/16/-- 10:06.28    MCMDOPE MCMMOMA (3)


Armitage, Merle 12
Accepted 11-12-35. 3
Leica 697d. 61
Signed L.R. in pencil "Richard Day:.///  Not dated.///Inscribed L.L. in pencil by printer "Paul Rocher imp. 1933".///Titl
e: below C. in artist's hand. 55
Rocher, Paul 74
0               :#
- - - - - - - - - - - - - - - - - - - - - - - - - - - - - - - - - - - - - - - - - - - - - - - - - -


ELISE (Elise Seeds Armitage)`70
Print 36
United States 76
215.35 66
DESCENT. 30
(1933'. 83
+1933 82
+1933 84
Lithrograph, printed in black, 47
lithograph 48
paper 48
Comp. 8 11/16 x 6 15/16" (22.0 x 17.5 cm.). 51
Gift of Merle Armitage. 5
Armitage, Merle 12
Accepted 11-12-35. 3
Leica 700b. 61
Signed L.R. in pencil "elise".///Not dated.///Impression:"5/15" L.L. in pencil, artist's hand.///Title: L.R. in pencil,
artist's hand. 55
0
- - - - - - - - - - - - - - - - - - - - - - - - - - - - - - - - - - - - - - - - - - - - - - - - - -


ELISE (Elise Seeds Armitage) 70
```

FIG. 44. Example of logical unit record print-out

3. Column 3 contains the list of region numbers where the data in column 2 was found.

In figure 45, for example, the user requested that annotation class "68" (identified in the heading line of the report) be printed in order to check the recording of "artifact type name" in a selected number of records in the collection master file. The following observations may be noted from the results:

1. Item 1 appears to be the correct way of recording the "Baytown" artifact name. It was recorded 43 times in the manner shown in column 2 of the report.

2. Items 2, 3, and 4 illustrate an inconsistency of recording the artifact type name, each having been recorded only once in their respective manner.

3. Item 5 appears to be the correct way of recording the ceramic type known as "Mississippi Plain."

4. Item 6 illustrates how the content of two data categories becomes intermixed when a field separator is incorrectly recorded (note next to last line: 35= in place of 35==).

File maintenance processing. File maintenance processing entails the clerical review of proof and editing type reports, and preparation of correction transactions for updating the master file records that

1

68 MCNDOPE   MCNSTR1   MCNSTR2   11/22/71 20:29.20

	1	2	3	4	5	6	7	8	9	10
(1) 43 BAYTOWN PLAIN, VAR. BAYTOWN	1	2	3	4	5	6	7	8	9	10
	12	13	14	15	16	17	18	32	33	34
	35	36	37	38	39	40	41	42	43	46
	47	48	49	50	51	53	54	55	57	58
	59	60	61							
(2) 1 BAYTOWN PLAIN, VAR. VAYTOWN	44									
(3) 1 BAYTOWN PLAIN VAR. BAYTOWN	30									
(4) 1 BAYTOWNPLAIN, VAR. BAYTOWN	11									
(5) 7 MISSISSIPPI PLAIN, VAR. MOUND FIELD	19	21	22	24	25	26	27			
(6) 1 (see note below)	28									

(6) THERE SEEMS LITTLE REASON TO PLACE THESE IN VAR. UNSPECIFIED INSTEAD OF WITH THE REST OF THE SHELL-TEMPERED WARE AS VAR. MOUND FIELD, EXCEPT FOR THE THICKNESS OF THESE SHERDS WHICH REMOVES THEM FROM ANY CONSIDERATION AS "THIN WARE." ASIDE FROM THIS, THEY CONFORM TO THE DESCRIPTION ON CARD 70-32-2. 35= MISSISSIPPI PLAIN, VAR. UNSPECIFIED

FIG. 45. An example of a frequency dictionary report

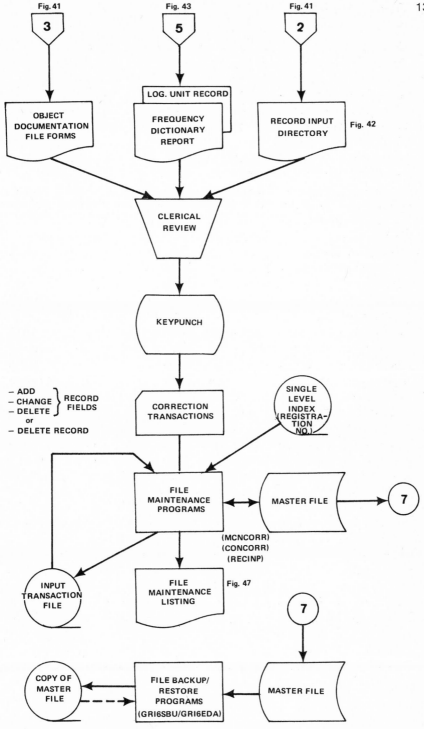

FIG. 46. File maintenance process flow chart

are in error. This process is illustrated by the flow chart in figure 46. The frequency dictionary, the logical unit record reports, and the object documentation forms used for the input data provide information to the GRIPHOS user to manually proof and edit records added to the master file. If errors are found during this clerical review, correction transactions are prepared to correct the file record data. The correction options available are to: (1) add a field to a record, (2) change a given field within a record, (3) delete a field from a record, and (4) delete an entire record.

In addition to showing the data to be corrected, correction transactions must also identify the record to be changed and the storage address (region) of the record in the master file. The record input directory prepared by the file update program MCNIN01 (figure 42) provides a reference for this purpose. The file maintenance program MCNCORR produces a file maintenance correction listing that describes correction requests and the file updating that occurred (figure 47).

The file maintenance program CONCORR enables the user to make mass changes to the master (changing a specific data condition wherever it exists in the file). The program searches the master for the mass change condition and prepares an input transaction file record (see figure 46) wherever changes to the master file are required. The input correction transaction file is then processed by program MCNCORR to affect the changes to the master file.

The file maintenance program RECINP may be used to update a master file if a single-level index file has been created by registration number. The S.L.I. enables the user to avoid the task of manually determining record addresses to put into the file maintenance transactions, as must be done when using program MCNCORR.

As part of the file maintenance processing, GRIPHOS provides two additional programs (see figure 46). One program, called GRI6SBU (GRIPHOS sequential backup), copies the master file onto magnetic tape to back up the data stored on the direct access file. In the event that an equipment malfunction or operator error invalidates the collection master file stored on the direct access storage unit, this data can be restored by processing the most recent copy of the master file on magnetic tape by using program GRI6EDA (GRIPHOS establish direct access file).

Data retrieval processing. Up to this point the functions of gathering data and building the data file were illustrated in describing computerized cataloging using GRIPHOS. Data retrieval processing

1

CORRECTIONS AND ADDITIONS   MCNDOPE   AASA1   09/02/72 08:26.16

CHA CORRECTION REQUESTED ON PATH STARTING AT 1978.
ANOTATION CLASS IS 48
OLD STRING IS   CERAMICO

NEW STRING IS 'CERAMICS'.
OLD UNIT IS   00040 480008CERAMICO

NEW UNIT IS '00040 480008CERAMICS'.

CHANGE MADE
- -

DPH CORRECTION REQUESTED ON PATH STARTING AT 1563.
ANOTATION CLASS IS 176
OLD STRING IS   3AR47
OLD UNIT IS   00050 17600053AR47

PATH DELETED
- -

DPH CORRECTION REQUESTED ON PATH STARTING AT 2800.
ANOTATION CLASS IS 176
OLD STRING IS   3AR47
OLD UNIT IS   00050 17600053AR47

PATH DELETED
- -

DPH CORRECTION REQUESTED ON PATH STARTING AT 2946.
ANOTATION CLASS IS 176
OLD STRING IS   3AR47
OLD UNIT IS   00050 17600053AR47

PATH DELETED
- -

DPH CORRECTION REQUESTED ON PATH STARTING AT 3018.
ANOTATION CLASS IS 176
OLD STRING IS   3AR47

FIG. 47. Example of file maintenance listing

entails the query and retrieval of data stored in the collection master files; and the preparation of retrieved data for the museum's object documentation needs.

The data retrieval process illustrated in figure 48 includes five levels of processing when using the GRIPHOS system:

1. Request. Entails submitting and preparing requests for searching the master file for the information specified by the query. If a collection master file is being queried, for example, the requests may be for catalog cards, an accession log book, and specimen labels, all from information about new objects added to the data base.

2. Search. GRIPHOS programs named REQST are designed to process general request specifications and generate a work file of record addresses that satisfy the request. No output listings that provide information about the records selected for retrieval are generated by the GRIPHOS REQST programs. There are four optional REQST programs which the user may specify depending on that which best suits the documentation need:

    a. REQST 2. Will accept general requests by searching the entire data base file and generate a storage file containing file addresses of records whose data satisfies the request specifications. Logical operators may be used for data comparison such as: exact match, or match beginning word or any word within record; greater than; less than; AND, OR.

    b. REQST 3, 4, 5. Will accept general request statements by searching an inverted file indexed to a master file. This will often speed up the REQST programs by avoiding searching the entire master file for those records that satisfy the query as in REQST 2. Inverted files are useful when the general request specifies exact string matches.

3. Retrieve. GRIPHOS programs named PERMIN(n) retrieve specified fields from records in a master file and store the information to allow the PRINT program to generate reports from this information. One of the PERMIN programs is designed to accept a work file of file addresses compiled by a REQST program from a unit record file using logical operators for data comparisons. The PERMIN program retrieves specified fields of data from the records that are determined by the REQST program to satisfy the request specifications. The flow chart in figure 48 illustrates a specialized retrieval request that required the use of the REQST program to generate a retrieval work file, from which the PERMIN program performed a retrieval from the master file.

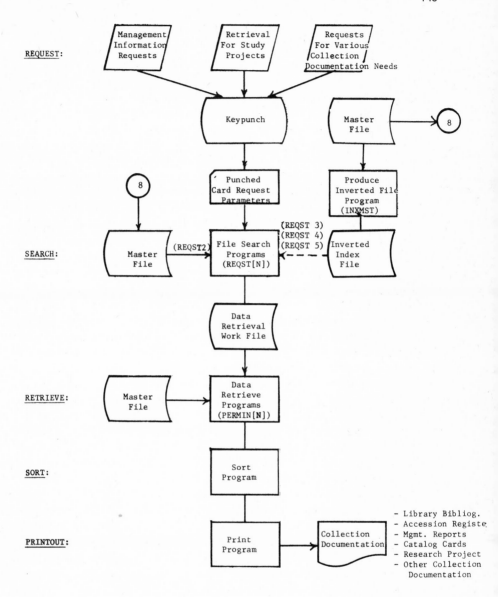

FIG. 48. Data retrieval process flow chart

There is also a type of retrieval need the user may have that avoids the REQST programs entirely. For this purpose there is a PERMIN program designed to retrieve fields of data from unit records within an address range in a master file. For example, PERMIN4 used with the SORT and PRINT programs produces catalog reports from given sets of tags from given regions in a master file.

At the present time there are four alternative PERMIN programs. In addition to the programs described above there are two for retrieving data from tree-structured (hierarchical) files: one a PERMIN program that retrieves within address ranges and one that retrieves from addresses in a work file.

4. Sort. The data retrieved from the data base may be sorted in the manner to properly classify the data for the output reports. The program used is the IBM SORT program that is part of the user's operating system (OS).

5. Print-out. The GRIPHOS program named PRINT is used to print output in multiple column, multiple row form from each set of data fields generated by the PERMIN programs (figure 49). In addition to the data, specifications may be input to the program for titling and page formatting as needed for the type output report being generated. For example, specimen labels are unique in the variety of labels that may be required for different classifications of objects. These formatting requirements will differ for management reports, research projects, and various collections documentation requirements. The GRIPHOS PRINT program provides several options to accommodate the needs of various report output types:

1. Special character editing and spacing.
2. Upper and lower case printing.
3. Underlining of characters.
4. Selective printing of page and column headings.
5. Variable number of lines per page.
6. Page numbering in roman numerals.
7. Compute mean average, minimum and maximum values, and the standard deviation for quantitative information included in a report.
8. Centering of data fields within report columns.

The GRIPHOS VANCEPRINT program enables the user to print a collection catalog card from data in the master file (see figure 50).

Data indexing functions. As previously noted, GRIPHOS storage files are organized for direct access processing. Each record is assigned a file address by which its data may be accessed. When new records are added to the data base, the input processing program assigns the record to a region number. Further access to a specific record for maintenance or other reference requires using the file address.

Based on the user's data retrieval requirements, he has the option of generating inverted files for selected annotation classes from a collection master file. As noted in figure 40, program CREINV is used to initialize the index file for use on a direct access storage unit. Program CRESINV further initializes the index file by assigning

18
BLUE SPRINGS - 3CR4   10/ /
ARTIFACTS FROM 7S10E

PROVENIENCE	OBJECT	MATERIAL	TYPE	QUANTITY	CAT. NO.
7S10E 33-20 CM AD	MAT UN	BONE AN LUMB VERT ODOCOILEUS SP			70-206-15-9
7S10E 33-20 CM AD	MAT UN	ELLIPTIO SP SHELL		22	70-206-15-1
7S10E 33-20 CM AD	MAT UN	GLASS CLEAR			70-206-15-15
7S10E 33-20 CM AD	MAT UN	GONIOBASIS SP SHELL			70-206-15-3
7S10E 33-20 CM AD	MAT UN	QUADRULA SP SHELL		12	70-206-15-2
7S10E 33-20 CM AD	MAT UN	SANDSTONE STONE		3	70-206-14-6
7S10E 33-20 CM AD	MAT UN	SHELL UNID		27	70-206-15-5
7S10E 33-20 CM AD	POINT	CHERT STONE	SCALLORN (SCHOLTZ J)		70-206-17
7S10E 33-20 CM AD	SHERD,BODY	POTTERY TEMPER SHELL	WOODWARD PLAIN (? COBB)	2	70-206-16-1
7S10E 33-20 CM AD	SHERD,RIM	POTTERY TEMPER SHELL	WOODWARD PLAIN (? COBB)		70-206-16-2
7S10E 40-50 CM	CORE	CHERT STONE		2	70-206-66-13
7S10E 40-50 CM	FLAKE,UNWORKED	CHERT STONE		89	70-206-66-11
7S10E 40-50 CM	FLAKE,UNWORKED	CHERT STONE			70-206-65-13
7S10E 40-50 CM	FLAKE,WORKED	CHERT STONE		12	70-206-66-12
7S10E 40-50 CM	MAT MOD UN	CHERT STONE		5	70-206-66-6
7S10E 40-50 CM	MAT UN	BONE AN HUM R ODOCOILEUS SP			70-206-66-11
7S10E 40-50 CM	MAT UN	BONE AN UNID		3	70-206-66-10
7S10E 40-50 CM	MAT UN	BONE BIRD UNID			70-206-66-8

FIG. 49. Example of report using PRINT program

```
┌─────────────────────────────────────────────────────────────┐
│  CONSTANT, George    Print - United States        707.40     │
│                                                        .I     │
│  PORTRAIT OF A. BAYLINSON. 1931.                              │
│  Drypoint, printed in black,                                 │
│                                                               │
│  Plate 11 13/16 x 8 3/4" (30.0 x 22.2 cm.),                   │
│                                                               │
│  Gift of Abby Aldrich Rockefeller.                           │
│                                                               │
│  Accepted 4-5-40.                                            │
│  Purchased from Downtown Gallery, N.Y.                        │
│                                                               │
│  Signed L.R. and original mat in brown                       │
│   crayon "G. Constant".                                      │
│  Dated on plate "(19)31".                                    │
│  Impression: "1/20" L.L., brown crayon.                       │
│                                                               │
│  Paper: wove, white.                                         │
│  Watermark:"(J. What)man 1930"; "England".                   │
│                                                               │
│                              MOMACTLG 3533       711029       │
│  CONSTANT, George   PORTRAIT OF A. ...   (PR)    707.40       │
└─────────────────────────────────────────────────────────────┘
```

FIG. 50. Example of catalog card prepared by GRIPHOS. One of the 25,000 catalog cards formatted and printed under computer control for the Museum of Modern Art, New York. The card program selects from the museum's data bank all those and only those items of information desired for master catalog cards for use by the public, arranges it in the museum's standard card format and prints the cards in the sequence in which they are filed, in this case by artist, title, and accession number. Since these cards are intended for a tray file, in which only the bottom line is exposed, the filing data are repeated on the bottom line. Numbers in the lower right, above the accession number, are the computer-assigned file address of the record and the date the card was generated, in this case October 29, 1971. (Reprinted from "Museum Computer Network: The Third Phase," by David Vance, in *Museum News* 51, No. 8 [April 1973]:24–27.)

its use to a specific master file. GRIPHOS program INXMST is then used to update (build) data to the index file; also, to add records to an index file as the related master file is updated. However, when adding, changing, or deleting records (file maintenance) to a master file, there is no corresponding program that will perform a similar file maintenance function to an index file. A new index file must be generated from a new master file by GRIPHOS index program INXMST (note the Search step in figure 48) when the number of changes made to the master file makes the continued use of the old index no longer effective.

The inverted files are used by the REQST programs, 3, 4, and 5 to search for data categories in a manner that is far more rapid than a sequential search of the data base directly. Single-level indexes can be generated for quick reference or cross-reference to the location of records in the master file. It is common for a GRIPHOS user to build a single-level index file on registration number, particularly, when program RECINP is used in the file maintenance process (figure 46).

Data within annotation classes are generally stored in a free-form text manner. The option is available to the user when establishing an inverted file to employ a "hashing" option, which in effect creates subfield levels within the annotation classes and sorts them alphabetically within the annotation class.

The GRIPHOS retrieval processing function as discussed earlier in this section (figure 48) provides the user with the capability to retrieve file output only in documentation form. GRIPHOS does, however, permit the user to produce fixed field, sequential files of data from existing GRIPHOS master files for use with non-GRIPHOS programs. The program FORMSEQ develops a data file from a PERMIN(n) work file, for use with such statistical packages as SPSS, CROSSTABS, BMD, and DATATEXT. These packages utilize quantitative data for analytical cross-tabulation and statistical summaries.

Implementation and Future Support

The GRIPHOS computer programs, documentation of programs, and technical support are made available through subscription and membership in the Museum Computer Network, Inc. Administrative and technical matters associated with the use of GRIPHOS are handled by Mr. David Vance, President, MCN, Inc. Dr. Jack Heller, the developer of the GRIPHOS package, is the technical advisor to MCN and is responsible for all new developments of the package.

The computer programs and their documentation are the principal support given to the GRIPHOS user. There is limited Museum Computer Network personnel to assist users with implementation matters. Assistance is given primarily by telephone or when the user travels to meet with Messrs. Vance or Heller.

Periodic updates of the program library and documentation are given the user. The program tape received by the user has an annual expiration date and deactivates itself when used beyond expiration. The program documentation received by the user provides detailed program specifications. The documentation is somewhat difficult to follow until the new user is oriented by an experienced GRIPHOS user and becomes familiar with the content and format approach used. The lack of descriptive systems content and general specifications is a chief drawback of the GRIPHOS documentation. It is difficult for the uninitiated user to understand readily the interrelationship and significance of the individual programs.

System improvements. It was noted earlier in this report that GRIPHOS is designed to operate only in a job-oriented (batch) computer operating environment. Future plans are to develop a terminal-oriented operation for parts of GRIPHOS. Present planning is to apply the use of terminals and data communications to the processing of the following GRIPHOS programs:

1. MCNCORR, file maintenance.
2. PRILGUN, file record print.
3. REQST 3, file search with index file.

The remote job entry approach being considered is that the terminal would be used for entering data and job control parameter cards (JCL) to initiate the processing of the above GRIPHOS programs and to receive back printed messages. The full reports and output documentation would be printed on the high-speed printers at the computer center.

Future plans are to permit GRIPHOS users to write their own programs. Training sessions or workshops are planned to orient interested users, who already have had PL/I programming experience, with an understanding of the elements of the GRIPHOS superstructure; namely, the data manipulation language and file accessing methods used by GRIPHOS. This capability would provide the GRIPHOS user with more flexibility for adapting GRIPHOS to his individual needs.

Other considerations for system improvements at the present time relate to:

1. Developing one PERMIN (Permuted Index Retrieval) program to replace the four that are available.

2. Developing new types of query/request techniques that will apply more effectively to logical search questions, especially as they relate to the manner of searching hierarchically structured storage files.

The GRIPHOS system is used by Professor Heller and the Computer Sciences Department at State University of New York for educational purposes. New program developments occur from this form of use and frequently result in worthwhile enhancements to the GRIPHOS package and to the benefit of its users.

Adaptability of package to use standard data categories. The Museum Computer Network, Inc., has established and maintains a directory of standardized annotation classes that GRIPHOS subscribers may assign to their data categories. The list in figure 32 is an excerpt from this directory. It would appear that the data directory is sufficiently flexible to accept additional data categories whose coding is within the seven characters used by GRIPHOS.

Adaptability of package to interact with other packages. The GRIPHOS program FORMSEQ was designed to function as a metalanguage that would reformat GRIPHOS data bases for processing in any user requested fixed field form, or reformat data bases from other systems for processing by GRIPHOS programs. FORMSEQ has been used to translate GRIPHOS data for processing by SEL-GEM, TAXIR, SPSS, SSP, Data Text, Text/360, BMD, and CODA-SYL, and to translate SELGEM data for processing by GRIPHOS. Through this program GRIPHOS is completely adaptable to interact with other packages.

Cost Considerations

There are two major aspects of cost that should be considered when evaluating the use of GRIPHOS.

Subscription costs. Subscription costs are principally associated with the acquisition and on-going use of the computer programs. There is an annual subscription cost of $1,000 to use GRIPHOS: $250 for membership in the Museum Computer Network, Inc., and $750 for use of the GRIPHOS programs and receipt of program updates. The experience of GRIPHOS users has been that the program package can be installed within a short time. Therefore, the principal need for computer programming personnel is for someone with a reasonable familiarity with the operating system of IBM 360 or 370 computers. The cost of installation would be minimal.

Operational costs. Operational costs are recurring costs of the day-to-day computer processing in order to build and update collection master files, perform information inquiries on data in these files, and retrieve the data for collection documentation needs. For a discussion of the problems of estimating operational costs see pages 92–93.

GIPSY
Package Description

Background

GIPSY, an acronym for Generalized Information Processing SYstem, is a general data base oriented information retrieval system. It includes capabilities for both batch processing and for real-time interrogation of a data base via a communications terminal. The package was developed in 1968 under the direction of Dr. James W. Sweeney at the University of Oklahoma Research Institute and Merrick Computer Center. The system was patented in October, 1971 (USP No. 3,614,744) by the University of Oklahoma.

GIPSY as a generalized type system offers museum users the flexibility to build and maintain an object collection data base, and to retrieve information to effectively utilize the computerized data. The first use of GIPSY in museums was a project for the development of an ethnographic data bank at the University of Oklahoma during 1968. The University of Missouri also used GIPSY to develop its own ethnographic data banks. The project has since become inactive at the University of Oklahoma; however, the Oklahoma Biological Survey has used the system for the development of a data bank of biological specimens. This project includes the records on 60,000 fish, 50,000 amphibians, 30,000 reptiles, 8,000 birds, and 4,000 grasses. Emphasis of the project has been to collect environmental data, and longitude/latitude coordinates, so as to facilitate retrieval for environmental impact statements.

Several agencies of the government (Department of Transportation, Department of Commerce, Federal Power Commission, U.S. Geological Survey, Department of the Interior), several departments within the University of Oklahoma (schools of medicine, geology, biology), the Oil and Gas Institute, and the Special Projects Program (linguistics studies) of the National Science Foundation represent the major types of GIPSY users at the present.

Administration of GIPSY to nonprofit organizations outside the University of Oklahoma is under the direction of Mr. Jack L. Morrison, Director, Information Systems Programs, Office of Research Administration (formerly the University of Oklahoma Research Institute). Dr. James Sweeney, now at Georgia Institute of Technology, also has a license to market GIPSY for commercial use.

The operation of the GIPSY package at nonprofit organizations outside the University of Oklahoma (Merrick Computer Center) is presently limited to the U.S. Geological Survey, Washington, D.C., Oklahoma State University, and Georgia Institute of Technology.

The GIPSY computer programs are written in IBM System/360 Assembler Language using the full Operating System (OS/360) software. The programs will operate on an IBM 360/40 or larger computer, with more than a 65K memory, and at least two IBM 2311 disk drives or equivalent direct-access device capacity. The on-line communications part of GIPSY uses the IBM 1050 data communications system and either IBM 2741 communications terminals or other manufacturers equivalent equipment.

System Description

The description of GIPSY will include several elements that make up the processing system: file types and data structures, functions of the computer programs that constitute the system, and the GIPSY information processing flow to illustrate the interrelationship of the various programs.

An overview of GIPSY is illustrated by the schematic chart in figure 51. The chart illustrates that GIPSY is made up of a data base that consists of three types of files: dictionary files, master files, and selected records files. The GIPSY programs may be classified by their processing functions: initialize programs, file build programs, file maintenance programs, print utility programs, and retrieval programs (QUESTRAN).

File types and data structures. The GIPSY package utilizes computerized files on both direct access devices and magnetic tape. Files used for data storage and retrieval are on direct access devices. Files used for master file back up, for temporary storage, and for interface with non-GIPSY packages are placed on magnetic tape. The principal storage type files include the following:

1. Dictionary file. A feature of GIPSY is the dictionary file. Its purpose is to catalog specifications from the object documentation forms that are used as source data for updating master files. Master file input data may originate from one or more forms such as that illustrated in figure 52. Data specifications for each object documentation form would be recorded in the dictionary file. It performs the function of data validation for the master file updating process when data is added to the file. It maintains the fields within the master file record in an ordered manner, thereby allowing the user to input data to the master file in an unordered manner. The dictionary file also controls the manner in which data in the master file records are displayed when retrieved for output documentation.

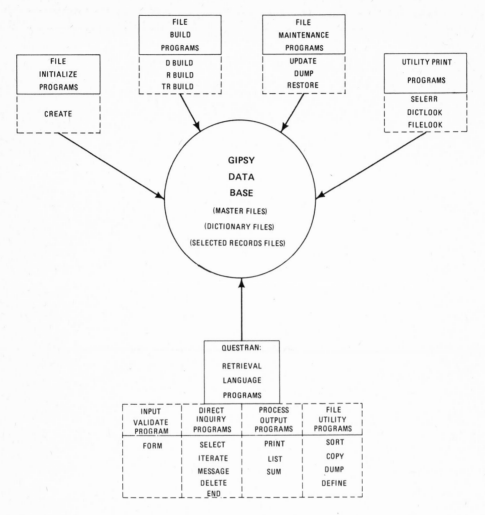

FIG. 51. Overview of GIPSY

The cataloging of a new object documentation form into the dictionary file requires the preparation of a specification sheet. Specifications for the form shown in figure 52 have been partially recorded on the dictionary file specification sheet illustrated in table 8. In table 8 are explanations of the data fields and codes that make up the specifications to be entered into the dictionary file.

FORM 100001

S.   SCHOOL INFORMATION SHEET

SA.   Location

    SA1.   Community < _____ >
    SA2.   County < _____ >
    SA3.   Map ID < _____ >
    SA4.   Date
           SA4A.   Day   < _____ >
           SA4B.   Month < _____ >
           SA4C.   Year   < _____ >
    SA5.   School District < _____ >

Identification and Description of Facility

    SD1.   Name of School < _____ >
    SD2.   Type of School
           SD2A1.   Public Elementary
           SD2A2.   Public Junior High
           SD2A3.   Public Senior High
           SD2A4.   Public Junior & Senior High
           SD2A5.   Public Other < _____ >

           SD3B1.   Private Elementary
           SD3B2.   Private Junior High
           SD3B3.   Private Senior High
           SD3B4.   Private Junior & Senior High
           SD3B5.   Private Other < _____ >

    SE.   Attendance: Total School < _____ >
    SF.   School Year < _____ >
    SJ.   Total Attendance Capacity of Existing Facility < ____ >
    SK.   Date Physical Plant Constructed < _____ >
    SL.   Additions to Original (if any) < _____ >
    SM.   Scheduled Expansion (if any) < _____
          _____ >

Number of Teaching Rooms by Type/School

    SG1.   Classrooms < _____ >   SG6.   Other < _____
    SG2.   Library   < _____ >   _____
    SG3.   Auditorium < _____ >   _____
    SG4.   Gymnasium < _____ >   _____
    SG5.   Laboratory < _____ >   _____ >
                                        SG7.   Portable Classrooms < __ >
                                        SG8.   Cafetorium < _____ >

FIG. 52. Sample of object documentation form

Table 8
Dictionary File Specification Sheet

Label (1)	Spacing and Level Code (2)	Print		Internal Format Code (5)	Item Description (6)
		Option Code (3)	Spacing Code (4)		
S	02	1	b	10	SCHOOL INFORMATION SHEET
SA	04	1	0	15	LOCATION
SA1	06	1		20	COMMUNITY
SA2	06	1		30	COUNTY
SA3	06	1		40	MAP ID
SA4	06	1		50	DATE
SA4A	08	1		60	DAY
SA4B	16	1	+	70	MONTH

Explanation of Codes:

(1) Mnemonic assigned to each field in the master file record. The object documentation form provides the data content for each file.

(2) The number of spaces from the left margin that item description and data content would be printed.

(3) Code 1 = Print item description and data content on same line.

(4) b = single spacing, O = double spacing, + = suppress spacing.

(5) Numeric code stored in the master file record, which corresponds to the mnemonic label of the field.

(6) Description assigned to the data field. Prints out on object documentation when data is displayed.

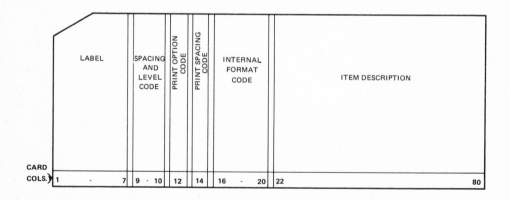

FIG. 53. Dictionary file input transaction card

The dictionary file specification sheet is used for keypunching input transactions for updating (building) the dictionary file. Figure 53 is an illustration of a dictionary file input transaction card format. Each transaction card contains the specifications for one field of data contained within a master file record. Figure 54 illustrates the content of a dictionary file record after it has been built from the object documentation form specifications.

| G I P S Y | DICTIONARY BUILD | FORM – 100001 | 70020 | UNIVERSITY OF OKLAHOMA | PAGE | 1 |

LABEL	SP	O	V	I.F.	CLEAR TEXT
S	02	1		10	SCHOOL FACILITY INFORMATION
SA	04	1	0	15	LOCATION
SA1	06	1		20	COMMUNITY:
SA2	06	1		30	COUNTY:
SA3	06	1		40	MAP ID:
SA4	06	1		50	DATE
SA4A	08	1		60	DAY
SA4B	16	1	+	70	MONTH
SA4C	26	1	+	80	YEAR
SF	04	1	0	81	SCHOOL YEAR:
SD	04	1	0	100	SCHOOL IDENTIFICATION
SD1	05	3		110	NAME OF SCHOOL
SA5	05	1		115	SCHOOL DISTRICT:
SD2	04	3		120	TYPE OF SCHOOL
SD2A1	06	1		121	PUBLIC ELEMENTARY SCHOOL
SD2A2	06	1		122	PUBLIC JUNIOR HIGH
SD2A3	06	1		123	PUBLIC SENIOR HIGH
SD2A4	06	1		124	PUBLIC JUNIOR AND SENIOR HIGH
SD2A5	06	1		125	PUBLIC
SD2B1	06	1		126	PRIVATE ELEMENTARY
SD2B2	06	1		127	PRIVATE JUNIOR HIGH
SD2B3	06	1		128	PRIVATE SENIOR HIGH
SD2B4	06	1		129	PRIVATE JUNIOR AND SENIOR HIGH
SD2B5	06	1		130	PRIVATE
SE	C4	1	0	150	ATTENDANCE: TOTAL/SCHOOL:
SG	04	1	0	200	NUMBER OF TEACHING ROOMS: BY TYPE
SG1	C6	1		210	CLASSROOMS
SG2	06	1		220	LIBRARY

FIG. 54. Example of dictionary file record print-out

FORM 100001

SCHOOL INFORMATION SHEET

Location

SA1. Community < *Oklahoma City   I-89* >
SA2. County < *Oklahoma* >
SA3. Map ID < *19216A3D* >
SA4. Date
    SA4A. Day < *14* >
    SA4B. Month < *03* >
    SA4C. Year < *1968* >
SA5. School District < >

Identification and Description of Facility

SD1. Name of School < *Dunjee* >
SD2. Type of School
    (SD2A1) Public Elementary
    SD2A2. Public Junior High
    SD2A3. Public Senior High
    SD2A4. Public Junior & Senior High
    SD2A5. Public Other < >

    SD3B1. Private Elementary
    SD3B2. Private Junior High
    SD3B3. Private Senior High
    SD3B4. Private Junior & Senior High
    SD3B5. Private Other < >

SE. Attendance: Total School < *789* >
SF. School Year < *67-68* >
SJ. Total Attendance Capacity of Existing Facility < *690* >
SK. Date Physical Plant Constructed < *13 years* >
SL. Additions to Original (if any) < *1964* >
SM. Scheduled Expansion (if any) < >

Number of Teaching Rooms by Type/School

SG1. Classrooms < *11* >   SG6. Other < *1KD27* >
SG2. Library < >   *2 Administrative*
SG3. Auditorium < >   *Rooms*
SG4. Gymnasium < >
SG5. Laboratory < >   < >
                                SG7. Portable Classrooms < *9* >
                                SG8. Cafetorium < *1* >

FIG. 55. Example of object documentation form (with data recorded)

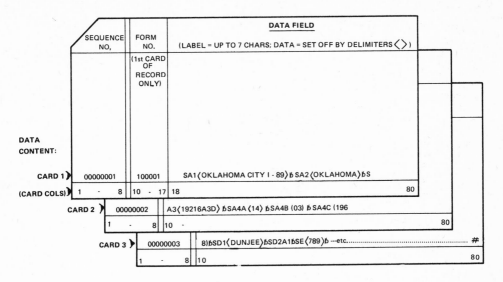

FIG. 56. Master file update input transaction

2. Master file. The master file is used for the permanent storage and maintenance of object documentation file data on direct access devices. This file is updated by means of input transactions that are keypunched from object documentation forms. Figure 55 is the same object documentation form as figure 52 with data recorded on it for keypunching.

The input transactions to update a master file are formatted for punched cards in the manner illustrated by figure 56. The first field in each card contains a sequence number that is used to keep the transactions in sequence. This sequence is important for correct file updating because data fields can continue from one card to the next. Figure 56 shows three cards whose illustrated data content is from the form in figure 55. The form number field in the transaction card identifies the dictionary file record where the specifications for this input transaction have been cataloged. The data field of the input transaction is used to record the data field label and the data content of the field. The size of the data content fields are variable in length and therefore are set off with delimiters < >, so as to distinguish data content from the field label. Data fields may overflow from one card to the next. The end of a record is identified by a single, unique character (e.g., # as in figure 56). The next object documentation form to be keypunched would begin with a new input card.

The input transaction to change a master file record is formatted differently from the transaction format for adding a new record to a master file. The data is formatted for punched cards in the manner illustrated in figure 57.

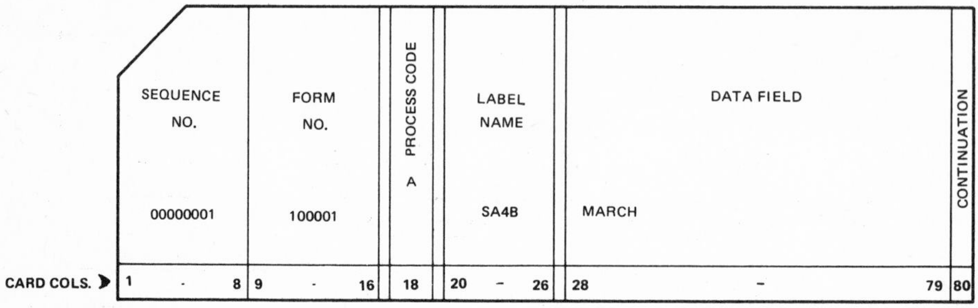

SEQUENCE NO.	FORM NO.	PROCESS CODE	LABEL NAME	DATA FIELD		CONTINUATION
00000001	100001	A	SA4B	MARCH		

CARD COLS. ➤ 1 - 8 │ 9 - 16 │ 18 │ 20 - 26 │ 28 - 79 │ 80

Process Code:

A = Add or replace label name and data content
D = Delete label name and data content
E = Add (extend) to existing text
P = Delete record text

FIG. 57. Master file maintenance input transaction

The file maintenance input transaction card is formatted to carry the data to affect only one master file data field. The data content of the transaction card may be variable in length. If the size of the data content is larger than one transaction card provides (52 characters), the balance of the data can be continued into the next card. The continuation field, column 80, when punched, signals that another card follows with the same label identifier and whose sequence number field value is one number higher. A process code in card column 18 identifies the processing that is to take place. The code options are shown in figure 57.

The data structure of the master file record differs from the data structures of the input transactions illustrated in figures 56 and 57. The format of the master file is referred to by GIPSY users as the "internal" data structure. The master file is built from input transaction data using a GIPSY file build program (refer back to figure 51). The internal data structure of the master file is illustrated in figure 58.

The format of the master file consists of three segments: *(a)* the record header, 16 bytes in length, which precede each master file record; *(b)* field designator segments, 6 bytes for each data field in

RECORD LENGTH	SPAN TRACK DESIG.	RELATIVE LOCATION 1st DATA FIELD	FORM NUMBER	INTERNAL FORMAT CODE	RELATIVE LOCATION OF DATA FIELD	LENGTH OF DATA FIELD	INTERNAL FORMAT CODE	RELATIVE LOCATION OF DATA FIELD	LENGTH OF DATA FIELD
1 - 2	3 - 4	5 - 6	7 - 14	17 - 18	19 - 20	21 - 22	23 - 24	25 - 26	27 - 28

LENGTH OF DATA FIELD	1ST DATA FIELD	2ND DATA FIELD	3rd DA
- 88			

FIG. 58. Master file data structure

the record [19]; and *(c)* data field segments that are variable length fields whose length is defined in a corresponding field designator segment.

The maximum length of master file records is 32,000 characters. (This limitation is imposed by the IBM operating system OS/360.) The order in which the fields are recorded in the master file record is determined by the corresponding specifications for the input data cataloged in the dictionary file (see figure 54). As the reader may have noted, the internal format code shown in the master file (figure 58), is not part of the input transaction data. The RBUILD program gets this data from the dictionary file by matching the label field in the transaction data with the corresponding label in the dictionary file record.

3. Select records file. The select records file is a temporary type file used as an index for the GIPSY information retrieval QUES-TRAN programs. During a search process, records meeting search criteria are selected for storage of their addresses and unique identifier labels (of the field in which the accession number is stored) in the selected records file. This file type is also used during the master file update process. During file maintenance processing, the selected records file provides access to the master file records, which are usually in random order.

The hierarchical structuring of master file records is only implied within GIPSY. The means of ordering the sequence of data fields within a record is through the "internal format code" code assigned to each data field in a record (refer back to description of the dictionary file). The internal format code determines the order in which the data fields would be presented by the print program for display. The value of the number placed in the internal format code for a data field would be inverse to the hierarchical position of the data field within a record. Table 8, referenced earlier, illustrates the intrarecord relationship of the internal format code. This internal format code does not permit joining multiple records for display of their hierarchical relationship.

Program descriptions. The types of computer programs that make up the GIPSY package are illustrated in Figure 51. The programs shown in the upper portion of this chart perform such functions as: file initializing, file building, file maintenance, and utility printing. These are individual programs performing unique functions. These programs are interrelated as a system by the GIPSY user to perform a series of processing functions. Several such system functions will be illustrated in the next section on information processing flow.

The QUESTRAN program, however, is structured differently from the aforementioned types of programs. QUESTRAN, the GIPSY retrieval language program, is comprised of the several command modules shown in figure 51 and performs such functions as input validation, direct inquiry, process output, and file utility.

Table 9 lists a glossary of the various GIPSY programs and QUESTRAN commands that perform a unique information processing function. They do not represent the entire library of GIPSY programs, but they are the widely used programs in the GIPSY package. This glossary should provide a convenient reference to GIPSY programs as they are referenced in the following description of information processing flow.

Table 9

GIPSY Programs

Name	Program Description
BACK	QUESTRAN program command used to return to a previous selected records file subset during the search and retrieve iterations
COPY	QUESTRAN program command used to construct fixed-field, fixed-length records on terminal, tape, disk, or printer
CREATE	Initializes direct-access files for acceptance of input data: master files, file dictionary, and selected records file
DBUILD	Used to catalog object documentation file forms descriptions in the dictionary. Builds or adds descriptions to the dictionary file

DEFINE	QUESTRAN program command permits the terminal display of names and contents of forms cataloged in the dictionary
DELETE	QUESTRAN program command flags records for deletion from a master file that have been selected to a selected records file; may be used only in a batch operation mode
DICTLOOK	Used to print a listing of form descriptions cataloged in the dictionary file
DUMP	Used to write GIPSY records from a direct-access file to a tape file. Prepares backup tapes and transfers data from one master file to another
END	QUESTRAN program command used to close out operation of GIPSY from a terminal
FILELOOK	Displays the extent that allocated space on a master file is utilized
FORM	QUESTRAN program command used to validate use of correct file prior to initiating an inquiry process
ITERATE	QUESTRAN program command used to restrict the number of records searched during an inquiry, by having the next inquiry iteration search against a selected records file
LIST	QUESTRAN program command designates portions of selected records from the master file instead of entire record
MESSAGE	QUESTRAN program command permits the sending of messages from the terminal to the computer console
PRINT	QUESTRAN program command used to print selected records from the master file on the terminal or high-speed printer. There are no parameters for specifying format other than a report heading
RBUILD	Used to add new records to a master file on a direct-access device
RESTORE	Used to restore a tape file created by the DUMP program to a specified master file on a direct-access device
SELECT	QUESTRAN program command used to initiate an inquiry to a master file once the input file is validated
SELLERR	Used to select the errors that result during a master file build or file maintenance process and display the error information on an output report
SORT	QUESTRAN program command used to sort selected records and reconstruct a selected records file in the desired sequence
SUM	QUESTRAN program command used to compute the following information from numerical values in selected records: the number of occurrences, the arithmetic mean, the algebraic sum, the maximum value of the item, and minimum value of the item
TRBUILD	Same as RBUILD except it creates nonsearchable records in internal format on a sequential magnetic tape. This file may be used with the RESTORE program to load file back to a direct-access device
UPDATE	Used for file maintenance to change or extend existing records on a master file

Information processing flow. The GIPSY processing flow includes the following system functions:

1. File initializing. Figure 59 illustrates the use of program CREATE to initialize each of the three types of files used in GIPSY. This program allocates the amount of direct access file storage estimated for the data and formats the data set for subsequent storage in the file.

2. Dictionary file build. Figure 60 illustrates the use of program DBUILD to build and add new records to the dictionary file. When a new object documentation file form (figure 52) is designed for adding records to a master file, specifications (table 8) are prepared for cataloging the object form into the dictionary file. The specification sheet is keypunched to prepare input transactions (figure 53) for processing by the dictionary build program DBUILD. A utility print program DICTLOOK may be used to produce a print-out of the

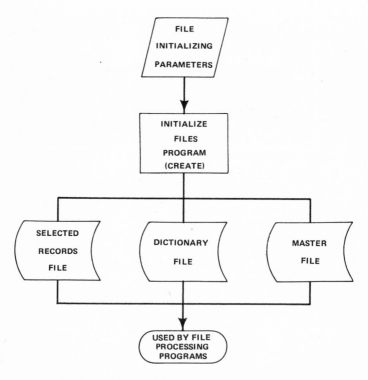

FIG. 59. File initializing program flow chart

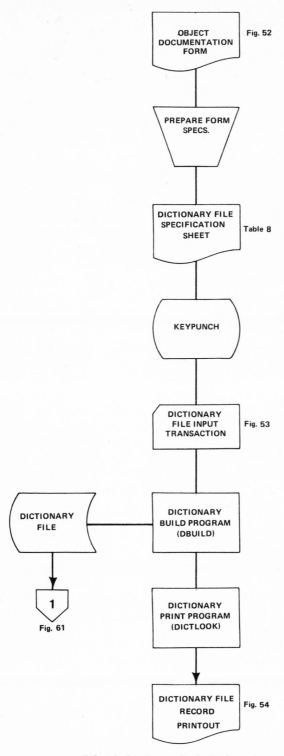

FIG. 60. Dictionary file build flow chart

object form record added to the dictionary file (figure 54). The up-dated dictionary file will subsequently be used by the master file update program (figure 61) when new records are added to the master file.

3. Master file build. Figure 61 illustrates the use of program RBUILD to build and add new records to a GIPSY master file. The object documentation file form recorded with data (figure 55) is keypunched to prepare input transactions (figure 56) for updating the master file by program RBUILD. The dictionary file serves to validate the input data as the master file is updated. A transaction listing of the new records added to the master is prepared by program RBUILD. Errors that occur as a result of the updating process are printed out by the utility print program SELERR. The program also punches transaction cards that may be used to correct the original updating errors. Errors may be due to "label not in dic-tionary," "too many labels," "invalid characters," "missing de-limiters," etc.

4. Master file maintenance. Figure 62 illustrates the use of program UPDATE to correct records in the master file. Parameters for the records to be changed or corrected are input to the QUESTRAN program SELECT command module, which generates a selected record index file of the master file records to be corrected. The selected records file is sorted to the input transaction sequence and copied to magnetic tape by QUESTRAN program command modules SORT and COPY. The master file correction transaction form is keypunched to prepare input transactions (figure 57) for processing by file mainte-nance program UPDATE. This program prepares a transaction listing of the master file records that were corrected. Errors that occur as a result of the file maintenance processing are printed out by the utility print program SELERR, and errors are corrected and reen-tered for processing.

5. Data retrieval. The search and retrieval function is a principal processing feature of the GIPSY package. Its process flow is illus-trated in figure 63. The GIPSY search function has iterative process-ing capability that permits repetitive decision points throughout the execution of the search. The program called QUESTRAN performs the following processing steps:

(a) Formulate the search statement.
(b) Formulate the search strategy (logical relationship of the variables in the search statement).
(c) Perform the file search.

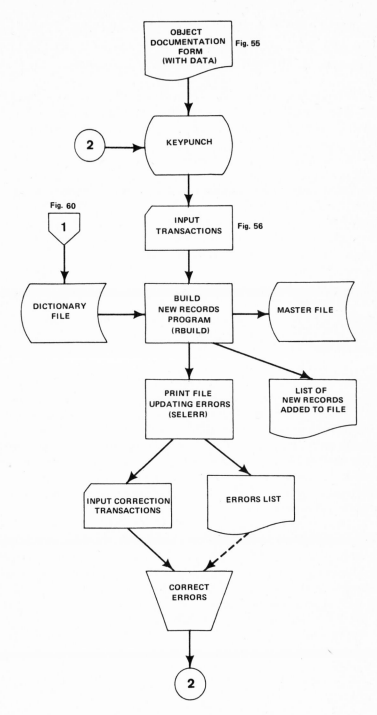

FIG. 61. Master file build flow chart

166

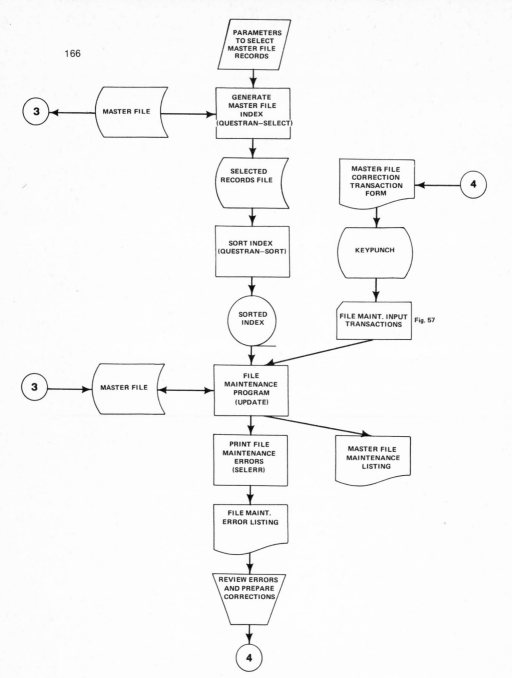

FIG. 62. Master file maintenance flow chart

(d) Display search statistics and evaluate further need to formulate the question.

(e) Display search results.

(f) Further decision point—evaluate results and need for further iteration.

Data records can be searched on the basis of comparing textual word data for certain conditions such as particular words, parts of words, phrases, or word ranges. Numeric data in records can be searched using relational operators such as "equal to," "greater than," "less than." Logical operators "and," "or," "not" may be used to specify logical association of the variables specified in the search statement.

Search statistics displayed (figure 63) are (1) the number of records searched, (2) the number of records selected, (3) the number of records that satisfied each variable in the search statement, (4) the number of records that satisfied the relationships of the entire search statement.

Retrieved records may be sorted by the GIPSY program SORT on any data element in ascending or descending order before displaying the data.

Search output such as illustrated in figure 64 may, at the option of the terminal operator, be displayed at the terminal, printed on the high-speed printer at the computer center, or transferred to an output file in any predefined format (fixed-field, fixed-length records) for use in a non-GIPSY program.

Implementation and Future Support

The GIPSY computer programs, documentation of programs, and technical support are made available through the University of Oklahoma, Office of Research Administration. Mr. Jack L. Morrison, Director, Information Systems Programs, is responsible for administering the use of GIPSY. There are two programmers on Mr. Morrison's staff who maintain the GIPSY computer programs and support its application. Dr. James Sweeney, the GIPSY developer, is now located at Georgia Institute of Technology.

Until July, 1973, there had been no formal plans for marketing the installation of the GIPSY program package at new user locations. There now appears to be an interest in marketing the GIPSY package by the University of Oklahoma. Steps are being taken to improve the support to GIPSY users: An information newsletter is being published periodically; a users' group meets periodically to discuss

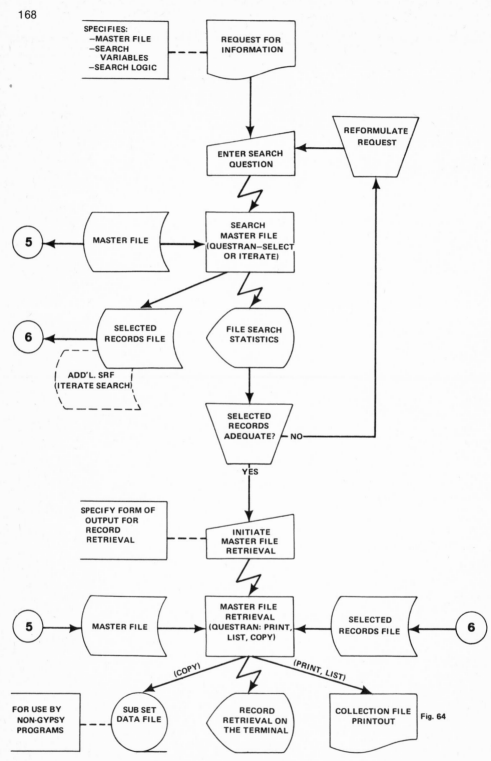

FIG. 63. Data retrieval flow chart

```
SCHOOL INFORMATION

  LOCATION
    COMMUNITY--- OKLAHOMA CITY I-89
    COUNTY---   OKLA.
    MAP ID---   19216A3D
    DATE
      DAY  14
      MONTH  03
      YEAR 1968

  SCHOOL YEAR- 67-68

  IDENTIFICATION
   NAME OF SCHOOL
     DUNJEE
  TYPE OF SCHOOL
   ELEM. SCHOOL

  ATTENDANCE: TOTAL/SCHOOL---   789

  NUMBER OF TEACHING ROOMS: BY TYPE
    CLASSROOMS 11
    PORTABLE CLASSROOMS   9
    CAFETORIUM 1
    OTHER
      1 KDGT 2 ADMINISTRATIVE ROOMS

  NUMBER OF CLASSROOMS: BY GRADE
    ELEMENTARY
      FIRST   3
      SECOND  3
      THIRD   4
      FOURTH  3
      FIFTH   3
      SIXTH   4
      KINDERGARDEN 1

  ATTENDANCE BY GRADE
    FIRST   94
    SECOND  110
    THIRD   124
    FOURTH  109
    FIFTH   120
    SIXTH   128
    KINDERGARDEN 104

  TOTAL ATTENDANCE CAPACITY OF EXISTING FACILITY---   690

  AGE OF PHYSICAL PLANT (IN YEARS) OR CONSTRUCTION DATE--- 13 YRS
  ADDITIONS TO ORIGINAL PLANT
    1964
```

FIG. 64. Example of a GIPSY master file print-out (see figure 55)

such matters as user problems, needs for enhancing the capabilities of programs, and potential new applications for the package; and the documentation is being updated at the systems, programming, and operational levels. At this time there are no plans formalized for adding any new features or changing the design of the GIPSY package.

Adaptability of GIPSY to use standard data categories. There has been no attempt on the part of GIPSY developers to enforce or recommend any standardization of data categories or uniform manner of labeling data. However, the dictionary file building feature of GIPSY makes the package readily adaptable to use standard data categories as they are developed in the future.

Adaptability of GIPSY to interact with other packages. The GIPSY package appears to offer the capability to interact with other packages on a file-to-program basis. Data can be retrieved and converted to standardized or preestablished file specifications for processing by other computerized information systems.

Cost Considerations

There are two major aspects of cost that should be considered when evaluating the use of GIPSY.

Subscription costs. Subscription costs are principally costs associated with the acquisition, installation, and on-going use of the computer programs. These costs for the GIPSY package are as follows:

One-time charge per location for installation and training	$1,400
Monthly rental charge, first location of installation, during first twelve months of use	550
Monthly rental charge, each secondary location of installation, during first twelve months of use	400
Monthly maintenance, service, and updating charge, per location, during first twelve months of use	—
Monthly rental charge, per location, after twelve months of use	—
Monthly maintenance, service, and updating charge, per location after twelve months of rental charge	150

Operational costs. Operational costs are recurring costs associated with the day-to-day computer processing required to build and maintain collection master files, to perform inquiries on data in these master files, and to retrieve data for collection documentation needs.

There is not sufficient information presently available at the office of Information Systems Programs to evaluate the GIPSY cost of operation.

TAXIR (STIRS)
Package Description

Background

TAXIR, an acronym for TAXonomic Information Retrieval, is a generalized information system designed to store data for query and information retrieval. STIRS (Set Theoretic Information Retrieval System) is the name given to the version of TAXIR currently in use at the University of Colorado, and it is STIRS that will be described here. In addition to STIRS, several other information systems (e.g., INVER, the system used by the Gulf Universities Research Consortium) are reported to be based upon the original TAXIR concepts and programs.

TAXIR was developed originally under the direction of David J. Rogers, taxonomist at the University of Colorado, and a team comprised of George Estabrook, mathematician, and Robert C. Brill, computer specialist. The package was funded by a National Science Foundation grant to develop a computerized system for systematic biology. Use of the package was to facilitate the curation of botanical and zoological collections. The design of the package was planned to be general in application for the scientific and business user requiring information retrieval from large masses of computer-stored data. The package is described as a generalized system because its retrieval processing is independent of the type of information stored in its master files. The system employs a limited range of file maintenance functions but is highly effective in its data retrieval capability with large, relatively static master files.

The TAXIR package is currently in use under the auspices of a well-known botanical institution for a land-use planning project and by a university for geographical mapping of biological data for designated land regions. The most accessible version of TAXIR, which is now STIRS, is available from the University of Colorado Computing Center. Subscribers have used the STIRS package for educational purposes within the School of Business at the University of Colorado;

for a system to inventory bridge structures for the State Highway Department; and for recording historical data on earthquake occurrences for an environmental information service by the National Oceanic and Atmospheric Administration (U.S. Department of Commerce). In the future STIRS is to be used for a project under the auspices of the United Nations to set up an international information system on genetic resource conservation in Rome, Italy. David Rogers will be the director of the project.

The STIRS package as presently available is limited to use on a Control Data Corporation (CDC) 6400 large-scale computer, utilizing the KRONOS CDC disk operating system. The programs are written in FORTRAN and CDC assembly language and COM-PASS(CDC) macro subroutines. The package permits the user to access his master files for processing in either a batch mode or in a teleprocessing mode from a remote-located terminal. The package uses an interactive command language that guides the user through the steps of inquiry and informational retrieval.

System Description

The description of STIRS will include the several processing elements that make up the system: file types and data structures, functions of the computer commands that comprise the system, and the STIRS information processing flow to illustrate the principal processing characteristics of the various program commands.

The organization of data stored and processed by the system is based on the principle of set theory, which is defined as the application of data groups or sets resulting from classifying items by characteristic or property. Data structured in the STIRS system is referenced by the following terminology:

1. Set. A collection of items or group of objects, whose data would ordinarily be grouped into a master file.

2. Item (record). An element of a master file and its corresponding pertinent information; an object (museum specimen) and the recorded data in the data bank concerning the object.

3. Descriptor (field). An information category describing pieces of information about an item, the criterion for dividing items of a master file into mutually exclusive subsets.

4. Descriptor state (data). The data content of a mutually exclusive subset (e.g., color of a flower).

As a system, STIRS embodies a data base whose processing is controlled by a series of program control statements. The control statements function to produce information print-outs from the data base as illustrated by the schematic chart in figure 65. The data base may consist of three file types: master files, control vocabulary, and original input data files. The STIRS control statements may be classified into the following processing functions: file build, query and retrieval, file update, and miscellaneous processing.

File types. The STIRS package utilizes direct-access and magnetic tape devices for the off-line storage of the three types of data files used by the system. Data files when used for query, retrieval, or update processing are loaded into the memory unit of the computer from the off-line storage devices. When processing is completed, the data files resident in the computer memory are returned to the off-line storage devices for future use.

The three types of STIRS files are:

1. Input files. The STIRS package accepts data in the form of punched cards, magnetic tape, or disk files. When magnetic tape or direct-access devices are used for the input files, the records must be in an 80-column format and in BCD (binary coded decimal) mode.

Figure 66 is a simplified example of an input file. The first card contains a STIRS program control statement, DEFINE ITEMS, describing the source and physical layout of the data record. In the illustration the input data is in free format (in contrast to the fixed field option), and the order of the predefined field numbers is indicated: fields 1,2,3,6,7,5 etc. Cards 2 to 7 are data cards. Data fields are separated by commas, and records are separated by asterisks. Each record begins on a new card, but a record may consist of more than one card. The definition for each field is described by the STIRS program control statement DEFINE DESCRIPTORS, which is described below.

2. Control vocabulary. This file defines the structure of the master file by defining the characteristics of each data field: name (descriptor), type of data content (state), and order of the data. The control vocabulary is a separate file but functions in an integral manner with the master file. The functions of the file are to interpret and control the data that are entered into the master file.

Figure 67 is an example of data prepared for input to a control vocabulary file to be used with the input shown in figure 66. The data for this example was punched into ten cards. The DEFINE DESCRIPTORS control statement appearing at the beginning of the first card identifies to STIRS that the data to follow are to be entered into the control vocabulary, and that in this example 15 data fields are being defined. The first field (TRANSACTION NO.)

~∫TIR∫ ~

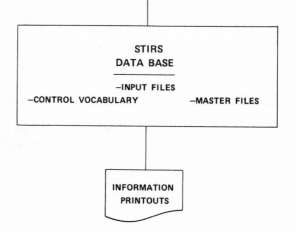

TYPES OF CONTROL STATEMENTS			
FILE BUILD	**QUERY & RETRIEVAL**	**FILE UPDATE**	**MISCELLANEOUS**
—DEFINE DESCRIPTORS —DEFINE ITEMS —DEFINE AND PRINT ITEMS —END OF ITEMS	—HOW MANY —PRINT —GENERATE —STATISTICS —CONTROL VOCABULARY —ID	—CORRECTION —DELETE STATE —DELETE ITEM —DEFINE MORE DESCRIPTORS	—END —TIME —MEMO —READ DATA BANK —WRITE DATA BANK

STIRS
DATA BASE

—INPUT FILES
—CONTROL VOCABULARY   —MASTER FILES

INFORMATION
PRINTOUTS

FIG. 65. Overview of STIRS

will be numeric with a range from 1 to 50,000. The option ORDER
FROM TO specifies the data may be retrieved in the numerical
sequence of TRANSACTION NO. Other data options illustrated in
figure 67 are:

(a) Field 2 in cards (1) and (2) is called TRANSACTING
PARTY. The NAME option indicates an unordered list of
alpha-numeric names. The 2000 indicates the maximum estimated number of names this field may have.

CARD NO.	CARD CONTENT
(1)	DEFINE ITEMS FROM CARDS, FORMAT FREE 1-3, 6, 7, 5, 4, 8-12, 14, 15, 13*
(2)	14616, CUTRATE FURNITURE CO., 415 KNOTHOLE ST., MAY, 15, 1960, EXPENSE, 3 DESKS
(3)	WITH CHAIRS, DELIVERED, 180.79, UNPAID, 0, JULY, 15, 1960*
(4)	14617, ECONOMO DRUGS, 800 BONGO DRIVE, MAY, 15, 1960, 1, 6, VANILLA + 2 CHOCOLATE
(5)	ICE CREAM SANDWICHES, 1, 1.29, PAID, 1.29,,,*
(6)	14618, J.W. SWINDLER, 99 CREDIT CARD BLVD., 5, 15, 1960, INCOME, 2 XYZ END OF ITE
(7)	MS SPECIALS, 3, 4.99, 2, 1.00, JUNE, 10, 1960*
(8)	END OF ITEMS

FIG. 66. Example of STIRS input file

(b) Field 6 in cards (4) and (5) is called MONTH OF TRANS-
ACTION. The ORDER option used for this field indicates
specific names that will appear in this data field; it also
indicates that the data may be retrieved in the order specified
in the control statement (January, February, March, etc.).

(c) Field 10 in card (7) is called TOTAL AMOUNT. The ORDER
option indicates the amounts may range in value from 1 to
10,000 in increments of .01 and the unit of measure is "$"
when displaying the data.

(d) Field 14 in card (9) is called MONTH DUE. The equals (=)
option indicates that the contents of field 14 may be set to
the same contents as field 6 (MONTH OF TRANSACTION)
whenever data field 14 is omitted in the input file. (Note
that in card (5) figure 66, the last three data fields for month,
date, and year due were left blank).

3. Master file. The master file is the principal element of the
STIRS data base. The STIRS functions of file build, query and
retrieval, and file update are performed by using the master file while
it is resident in the computer memory. The master file is similar
to an index or inverted file. The difference is that STIRS reorganizes
the original input data and creates a compressed, inverted file with
binary bit strings (internal machine codes) from which all STIRS
data retrieval functions are performed. All the data fields that are
input as part of a data record are retained in the master file in a

CARD NO.	CARD CONTENT
(1)	DEFINE DESCRIPTORS 15 TRANSACTION NO.(1, ORDER FROM 1 TO 50000), TRANSACTING PARTY
(2)	(2, NAME, 2000), ADDRESS OF TRANSACTING PARTY (3, NAME, 2000), NATURE OF TRANSAC
(3)	TION(4, ORDER, EXPENSE, INCOME), YEAR OF TRANSACTION(5, ORDER FROM 1950 TO 1990)
(4)	, MONTH OF TRANSACTION(6, ORDER, JAN., FEB., MAR., APR., MAY, JUNE, JULY, AUG.,
(5)	SEPT., OCT., NOV., DEC.), DAY OF TRANSACTION(7, ORDER, 1 TO 31), DESCRIPTION OF
(6)	GOODS(8, NAME, 5000), DELIVERY STATUS(9, ORDER, DELIVERED, PARTLY DELIVERED,
(7)	UNDELIVERED), TOTAL AMOUNT(10, ORDER FROM 1 TO 10000 BY .01 IN $), PAYMENT
(8)	STATUS(11, ORDER, PAID, PARTLY PAID, UNPAID), AMOUNT PAID(12, = 10, YEAR DUE(13
(9)	, = YEAR OF TRANSACTION), MONTH DUE(14, = MONTH OF TRANSACTION), DAY DUE(15, =
(10)	DAY OF TRANSACTION)*

FIG. 67. Example of STIRS control vocabulary

compressed form, referred to by STIRS as Base Characteristic Functions (BCF). The extent that an input data file can be compressed may be a ratio ranging from 4 to 1 to 1,000 to 1; the greater the amount of data, the greater the ratio of data compression that is experienced.

Table 10
Example of STIRS Input File

Item I.D. Number	Flower Color	Leaf Venation	Geographical Location	Month of Flowering
100	Blue	Palmate	Vermont	April
102	Blue	Pinnate	Delaware	August
120	Red	Unknown	Maryland	May
116	White	Parallel	Virginia	June
103	Violet	Palmate	Maryland	June
114	Red	Palmate	Maryland	July
115	Pink	Parallel	New Jersey	April
106	Yellow	Pinnate	Virginia	May
110	Pink	Pinnate	Maryland	June
112	Blue	Pinnate	New York	August

Table 11
Control Vocabulary for Input File in Table 10

Descriptors	1. Flower color	2. Leaf venation	3. Geographical location	4. Month of flowering
Descriptor-states	1. Blue 2. Red 3. White 4. Violet 5. Pink 6. Yellow	1. Palmate 2. Pinnate 3. Parallel	1. Vermont 2. Delaware 3. Maryland 4. Virginia 5. New Jersey 6. New York	1. April 2. May 3. June 4. July 5. August

Table 12
Master File Developed from Input File in Table 10 and Control Vocabulary in Table 11

Base Characteristic Functions (Master File)

Item I.D.	▷	100	102	120	116	103	114	115	106	110	112
1. Flower color	c_{11}	1	1	0	1	0	0	1	0	1	1
	c_{12}	0	0	1	1	0	1	0	1	0	0
	c_{13}	0	0	0	0	1	0	1	1	1	0
2. Leaf venation	c_{21}	1	0	0	1	1	1	1	0	0	0
	c_{22}	0	1	0	1	0	0	1	1	1	1
3. Geographical location	c_{31}	1	0	1	0	1	1	1	0	1	0
	c_{32}	0	1	1	0	1	1	0	0	1	1
	c_{33}	0	0	0	1	0	0	1	1	0	1
4. Month of flowering	c_{41}	1	1	0	1	1	0	1	0	1	1
	c_{42}	0	0	1	1	1	0	0	1	1	0
	c_{43}	0	1	0	0	0	1	0	0	0	1

Data structure. The STIRS input file and control vocabulary structures were illustrated in the preceding section on file descriptions. However, the data structure of the master file is more complex to describe because of the mathematical principles associated with set theory and the manner they are used in the STIRS package to reorganize the master file from original input data.

The three basic file types are illustrated by the example in tables 10, 11, and 12.[20] Table 10 represents the input file in which ten items, each containing four descriptor states, are listed in the data bank. Table 11 represents a control vocabulary describing the descriptors (fields) and the descriptor states (field contents) for the data base example. Table 12 represents the master file reorganized from the input file in table 10. This master file, when resident in the computer memory, appears as a matrix: the master file records (items) across the horizontal axis, and the fields (descriptors) down the vertical axis. The contents of the matrix are represented by the bit strings (ones and zeroes). For example, the input data for Item I.D. number 100 (table 10) is: Flower color = blue, leaf venation = palmate, geographical location = Vermont, and month of flowering = April. STIRS would reorganize this data into the bit string '10010100100' (C_{11} –C_{43} under I.D. 100 in table 12). This bit string is logically developed by STIRS as follows:

1—because flower color is blue or white or pink
0—because flower color not red or white or yellow
0—because flower color not violet or pink or yellow
1—because leaf venation is palmate or parallel or undefined descriptor-state (UDS)
0—because leaf venation not pinnate or parallel or UDS
1—because geographical location is Vermont or Maryland or New Jersey
0—because geographical location not Delaware or Maryland or New York
0—because geographical location not Virginia or New Jersey or New York
1—because month of flowering is April or June or August
0—because month of flowering not May or June or UDS
0—because month of flowering not July or August or UDS

Hierarchical structuring of master file records in the STIRS system is accomplished by a sequential or ordered relationship of data fields and records within a master file (set). As noted earlier regarding the control vocabulary, the options available for coding input data (such as NAME, CODE) allow a hierarchical value to be internally assigned to the data. When the data is retrieved from the master file, the data is arranged according to the assigned hierarchical sequence.

Information processing flow. The STIRS system description is comprised of three principal processing functions: building master files, query and master file retrieval, and updating master files.

1. Master file build. This processing function includes the conversion of input data files to a master file. Figures 68*A* and 68*B* illustrate

this process flow. The user prepares specifications describing the data to be stored in the master file. Figure 67 is an illustration of specifications (descriptor definitions) for a master file. These specifications may be entered into the computer using a remote terminal to construct the control vocabulary, or the user may elect a batch-mode of processing by submitting the data directly to the computer center for processing. The user determines if the control vocabulary is adequate by requesting through the terminal a print-out of the control vocabulary (figure 68A) using the STIRS program control statement CONTROL VOCABULARY. The terminal display in figure 69 shows the use of several control statements: DEFINE DESCRIPTORS, DEFINE ITEMS, and CONTROL VOCABULARY. It will be noted that the sequence of using the latter two control statements differs with the flow chart in figures 68A and 68B, which allows for reviewing the control vocabulary before beginning the file building process.

The user gathers source input data for building the master file. The data is keypunched from the object documentation form for preparation of an input data file. The STIRS program will accept input data in the form of punched cards, magnetic tape, or disk file (figure 70).

When ready to load the input data and build the master file, the user from the remote terminal calls in the input data file, and using the control statement DEFINE ITEMS, instructs the STIRS program to build the master file. The user receives statistics back over the terminal as to the number of records in the new file and messages regarding any errors encountered in the processing. When loading of input data is completed, the new master file resident in the computer memory is saved for future use by copying it to a disk file. The STIRS control statement WRITE DATA BANK is used for this purpose. The control vocabulary is also stored on the disk file at the same time.

2. Query and master file retrieval. This processing function includes querying a master file concerning the stored data and retrieving the master file records for information reference. Figures 71A and 71B illustrate this process flow. Prior to making a query, the user first readies the master file by using the STIRS control statement READ DATA BANK to instruct the program to load the file into computer memory from the disk file. This task may be requested from his remote terminal.

The user proceeds to enter queries from his remote terminal using the STIRS control statement HOW MANY. Results of the master

180

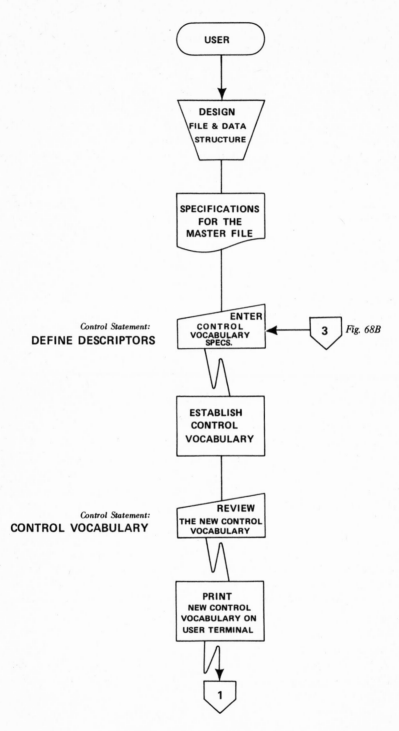

FIG. 68A. Master file build flow chart

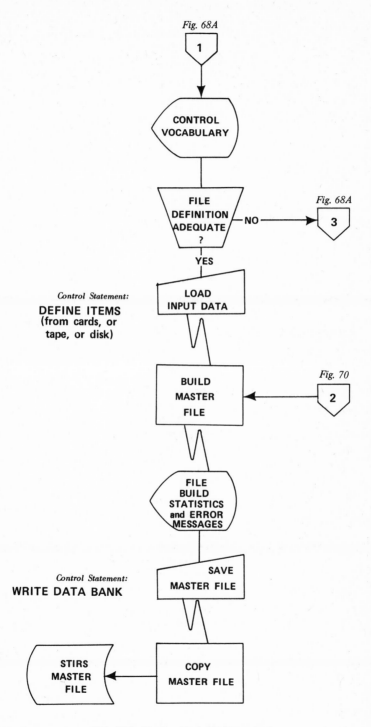

FIG. 68*B*. Master file build flow chart

```
ID      SAMPLE  PROBLEM 1   FOR   INVENTORY   OF   STRUCTURES

DEFINE DESCRIPTORS 5 COUNTY (1,ORDER FROM 1 TO 63)
  ,RT.NO.   (2,ORDER FROM 0 TO 1000),
LOGSL(3,    TEXT,1),
MINOR ST(4,ORDER FROM 0 TO 1), STR.NO.(5,NAME,50)*

DEFINE ITEMS FROM CARDS FIXED 21-23,31-35,47,53,54-60*

CONTROL VOCABULARY*

1. COUNTY
     NO. OF CHARACTERS IN LONGEST STATE:  3
     OPTION:  ORDER     NO. OF STATES:  63
       FROM 1
       TO 63
       BY 1
       NO LABEL

2. RT. NO.
     NO. OF CHARACTERS IN LONGEST STATE:  4
     OPTION:  ORDER     NO. OF STATES:  1001
       FROM 0
       TO 1000
       BY 1
       NO LABEL

3. LOGSL
     NO. OF CHARACTERS IN LONGEST STATE:  3
     OPTION:  TEXT

4. MINOR ST
     NO. OF CHARACTERS IN LONGEST STATE:  3
     OPTION:  ORDER     NO. OF STATES:  2
       FROM 0
       TO 1
       BY 1
       NO LABEL

5. STR.NO.
     NO. OF CHARACTERS IN LONGEST STATE:  7
     OPTION: NAME      NO. OF STATES:  12
                       NO. OF DELETED STATES:  0
                       NO. OF DICTIONARY ENTRIES RESERVED:  50
```

FIG. 69. Sample problem using control vocabulary statement

file search are written to a temporary disk file by the STIRS program, and file search statistics are printed at the user's remote terminal. If the statistics indicate the search was adequate, the user may elect

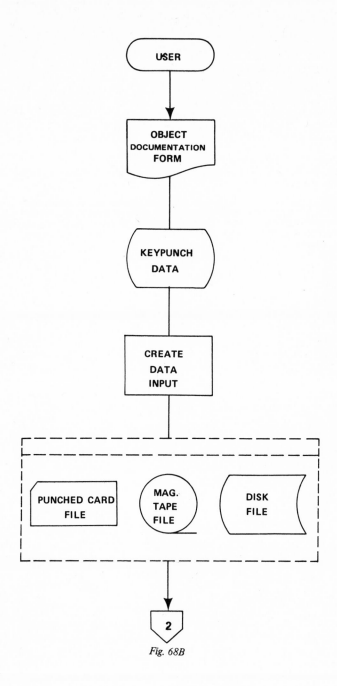

FIG. 70. Input preparation flow chart

184

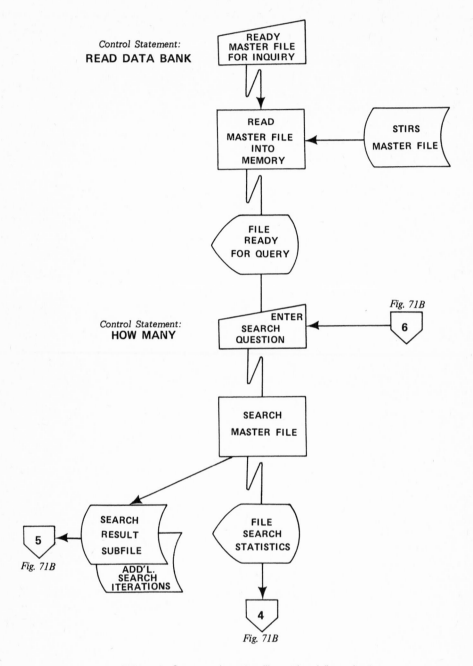

FIG. 71A, Query and master file retrieval flow chart

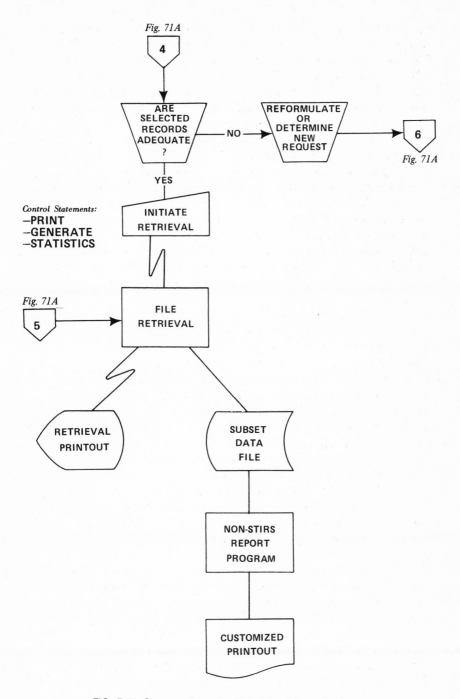

FIG. 71*B*. Query and master file retrieval flow chart

to have the retrieved results: (1) printed on his remote terminal using the STIRS control statement PRINT or (2) written on a temporary disk file using the STIRS control statement GENERATE for printing on a high-speed printer. The user might also elect to use this temporary disk file for further computer processing using a non-STIRS program, such as for customized formatting of output reports (figure 71B.) When the retrieved output data written to a temporary disk file is all in numeric form for further computer tabulating by a non-STIRS program, using the STIRS control statement STATIS-TICS, the data will be written as floating point values.

3. Update master file. This processing function is for the purpose of correcting data on the master file or adding additional records to the master file. Figures 72A and 72B illustrate this process flow. Prior to correcting or adding new data records, the user readies the master file by using the STIRS control statement READ DATA BANK to instruct the program to load the file into the computer memory from the disk file. This task may be requested from a remote terminal.

From the terminal the STIRS control statement CORRECTION may be used. The data fields (descriptors) in every record in the master file can be changed to a new value (state). The logical commands AND, OR, NOT, may be used in the correction control statement when a logical relationship can be expressed regarding the records to be changed. The STIRS control statement PRINT, as illustrated in figure 72B, may be used from the remote terminal to confirm the results of using the file change control statements. Other STIRS file change options include:

1. DELETE STATE. This control statement removes field name descriptions from the control vocabulary.

2. DELETE ITEMS. This control statement removes records from the master file. The logical commands AND, OR, NOT, can be used with this control statement when the records to be removed can be stated by a logical expression.

To add additional records to a master file, the DEFINE ITEMS control statement is used preceding the new item data records. If additional data fields are to be incorporated when adding new records to the master file, the STIRS control statement DEFINE MORE DESCRIPTORS should first be used for defining the additional fields. This expansion of the record definition continues where the previous DEFINE DESCRIPTORS control statement left off.

After updating of the master file is completed, the revised master file resident in the computer memory is saved for future use by

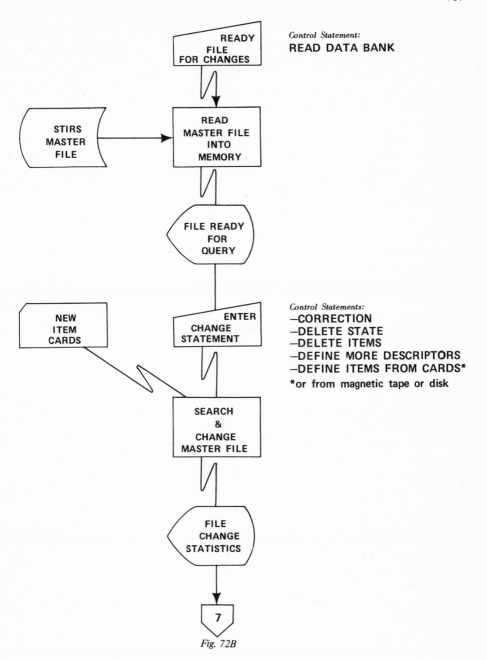

FIG. 72A. Update master file flow chart

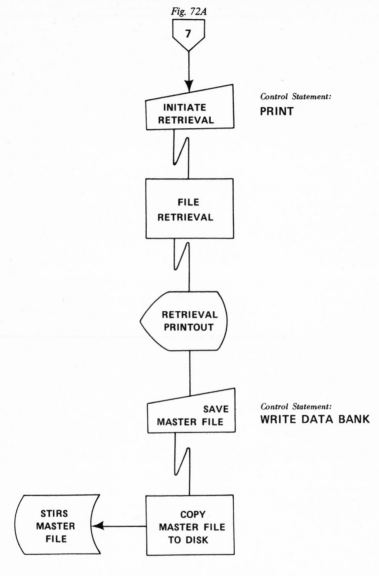

Fig. 72A

7

INITIATE
RETRIEVAL

Control Statement:
PRINT

FILE
RETRIEVAL

RETRIEVAL
PRINTOUT

SAVE
MASTER FILE

Control Statement:
WRITE DATA BANK

STIRS
MASTER
FILE

COPY
MASTER FILE
TO DISK

FIG. 72*B*. Update master file flow chart

copying it to a disk file. The STIRS control statement WRITE DATA
BANK is used for this purpose.

Implementation and Future Support

The STIRS computer program and documentation of the package is made available through the University of Colorado Computing Center. There is no charge for the programs other than the cost to copy it for a prospective user. Technical assistance with application orientation and the use of the computer programs has not been formally established. Dr. Claude McMillan, professor at the University of Colorado School of Business, is the principal contact regarding the use of STIRS. The original developers of the TAXIR program, from which STIRS is a variant, are no longer affiliated with the University or involved with the program.

The STIRS package will continue to be available at the University of Colorado Computing Center. System improvements for the STIRS package have been planned by Dr. McMillan. His objective is to redesign the system to make it adaptable to models of computers other than CDC.

The University of Colorado Computing Center can be subscribed to on a time-sharing basis, permitting the use of STIRS on a remote basis using a terminal and telecommunications equipment.

Adaptability of package to use standard data categories. The STIRS package is not designed to use a specific data set structure or coding system. Through the function of the STIRS control vocabulary and the DEFINE DESCRIPTORS control statement, the system appears readily adaptable to the use of standard data categories.

Adaptability of package to interact with other packages. STIRS has limited capability to interact with other packages. The system has the capability to produce data files from its master files by reversing the reorganization processing that is used to produce the compressed, binary string file matrix format. Additional computer programs would have to be developed to interface the STIRS data files produced with those produced by another package.

GIS
Package Description

Background

GIS, an acronym for Generalized Information System, is a generalized computer program product of IBM designed for building and maintaining a large collection of information, with the capability to query and retrieve the stored information. Because of the generalized nature of GIS, it has been adapted for use in a wide range of industrial and institutional applications. This package description concentrates principally on the application of GIS in the institutional area.

The principal user of GIS in the institutional area has been the Smithsonian Institution, Department of Botany, Washington, D.C., for the Flora North America (FNA) project. Though the project is not active at the present time and the use of GIS has been discontinued, the FNA project remains as a good example to describe the manner in which GIS was utilized.

GIS is a generalized system consisting of a high-level English-like command language. It contains approximately 72 control statements from which the user can write program routines to tailor the system to perform such functions as file create, file update, file modification, file query, and output report generation. The system permits the user to design highly structured data records and an interrelated network of master files.

The current version of the GIS package was developed by the International Business Machines Corporation in 1971. It is available to IBM customers on a monthly rental basis. The GIS package requires a medium-to-large-scale IBM computer, depending upon the user's selection of the several optional program features and operating system features associated with the package. However, the minimum configuration ranges between an IBM 360/40 with a 256K memory and an IBM 360/50 with a 512K memory. The use of teleprocessing with GIS, for example, would require the larger computer configuration. Disk file storage equivalent to four IBM 2311 drives are required. Essential peripheral equipment devices include card reader, tape drive, and printer. Equivalent models of the IBM 370 computers may also be used with GIS. The package operates in either a job-oriented (batch) mode or in a teleprocessing mode permitting access to its operation from remotely located terminal devices.

The operating system required for GIS is OS/MFT or OS/MVT. This is the IBM Operating System, using the multiprogramming feature that allows either a fixed or variable number of tasks to operate in the computer simultaneously.

The GIS package is written in IBM assembler language, but the user need only be concerned with the use of the GIS command language statements to design the master files and process data. If non-GIS programs are required by the user for specialized functions not within the specification of GIS, these programs would be written in an IBM language of the user's choice such as COBOL, PL/I, etc. It should also be obvious at this point that the operation of GIS is only available on IBM equipment.

System Description

The description of the GIS package will include several processing elements that describe the characteristics of the system: file types, data structuring, hierarchical record structuring, access methods, functions of the command language that make up the system, and the information processing flow to illustrate use of the system.

File types. GIS data files are organized and structured for processing on direct-access file storage devices. There are four types of data files used in GIS:

1. Data definition tables (DDT). The data definition table defines identification labels, the physical data characteristics of each data field, and the logical arrangement of segments into records. Error conditions are defined for the content of each field to permit error analysis during file building and file maintenance. A DDT file must be defined for each data file used (e.g., input files, master files, work files).

2. Input files. The GIS package accepts transaction data in fixed-field formats from punched cards, magnetic tape, or disk files. The input file is used as the data source for building and maintaining master files.

3. Master files. Master files are used for the permanent storage of data. The records are made up of data input from transactions in the input files and grouped into a logical record format by the GIS file create processing.

4. Work files. Work files are temporary storage type files used in intermediate processing steps when data will no longer be needed after completion of a processing phase.

Data structuring. The GIS package allows the user to design complex, logically structured formats for data files. The main requirement is that the file records must be made up of a set of fixed length, fixed position fields. The structuring of GIS data files includes the following elements:

1. Field. The basic unit for grouping of referable data that can be described in GIS. A field may contain up to 255 characters.

2. Segment. A grouping of fields. A given segment of data may appear once or many times depending on the type of information it contains.

3. Record. A grouping of segments. It is an identifiable hierarchy consisting of a single master segment and its subordinate segments, repeating segments that may recur a number of times.

Figure 73 illustrates a schematic of fields grouped into a segment of a record structure and examples of data that would appear in it. Figure 74 then illustrates a schematic of the fields and segments fitting together into a record structure.

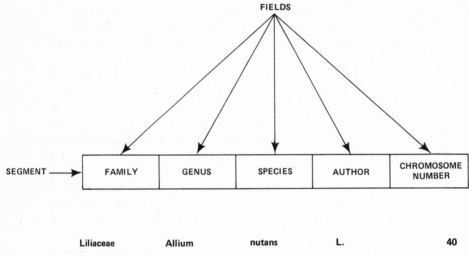

FIG. 73. Schematic of a typical segment structure

The definition of fields, segments, and files to GIS is the function of the data definition table. The DDT defines the layout or mapping of the data files. Figure 75 is an example of the GIS specification for a DDT FILE definition and the manner of preparing the information for entry into the system to initialize a file. In the example

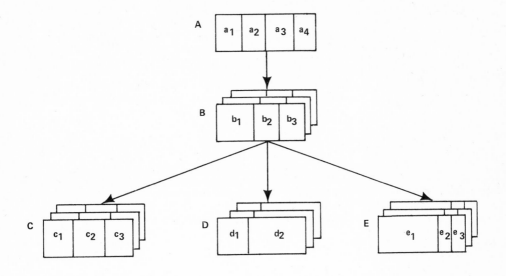

SEGMENTS: A, B, C, D, E

FIELDS: a_1, a_2, a_3, a_4, b_1, b_2, b_3, c_1, c_2, c_3, d_1, d_2, e_1, e_2, e_3,

FIG. 74. Schematic of a record structure

the file is called PERSONEX. Several fields of information must be provided in order to specify the manner of processing associated with the file. Figure 76 is an example of the GIS specification for a FIELD definition and the manner of its preparation for entry into the system to initialize a file. From figures 75 and 76 it may be noted that two optional formats are permitted for this DDT: comma format and column format. The comma format entails separating fields by commas, their order being predetermined by the DDT. When data entry transactions are prepared in the comma format, the data label precedes the data fields, which in turn are separated by commas. The column format entails entering the data into the predetermined columns of the transaction record. The DDT determines the record columns in which the data are entered. Figure 77 is an example of a complete DDT listing for a master file.

Hierarchical record structuring. GIS files can be organized in two basic ways, single level and multilevel.

Comma Format

FILE, PERSONEX, 001, 001, LDM M L L H L H L M L L   ...   L ;*

Column Format

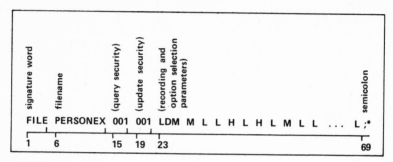

Column (Keyword)	Contents/Function
1 - 4 (FILE)	The signature word FILE
5	blank
6 - 13 (NAME)	The file name, left justified
14	blank
15 - 17 (MINFQS)	QUERY/MODIFY mode (Query) security access value (optional): a right-justified numeric value between 0 and 128 or blank. Blank and zero represent no security.
18	blank
19 - 21 (MINFUS)	UPDATE/CREATE mode (Update) security access value (optional): value limitations same as for query security above.
22	blank
23 - n (RCDLVL)	Recording-and-option-selection function. Each successive pair of positions in the field (23, 24; 25, 26; et seq.) represents a recording-and-option-selection event category.

1st position
Recording Importance

H - High
M - Moderate
L - Low
N - No recording
b - no recording

2nd position
Processing Option

A - Abort
D - Depart
C - Continue
b - Refer to Table 1 for default options

FIG. 75. A data definition table (DDT) statement

Comma Format

FLD, MANNO, EBCD, 6, , , , 001,001, L, EMPLOYEE NUMBER;

Column Format

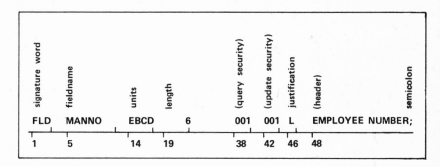

Column (Keyword)	Contents/Function
1 - 3 (FLD)	The signature word FLD
4	blank
5 - 12 (NAME)	Field name, left-justified
13	blank
14 - 17 (UNITS)	Type of data: EBCD or blanks for extended binary coded decimal, PACD for packed decimal, FLPT for floating point, or BINA for binary.
18	blank
41	blank
42 - 44 (USEC)	UPDATE/CREATE mode (Update) security; value limitations same as query security.
45	blank
46 (JUST)	Field justification and contents: R for right-justified numeric fields; L or blank for left-justified alphameric data. Blank for fields containing other than EBCDIC characters.
47	blank
48 - n (HEADER)	The output header. If this field is blank, the field name is used as a header. The maximum header length is 132 bytes.

FIG. 76. A data definition table (DDT) field statement

```
DDT ;
*******************************************************************************************
* THIS DDT WILL NOT COMPILE UNLESS THE HIERARCHIC FILE SUPPORT FEATURE HAS
* BEEN INSTALLED.
*******************************************************************************************
FILE:NAME=PERSONEX, RCDLVL=LDM M L L H L H L M L L L H L M L L L L L
FLD:NAME=RECDATE, LENGTH=6, UNITS=EBCD, JUST=L, HEADER=RECORD DATE
MASK:PATTRN= ZZ/ZZ/ZZ
RDFN:FIELDS=MONTH,2,DAY,2,YEAR,2;
FLD:NAME=MANNO, LENGTH=6, UNITS=EBCD, JUST=L, HEADER=EMPLOYEE NUMBER
FLD:NAME=NAME, LENGTH=20, UNITS=EBCD, JUST=L, HEADER=EMPLOYEE NAME
FLD:NAME=STREET, LENGTH=19, UNITS=EBCD, JUST=L
FLD:NAME=CITY, LENGTH=15, UNITS=EBCD, JUST=L
FLD:NAME=STATE, LENGTH=02, UNITS=EBCD, JUST=L
FLD:NAME=ZIPCODE, LENGTH=5, UNITS=EBCD, JUST=L
FLD:NAME=PHONE, LENGTH=10, UNITS=EBCD, JUST=L
MASK:PATTRN=ZZZ–ZZZ–ZZZZ
RDFN:FIELDS=AREACODE,3,EXCHANGE,3,NUMBER,4;
FLD:NAME=SEX, LENGTH=1, UNITS=EBCD, JUST=L
FLD:NAME=DOB, LENGTH=6, UNITS=EBCD, JUST=L, HEADER=BIRTH DATE(MO/DA/YR)
MASK:PATTRN= ZZ/ZZ/ZZ
FLD:NAME=PACDOB, LENGTH=4, UNITS=PACD, HEADER=BIRTH(YR/MO/DA);
FLD:NAME=MARSTAT, LENGTH=1, UNITS=EBCD, JUST=L, HEADER=MARITAL STATUS
DECD:TYPSPC=LKUP, LGTHA=1, LGTHF=8, EEDVAL=D,DIVORCED,M,MARRIED ,S,SINGLE  ,W,WI
⊬DOWED ;
FLD:NAME=NODEP, LENGTH=2, UNITS=EBCD, JUST=R, HEADER=⊬ OF DEPENDENTS
FLD:NAME=DOH, LENGTH=6, UNITS=EBCD, JUST=L, HEADER=DATE OF HIRE(MO/DA/YR)
MASK:PATTRN= ZZ/ZZ/ZZ
FLD:NAME=PACDOH, LENGTH=4, UNITS=PACD, HEADER=HIRE(YR/MO/DA);
FLD:NAME=POSCNT, LENGTH=2, UNITS=EBCD, JUST=R, HEADER=# OF POSITIONS
SEGM:NAME=MASTER, UNIND=Y, SORT=MANNO,A
DATM:DSORG=PS, CREATE=YES, ENTRIES=5, CATLG=YES, LRECL=339, BLKSIZE=8479, UNIT=2
⊬ 314, RECFM=VB, DSNAME=SYS1.EMPLOYEX, ALLOC=TRK, SPACE=6, INCRE=1, VOLUME=REF=GI
⊬ S;JOBLIB;
FLD:NAME=DEPT, LENGTH=3, UNITS=EBCD, JUST=L, HEADER=DEPARTMENT
FLD:NAME=LOCATION, LENGTH=3, UNITS=EBCD, JUST=L
FLD:NAME=POSCODE, LENGTH=3, UNITS=PACD, HEADER=POSITION
DECD:TYPSPC=LKUP, LGTHA=3, LGTHF=10, CONVA=D, EEDVAL=09151,ENGINEER   ,11784,PROG
⊬ RAMMER,12597,INSTRUCTOR,47239,OPERATOR   ,60648,ANALYST  ,70724,SECRETARY,,8081
⊬6,TECHNICIAN;
FLD:NAME=POSDATE, LENGTH=6. UNITS=EBCD, JUST=L, HEADER=DATE OF POSITION
FLD:NAME=SALARY, LENGTH=3, UNITS=PACD
MASK:PATTRN= ZZ,ZZZ
FLD:NAME=POSCNTR, LENGTH=1, UNITS=EBCD, JUST=L;
SEGM:NAME=JOB, LEVEL=01, TYPE=TRAILR, OPTION=CNT, OPTENM=POSCNT, UNIND=Y, SORT=P
⊬OSCNTR,A;
END
```

FIG. 77. Sample listing of a master file DDT

The single level is the simplest and probably most widely used approach. An entire record is described by a single segment, the master record segment, and every record in the file conforms to the one segment format. The single level file is available to all GIS users as part of the basic retrieval package. Figure 78 illustrates the single level file.

In the multifile structure, (figure 79) two or more segments may exist as part of one record. Level numbers are used to define the hierarchy of these segments within a record. There is one master segment per record, which is hierarchically superior to all the other segments in the record. A count field, which reflects the number of occurrences for a particular segment of a record, is maintained

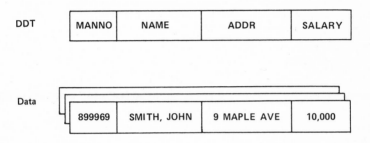

FIG. 78. Schematic of a single-level file structure

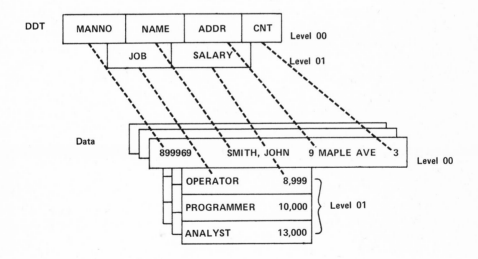

FIG. 79. Schematic of a multilevel file structure

for the user during file update, create, or modify tasks. The lowest level segment of a record does not require a counter field. In both single level and multilevel file records, a user may declare a field in a segment as a sort field to maintain the segments within a record in a specified sequence.

In a multilevel file only the lowest hierarchical level may contain different segment formats. Part A of figure 80 illustrates this form. It is allowed because the various segment formats (A, B, C) for level 03 data are found at the lowest level in the hierarchy of the file. Part B of figure 80 illustrates an invalid multilevel file structure form.

Access methods. The principal data set access methods processable by GIS are indexed sequential (IS) and physical sequential (PS).

Indexed sequential data sets reside on direct-access devices. These files are organized by an index, which contains key field values and their address pointers. The advantage of this file organization is that the records in the file may be retrieved in random order without a sequential, record-by-record search. However, the requirements made by the IBM operating system for space in which to maintain the index (independent overflow areas, and separate index areas) add to the required space for storage of actual data. Also, it can be difficult to maintain a backup copy of the file in the event of an error during file maintenance runs because IS organizes the "new" file in the space occupied by the old file. After a few file maintenance tasks have been run, the data set must be reorganized because the process of adding and deleting records in place has caused inefficient organization.

Indexed sequential organization is a good choice if most of the searches of the master file will cause a small number of "hits" (selected records) in proportion to the number of records in the file. The price paid for more efficient search techniques is the extra space required to maintain the index and overflow areas. This price may be too high for a small file. Ideally, an indexed sequential data set should be subject to a minimum of file maintenance (i.e., where new records are inserted or old ones deleted).

Physical sequential data sets can reside either on direct-access devices or on magnetic tape. These records are stored in the same sequence in which they are accessed. After a file maintenance run, the physical sequential data set is copied over in a new area so that the old or "original" remains intact as a backup copy of the file in case of erroneous processing.

A. VALID MULTI-LEVEL STRUCTURE:

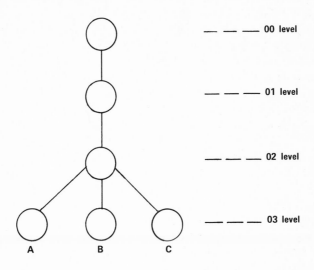

B. INVALID MULTI-LEVEL STRUCTURE:

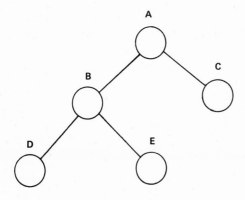

FIG. 80. Multilevel file structure examples

Physical sequential organization is an appropriate choice when most of the procedures against a file will cause a high number of "hits" (selected records) with respect to the number of records in the file. It is also a good choice when particular data cannot be retrieved without a record-by-record search. Runs that require the retrieval of every record in a file, as in a transaction file, might influence a decision to use physical sequential organization. For files subject to frequent updating, the physical sequential organization may be desirable because it facilitates recovery and restart.

Functions of the command language. The command language for writing GIS programs is an English-like procedural language. It has a hierarchy consisting of "subprocedure declaration" statements and "task specification logic" statements. The subprocedure declaration is a GIS language statement that initiates a major processing subroutine within a program; the task specification logic words are verbs used within a subroutine to describe specific logical steps.

The four major subprocedure declaration statements are the following:

1. QUERY. A master file inquiry control verb that initiates an information retrieval process.

2. MODIFY. A master file maintenance control verb that signals a request for modification of a file. Typical use involves updating of field values or deletion of obsolete or invalid records. Up to three master and source (input) files may be named in one statement.

3. UPDATE. A statement to signal that updating of an existing file is to take place. Only one master and one input file may be named in one statement.

4. CREATE. A request to build a new data file (master, input, or work file). As source data entries are read, master file records are created.

Task specification logic key words, to perform such functions as data selection, data manipulation, and data presentation (print-out), are listed in table 13.

Figure 81 is an example of a multiprocedure program subroutine using both subprocedure declaration statements and task specification logic key words. The following steps describe the tasks in the subroutine: *(a)* performs a master file inquiry on the PERSONNEL file and holds the selected records in a work file (HOLDFL1), *(b)* rearranges the selected records by the field in each record entitled DEPT, *(c)* creates a new master file (JOBFILE) from the sorted work file, and *(d)* prepares a listing of the newly created work file.

Information processing flow. The application of GIS to an information storage and retrieval system is described in the sequence of its information processing flow. The processing functions that are

Table 13
Task Specification Logic Key Words

AFTER	IFn	SNAPA
APPEND	IGNORE	SNAPB
AVERAGE	IN	SNAPX
AVERAGEn	IN DEBUG MODE	SORT
CHANGE	INCLUDE	SORTnn
COUNT	INCLUDEF	SPACE
COUNTn	INCREASE	SPACEn
CREATE	INFORM	STORE
DECREASE	INSERT	STRUCTURE
DEFINE	KEEP	SUBAVERAGE
DELETE	LINK	SUBCOUNT
DETAIL	LIST	SUBTOTAL
DIVIDE	LITERALn	SUMMARY
EJECT	LOCATE	TALLYn
ELSE	MLIST	TITLE
END	MODIFY	TOTAL
EQUATE	MULTIPLY	TOTALn
ERASE	QUERY	TRACE
EXCEPT	READ	TRAILER
EXHAUST	REMOVE	UNICOUNT
FINALLY	REPLACE	UNICOUNTn
FOR	REPLACEF	UPDATE
GOTO	REPORT	VARIABLEn
HALT	RESET	WHEN
HEADER	RETURN	XMODMAP
HOLD	RUN	
IF	SET	

described include: data preparation, data editing, master file create/update, and data retrieval. Throughout this processing description, reference will be made to the Flora North America (FNA) project as a means of illustrating the system application of GIS. Figure 82 is a schematic to illustrate an overview of the FNA system using GIS.

Data preparation. Includes the gathering of data recorded on object documentation, technical review of the information, converting the information to machine-readable form, and storing the data on an input data file for computer processing. These steps are illustrated by the flow chart in figure 83. The museum user employing the GIS package is able to perform these data preparation steps at a site remotely located from the computer.

Data editing. Includes validation of the input data (gathered in the data preparation step), reviewing errors diagnosed by the com-

```
a)  QUERY PERSONNEL;
    WHEN JOBCODE EQ '555';
    HOLD HOLDFL1 RECORD;

b)  SORT HOLDFL1 DEPT;

c)  CREATE JOBFILE FROM HOLDFL1;
    STRUCTURE JOBFILE:  SEGOO FROM HOLDFL1:  SEGOO; (note 1)
    INSERT JOBFILE:  SEGOO;  (note 2)

d)  QUERY JOBFILE;
    LOCATE RECORD; (note 3)
    LIST RECORD;
    EXHAUST RECORD; (note 4)
    END PROCEDURE;
```

Notes:

(1) This statement is a mapping function which structures the configuration of corresponding data fields of the new data file from its source file.

(2) This statement is the updating action involving the movement of data from the source file into the new data file.

(3) This statement identifies the segment of the data file to be made available for the subsequent processing commands.

(4) This statement is a signal to obtain the next record of the data file for listing until the end of file is reached.

FIG. 81. Example of a GIS program subroutine

puter, correcting and resubmitting the data for further computer processing. These steps are illustrated by the flow chart in Figure 84. The preprocessor validation program shown is a non-GIS program in the FNA application because of the unique editing requirements imposed upon the input data. The FNA Data Bank (figure 82) is comprised of a series of authority files containing reference data in specialized categories to which the input data must conform. The following briefly describes these authority files and the basis for their edit control over input data:

1. Morphological and ecological vocabulary. A dictionary of approved morphological and ecological terminology for the systematic botanist.
2. Type register. The first reported or authoritative specimens that have been accepted for purposes of type definition and naming.

FNA DATA BANK

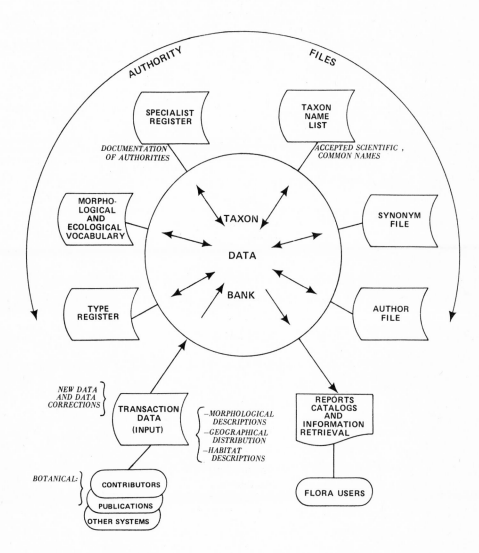

FIG. 82. Schematic overview of FNA system using GIS

3. Specialist register. A registry of plant systematists; biographical information on contributors to the FNA Data Bank.

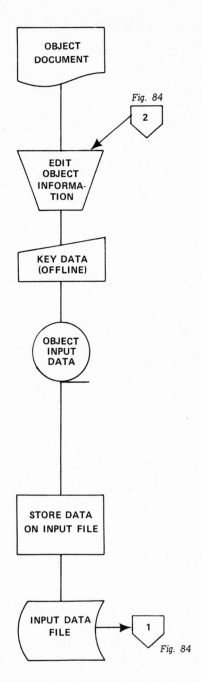

FIG. 83. Data preparation flow chart

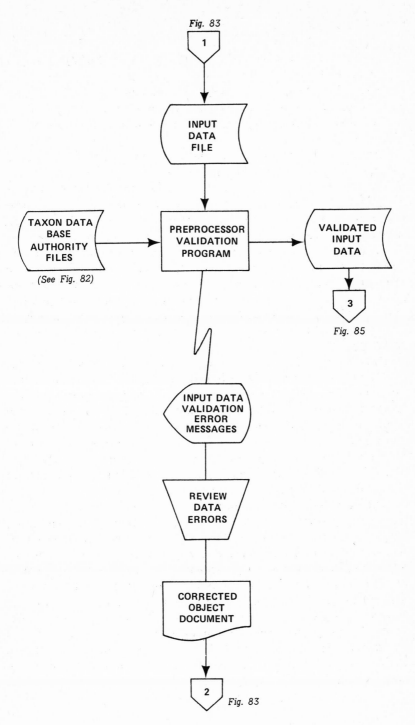

FIG. 84. Data editing flow chart

4. Taxon name list. An authoritative checklist of species accepted for inclusion in FNA.

5. Author. An authority file of authors who have named plants, biographical data, notes, abbreviations, etc.

6. Synonym. A file of synonyms of scientific names used in the taxon name list file.

Master file create/update. Includes the preparation and entry of data definition tables and the processing of input data to create a new master file. These steps are illustrated by the flow chart in figure 85. A similar processing flow would occur for updating an existing master file as illustrated here for creating a new master file, namely, validated file maintenance data would be included in the validated input data file as a result of the aforementioned data preparation and data editing processing procedures, and the appropriate GIS command language statements (MODIFY or UPDATE) would be used in the users file maintenance program routine. This program may include routines for adding or deleting complete records, adding or deleting segments from existing records, or changing individual field values.

Data retrieval. Includes the entry of an inquiry to a GIS master file, sorting the selected records into an output data arrangement, preparing the selected data for a formal output report, and the print-out of query results on a terminal device or the preparation of an additional data file for processing by a non-GIS program (figure 86). Figure 87 illustrates a typical GIS query process. The master file named TAXON is queried for records containing the states of MD (Maryland) or VA (Virginia) and a listing is printed from data in the selected records.

The GIS command language is used to communicate with the program to perform the selection, processing, and output preparation functions on the master file data. File search is performed either sequentially or by index, depending upon which is the more efficient for the particular search requirement. A query search may involve access to multiple files and accumulating data together from several files (as in the illustration of the Taxon Data Bank in figure 82). Selected records may be sorted on any of the data fields for output.

A wide range of output formatting and processing capability is afforded by GIS, from simple tabular listings to formal report formats. Multiple reports may be produced from records selected from single query searches.

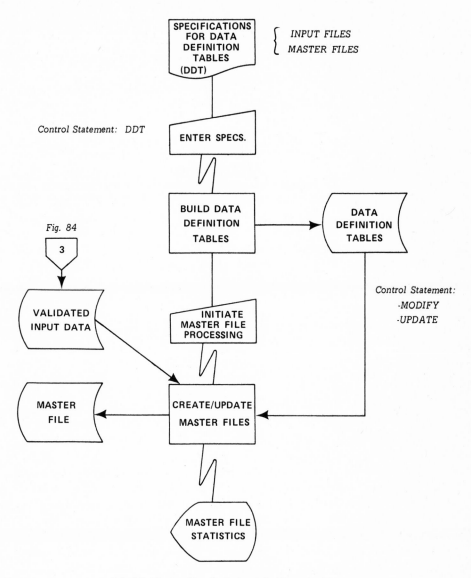

FIG. 85. Master file create/update flow chart

Implementation and Future Support

GIS is an IBM program product available under license for a monthly charge. Prior to 1971 IBM introduced the first version of

208

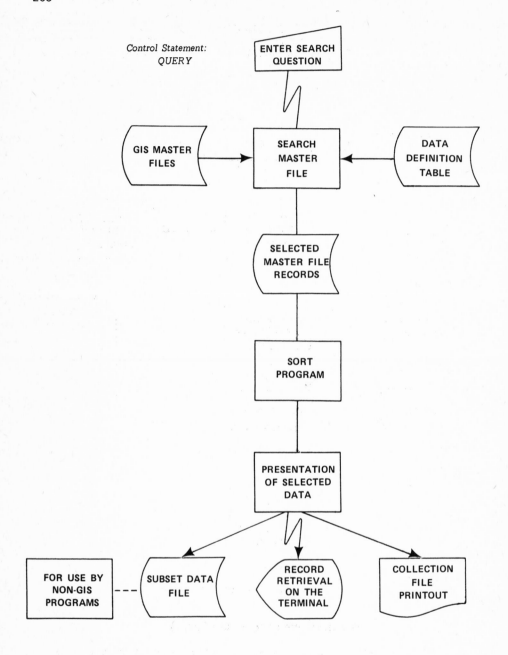

FIG. 86. Data retrieval flow chart

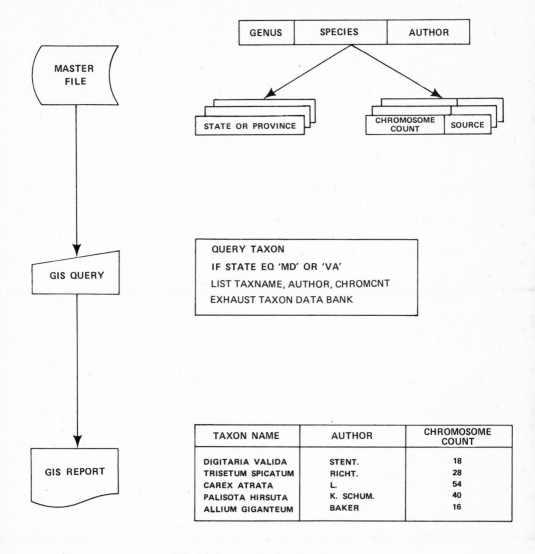

| GENUS | SPECIES | AUTHOR |

| STATE OR PROVINCE |

| CHROMOSOME COUNT | SOURCE |

MASTER FILE

GIS QUERY

QUERY TAXON

IF STATE EQ 'MD' OR 'VA'

LIST TAXNAME, AUTHOR, CHROMCNT

EXHAUST TAXON DATA BANK

GIS REPORT

TAXON NAME	AUTHOR	CHROMOSOME COUNT
DIGITARIA VALIDA	STENT.	18
TRISETUM SPICATUM	RICHT.	28
CAREX ATRATA	L.	54
PALISOTA HIRSUTA	K. SCHUM.	40
ALLIUM GIGANTEUM	BAKER	16

FIG. 87. Data retrieval schematic

GIS (GIS/1) and since then has continued support and development of the package. The current version of the package available to users is GIS/2. The package consists of a basic program, whose features have been described in this report. In addition, there are several features that a user has the option of selecting:

1. Formal report feature. Provides language extensions to support the generation of report programs within a GIS/2 procedure. This feature enhances the basic LIST command capability by permitting the specifications of a title page, page headers and trailers, summary lines conditioned on end of data and/or control field breaks and detail lines, all with the flexibility to control the horizontal and vertical spacing of the printed output.

2. Control statement feature. Provides language extensions to permit scanning of data fields, generation of procedure testable switches, and additional comparison operators for detecting increase or decrease of a field and absent or empty state of a field.

3. Utility feature. Provides language to save both external and compiled forms of GIS/2 language, perform corrections on saved language, execute a precompiled procedure or subprocedure and define the necessary data set formats to support the execution.

4. File modify feature. Provides the MODIFY verb and the associated file copy and security logic to perform field level file maintenance activities.

5. Arithmetic statement feature. Extends the language by providing four additional arithemtic verbs.

6. Processing statement feature. Extends the language to provide totaling, counting, averaging, and count of unique occurrences of data with both automatic and user controlled output. The control statement and arithmetic statement features must both be ordered as prerequisites to this feature.

7. Extended multifile support feature. Extends the system maximum of three files for concurrent operation to sixteen files in the areas of query and modify.

8. Teleprocessing support feature. Adds to program modules to interface to a QTAM or TCAM message control program. This feature is applicable to operation under MFT or MVT. When operating under MVT, GIS/2 provides a single monitor that handles both batch and terminal entered GIS procedures.

9. Hierarchic file support feature. Extends the file definition and processing support to provide for repeating groups of data. As many as fifteen levels of subordination may be specified, and at the most subordinate level there may be multiple formats of data.

10. File update and create feature. Extends the language to provide segment addressing verbs, automatic I/0 control, and implied data format translation for addition and replacement of data in file creation or general file maintenance activities.

11. Edit and encode feature. Extends the system processing by providing automatic data entry validation and conversion in file maintenance activities controlled from data description.

The rental cost of the Basic Retrieval System is $450 per month. The additional features may be acquired at the following additional rental cost:

Reporting—$100/month
Control statement feature—$40/month
Utilities—$75/month
File modification—$50/month
Arithmetic feature—$20/month
Processing feature—$40/month
Extended multifile support—$75/month
TP support—$50/month
Hierarchic file support—$125/month
File updating and creation—$400/month
Editing and encoding—$75/month

IBM provides a full range of support for GIS including the computer programs and latest system enhancements; systems, programming, and operational documentation manuals; training materials, and customer engineering service.

In general, GIS is quite expensive for a single user to rent. It has been possible for a user to gain access to the system through a service bureau that rents computer services. In such an operation the surcharges are added to the service bureau's standard processing rates. The FNA project gained considerable experience with the use of GIS in this manner. Mr. Stanwyn G. Shetler, Department of Botany, Smithsonian Institution, had administrative responsibility for the use of GIS in the FNA project. Mr. Shetler continues an information service and publication library relating to FNA and its data that is resident on computer master files.

Adaptability of package to use standard data categories. The GIS package is not designed to use a specific data set structure or coding system. However, the user through the function of the data definition table specifications has a high degree of flexibility in the design of data structure and file requirements. For example, on a data definition table (see figure 76) specification could be made to accept a standard data category number, such as 35 to indicate place of origin, in the NAME key word field (columns 5–12 of the DDT).

Adaptability of package to interact with other packages. GIS has limited capability to interact with other packages. Its operation is machine-dependent upon IBM. Additional computer programs would have to be developed to interface GIS data files with those produced by another package.

ELMS
Package Description

Background

ELMS, an acronym for Experimental Library Management System, is a package of generalized computer programs designed to perform most major library functions. Several computer systems have been developed for the automation of individual library functions such as circulation, but ELMS is considered by its developers to be the first total library system that integrates all the functions of ordering, receiving, cataloging, circulation, bibliographic search, etc.

The reasons for including a description of ELMS in this publication are (1) the library functions of cataloging and bibliographic search have direct analogies in the storage and retrieval of museum catalog data and (2) ELMS is the best example available of an integrated system that utilizes the cathode-ray tube terminal as the primary means of both creating files and retrieving data from files. This is an important attribute that must, in time, be integrated into information systems to be used for museum cataloging.

The ELMS system was developed at the Los Gatos Laboratory of the Advanced System Development Division of IBM Corporation. It was written initially to be run on a shared IBM System/360 Model 40 with 256K bytes of storage. It has been in operation at the laboratory's library since 1970, and on the basis of this day-to-day experience, modifications have been made, functions expanded, and interactive procedures refined. The ELMS system was marketed by IBM for some time as Library Access System. Recently LAS was taken off the market. However, ELMS is still an excellent system to illustrate the functions of cataloging and bibliographic search utilizing the cathode-ray tube terminal.

System Description

The ELMS system description is not the same as the other system descriptions included in this book. File designs, data structures, and the internal functioning of key programs that are part of the system will not be included. Rather an attempt will be made to give the reader the experiences of cataloging a new object and doing a search of the files using the interactive, conversational mode of entry and enquiry considered to be the unique contribution of the ELMS system. The reader should remember, however, that ELMS is a complete and integrated system and that the two functions of cataloging and bibliographic search are only those parts of the total system most directly applicable to computerized museum cataloging.

Introduction. The key element in the ELMS system, so far as the user is concerned, is the cathode-ray tube terminal (figure 88), although the system will work with other terminals as well. The terminal keyboard (figure 89), which is somewhat similar to a typewriter keyboard with a few extra keys, is the means by which the operator communicates with the information system; the cathode-ray

FIG. 88. IBM 3270 cathode-ray tube terminal

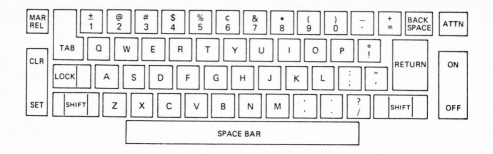

FIG. 89. IBM 2741 keyboard

tube above the keyboard is the means by which the system communicates with the operator. In the following pages the illustrations enclosed in rectangular boxes display the verbal data that would in each case appear on the cathode-ray tube at that particular point in the processing sequence.

The ELMS system is programmed to recognize three different kinds of users who identify themselves as such at the terminal: a library patron, a library visitor, or a librarian. The content of the data in the files can only be modified by those who identify themselves as librarians.

The first step in using the system, of course, is to turn on the terminal and allow it to warm up. When the SHIFT key and the ENTER key are depressed together [21] the system will display on the cathode-ray tube the information shown in the first line of figure 90. The information shown on the second line of figure 90 is what the librarian types in: his or her initials, the name of the system,

```
.SIGN ON, 07/11/72, 10:28
RBW,LMS,LBRRN
```

FIG. 90

and the code LBRRN. When the SHIFT/ENTER keys are again depressed, the first four lines of figure 91 will appear on the screen. The librarian responds this time by entering his or her name and identification number, and if changes are to be made to the file, the word UPDATE on the next line. Permission to update the file will be given only to someone who is identified as a librarian.

If the librarian is in the update mode, figure 92 would appear on the screen when the SHIFT/ENTER keys are depressed. (Note the instructions on the last line of figure 91.) If the user is a patron,

```
             THIS IS THE LIBRARY MANAGEMENT SYSTEM.        7/11/72

PLEASE ENTER YOUR NAME AND IDENTIFICATION CODE IN THE FOLLOWING FORM;
LAST NAME, INITIALS
IDENTIFICATION

   WINIK, R
796877
UPDATE
DEPRESS 'SHIFT' AND 'NEW LINE' KEYS TOGETHER TO START A NEW LINE.
DEPRESS 'SHIFT' AND 'ENTER' KEYS TOGETHER WHEN ENTRY COMPLETE
```

FIG. 91

a visitor, or a librarian not operating in update mode, figure 93 would appear on the screen rather than figure 92. The instructions given on the last line of figures 92 and 93 indicate how an operator, by

```
PLEASE SELECT THE FUNCTION YOU REQUIRE:
                                                STAND. CODES
    1 ORDERING                                    //ORDR/
    2 RECEIVING                                   //RECV/
    3 CATALOGING                                  //CATL/
    4 CIRCULATION                                 //CIRC/
    5 BIBLIOGRAPHIC SEARCH                        //BSCH/
    6 FILE REVIEW OR REVISION                     //FILE/
    7 REVIEW THE STANDARD CODES                   //SDCD/
    8 PRINTING                                    //PRNT/

       ENTER THE LINE NUMBER OF THE DESIRED FUNCTION
```

FIG. 92

```
PLEASE SELECT THE FUNCTION YOU REQUIRE:
                                                STAND. CODES
    1 DEVELOP A BIBLIOGRAPHIC RETRIEVAL SEARCH      //BSCB/
    2 REVIEW THE CATALOG FILES (AUTHORS, TITLES, ETC.)  //FILE/
    3 REVIEW THE STANDARD CODES                    //SDCD/
    4 REVIEW THE SYSTEM INSTRUCTIONS               //SYSI/

       ENTER THE LINE NUMBER OF THE DESIRED FUNCTION
```

FIG. 93

depressing a single key, branches to the computer program or programs necessary to perform the desired functions. Because they are most appropriate to the content of this book, the functions of cataloging and bibliographic search will be used to illustrate how the ELMS system works.

Cataloging. For illustrative purposes it will be assumed that the objective is to catalog a new document with bibliographic information as follows:

Author:	Zwicky, Fritz
Title:	Discovery, Invention, Research through the Morphological Approach
Publisher:	Macmillan 1969
Subject headings:	Science—Addresses, essays, lectures
	Science—Philosophy
Descriptors:	Scientific discovery
	Invention
	Morphological analysis
Catalog note:	Translation of Entdecken, Erfinden, Forschen im Morphologischen Weltbild
Call number:	Q 171 Z8
L. C. card number:	69-10785
Accession number:	020105
Report number:	MAC 137-2
Document type:	Book
Document form:	Hardcopy
Owning library:	A SDD LG
Location:	A SDD LG
Security:	Unclassified
Charge period:	Indef.
Primary language:	English
Secondary language:	None

From the alternatives available in the CRT display in figure 92, the librarian has selected number 3. The system responds by displaying the contents of figure 94. The operator depresses number 1 and the content of figure 95 appears on the screen.

The ELMS displays all follow the same general format shown on figure 95, namely: a one- or two-line heading, variable information, and at the bottom of the display, instructions. In the first line of the heading the first segment specifies the function; the second segment specifies the subfunction; the last segment is optional and, if present, labels the display itself. In the present case the paragraph numbers 1 through 7 are variable information that can be changed but are assumed to apply unless modified. If the information is

```
CATALOGING:

SELECT TYPE OF CATALOGING DESIRED:
1 CREATE A NEW DOCUMENT
2 EXISTING DOCUMENT—ALTER OR ADD FURTHER COPIES
3 PRINT SPINE/POCKET LABELS
4 ADD A DESCRIPTOR TO AUTHORITY LIST
5 ADD A SUBJECT HEADING TO AUTHORITY LIST
6 BUILD CROSS REFS./NOTES


ENTER THE LINE NUMBER OF THE DESIRED FUNCTION
```

FIG. 94

```
CATALOGING:    NEW DOCUMENT:    DOCUMENT INFORMATION    10/20/71

1 DOC. TYPE            BOOK             5 CHARGE PERIOD:       INDEF
2 DOC. FORM:           HARDCOPY         6 OWNING LIBRARY:      ASDD LG
3 SECURITY CLASS:      UNCLASSIFIED     7 LOCATION:           ASDD LG
4 COPIES:              1

        ENTER LINE NUMBER TO CHANGE AN ITEM
        Y = ACCEPT ABOVE INFORMATION
```

FIG. 95

acceptable, the letter Y is depressed and the contents of figure 96·
appear on the screen.

```
CATALOGING: NEW DOCUMENT: DOCUMENT INFORMATION—AUTHOR, 10/20/71

    ENTER FIRST AUTHOR:    (N = NONE)
```

FIG. 96

This requires the operator to enter some kind of author information,
even if it is the letter N to indicate that there is no author. In the
example being illustrated, Zwicky is a personal author, and the letters
ZWI are entered. The system responds by giving that portion of the
previously cataloged author file around the letters ZWI (figure 97).
Since the present author, Fritz Zwicky, is already in the file, the
numeral 7 is entered. Other alternatives are illustrated by the instructions at the bottom of figure 97.

After giving the operator an option of entering the author type
(e.g., editor, translator), the contents of figure 98 appear on the screen.
When the operator types in DISCOVERY, I (i.e., enough of the title

```
CATALOGING:     NEW DOCUMENT: DOCUMENT INFORMATION—AUTHOR, 10/20/71

1                              ZUBOV, V I
2                              ZULL, CAROLYN G
3                              ZWEIGBAUM, HAROLD
4                              ZWENG, CHARLES A
5                              ZWICK, CHARLES J
6                              ZWICK, JACK
7                              ZWICKY, FRITZ
8                              ZWIKKER, CORNELIS
        ENTER NUMBER TO SELECT AN ITEM     F = FORWARD   R = REVERSE
   S = NEW SEARCH TERM   M = MORE DETAIL   A = ADD AN AUTHOR   N = NONE
```

FIG. 97

```
CATALOGING:   NEW DOCUMENT:   DOCUMENT INFORMATION—TITLE. 10/20/71
AUTHOR: ZWICKY, FRITZ

ENTER FIRST TITLE: (N = NONE)
```

FIG. 98

to locate it in the permuted index of titles already present in the system), the system displays the contents of figure 99.

```
CATALOGING:   NEW DOCUMENT:   DOCUMENT INFORMATION—TITLE 10/20/71
AUTHOR: ZWICKY, FRITZ
1 *     PERSONAL ACCOUNT OF THE DISCOVERY OF THE STRUCTURE OF DNA
2                               DISCOVERY TRIPS IN OREGON
3 *              LEARNING BY DISCOVERY, A CRITICAL APPRAISAL, CONFE
4 *              PATTERNS OF DISCOVERY, AN INQUIRY INTO THE CONCEPT
5 *          MATHEMATICAL DISCOVERY, ON UNDERSTANDING, LEARN-
6 *                      DISCRETE AND CONTINUOUS BOUNDARY
7 *     EFFECT TRANSISTORS FOR DISCRETE AND INTEGRATED CIRCUIT
8     PROB INFORMATION THEORY, DISCRETE AND MEMORYLESS MODELS
        ENTER NUMBER TO SELECT AN ITEM   F = FORWARD   R = REVERSE
   S = NEW SEARCH TERM   M = MORE DETAIL   A = ADD A NEW TITLE   N = NONE
```

FIG. 99

The title desired is not there. However, the operator realizes that if the comma has been erroneously omitted, the title would be filed elsewhere in the title file. Therefore, the letter R is entered to check the preceding titles in the file. This produces figure 100 on the cathode-ray tube. Again the title is not in the file, so the letter A is entered to add it to the system. This produces figure 101 on the screen, and the title of the book is typed.

```
CATALOGING:  / NEW DOCUMENT:    DOCUMENT INFORMATION—TITLE. 10/20/71
AUTHOR: ZWICKY, FRITZ
1 *      |           OF FIRST HAPPENINGS, DISCOVERIES AND INVENTIONS IN THE UNIT
2 *                                   DISCOVERING BASIC, A PROBLEM SOLVING
3                LOGIC OF SCIENTIFIC DISCOVERY
4 *  MODELS OF FORM PERCEPTION AND DISCOVERY
5                CHANCE IN SCIENTIFIC DISCOVERY
6          TEACHING SCIENCE THROUGH DISCOVERY
7             PATTERN RECOGNITION, DISCOVERY AND LEARNING TECHNIQUES
8 *       CONDITIONS FOR SCIENTIFIC DISCOVERY AND TECHNICAL INVENTION
ENTER NUMBER TO SELECT AN ITEM F = FORWARD  R = REVERSE  S = NEW
     SEARCH TERM  M = MORE DETAIL  A = ADD A NEW TITLE  N = NONE
```

FIG. 100

```
CATALOGING:  NEW DOCUMENT:  DOCUMENT INFORMATION—TITLE.  10/20/71
AUTHOR: ZWICKY, FRITZ
ADD A NEW KEY TO TITLE FILE
MAKE ENTRY EXACTLY AS IT IS TO APPEAR IN THE SYSTEM          N = NONE
```

FIG. 101

This title is permuted automatically by the ELMS system and entered alphabetically in the title access point file.

After the title has been entered, ELMS summarizes the information that has been entered for this document so far on the first bibliographic summary screen (figure 102).

```
CATALOGING:    NEW DOCUMENT:     DOCUMENT INFORMATION    10/20/71
AUTHOR: ZWICKY, FRITZ
  1 AUTHORS                1        8 REPORT NUMBERS            0
  2 TITLES                 1        9 CONTRACT NUMBERS          0
  3 SERIES TITLES          0       10 PATENT NUMBERS            0
  4 PUBLISHERS             0       11 CATALOG NOTES             0
  5 COPYRIGHT DATE      NONE       12 LIBRARIAN NOTES           0
  6 SUBJECT HEADINGS       0       13 COLLATION              NONE
  7 DESCRIPTORS            0
          ENTER LINE NUMBER OF ITEM TO BE CHANGED
F = FORWARD  B = REVIEW COMPLETE BIBLIOGRAPHIC DETAIL
```

FIG. 102

By entering the appropriate line number on the keyboard, the subroutines appropriate to each category of catalog information are called forth and processed by the operator as necessary in order to produce the complete catalog entry. The entire procedure will not be illustrated here, but the way in which multiple entries are handled through a chain of commands can be illustrated with the following operator-system communication.

The first descriptor is entered with a command chain /7/SCIEN-TIFIC DIS/. This produces on the screen that portion of the descriptor file shown in figure 103.

```
CATALOGING:        NEW DOCUMENT:        DESCRIPTORS        10/20/71
REVIEW DESCRIPTOR FILE
1                   COLLECTING  SCIENTIFIC DATA
2                               SCIENTIFIC DATA CENTER
3                               SCIENTIFIC DEVELOPMENT
4                               SCIENTIFIC DICTIONARY
5                               SCIENTIFIC DISCOVERY
6                               SCIENTIFIC DOCUMENTATION
7                               SCIENTIFIC EDUCATION
8                               SCIENTIFIC ENCYCLOPEDIA
ENTER  NUMBER  TO  SELECT  AN  ITEM   F = FORWARD  R = REVERSE   S = NEW
                              SEARCH TERM
M = MORE DETAIL   D = DISPLAY CURRENT DESCRIPTORS   A = ADD NEW TERM
```

FIG. 103

Since the descriptor desired is already in the file, the number 5 is entered. The system then goes back to a descriptor summary display, and the second descriptor is added by a command chain /A/INVEN-TION/. This in turn produces that portion of the file around the term INVENTION. Since the word INVENTION by itself is already in the file, the operator has only to select the line number that appears opposite that word. This again produces the descriptor summary display, now with two entries shown. The further command chain /A/MORPHOLO/ is entered, and once again that portion of the file alphabetically closest to this term appears on the screen (figure 104).

```
CATALOGING:        NEW DOCUMENT:        DESCRIPTORS        10/20/71
REVIEW DESCRIPTOR FILE
1                   MICHELSON MORLEY EXPERIMENT
2                       ENGLISH MORPHEME
3              AUTOMATIC VERB MORPHEMICIZATION
4                               MORPHOGENESIS
5                               MORPHOLOGICAL ASTRONOMY
6                               MORPHOLOGICAL RESEARCH
7                               MORPHOLOGY
8                       CRYSTAL MORPHOLOGY
ENTER  NUMBER  TO  SELECT  AN  ITEM   F = FORWARD   R = REVERSE   S = NEW
                              SEARCH TERM
M = MORE DETAIL   D = DISPLAY CURRENT DESCRIPTORS   A = ADD NEW TERM
```

FIG. 104

Since the exact wording "morphological analysis" does not appear in the file, this time the operator enters the letter A. This in turn produces on the screen the contents of figure 105, and the new descriptor is then typed in exactly as it is wanted in the file.

```
CATALOGING:        NEW DOCUMENT:        DESCRIPTORS        10/20/71
REVIEW DESCRIPTOR FILE
ADD A NEW KEY TO DESCRIPTOR FILE
MAKE ENTRY EXACTLY AS IT IS TO APPEAR IN THE SYSTEM        N = NONE
```

FIG. 105

The system once again gives the summary of the descriptor terms that will call forth this book (figure 106), and since no more descriptors are to be added, an E is entered.

```
CATALOGING:        NEW DOCUMENT:        DESCRIPTORS        10/20/71
AUTHOR: ZWICKY, FRITZ
001 SCIENTIFIC DISCOVERY
002 INVENTION
003 MORPHOLOGICAL ANALYSIS

                                        A = ADD A TERM
                                        E = END OF DESCRIPTORS
ENTER LINE NUMBER FOR MORE DETAIL       D = DELETE A TERM
```

FIG. 106

In the discussion of the content of museum catalogs it was pointed out (page 49) that a data category expresses a classification of an object according to an attribute or dimension that is distinct from all other attributes or dimensions. It is a unique kind or type of observation that can be made about that object. A book is an object just as much as the artifacts in any other kind of a museum collection. The author of the book, the title of the book, the descriptors that are used in searching for the book, and in fact, all the different ways that a book is classified in the process of cataloging it (i.e., the list on page 216) become the content of a fixed list of data categories. The *principles* of cataloging are the same for a library and a museum even though the number and variety of data categories used may be quite different.

Bibliographic search. The cataloging of objects and/or books by computer involves the storage of information about those objects. The reason for cataloging objects is that the stored information may be eventually retrieved in the most usable form. The retrieval function in the parlance of librarians is called the function of bibliographic search, and it is this function more than any other that makes a discussion of the ELMS system appropriate to computerized museum cataloging.

From the list of functions available to the operator of the terminal (figures 92 and 93), if the bibliographic search function is chosen, the terminal display shown as figure 107 would appear on the CRT screen.

```
BIBLIOGRAPHIC SEARCH FUNCTION        FILE IDENTIFICATION        11/16/71

1 AUTHOR
2 TITLE
3 DESCRIPTOR
4 LC SUBJECT HEADING
5 REPORT NUMBER
6 CONTRACT NUMBER
7 PATENT NUMBER

        ENTER LINE NUMBER FOR DESIRED FILE
```

FIG. 107

If the operator wishes to search the author file first, the numeral 1 would be entered and the system then would ask for the search term (figure 108).

```
BIBLIOGRAPHIC SEARCH FUNCTION              AUTHOR          11/16/71
ENTER SEARCH TERM
```

FIG. 108

If the truncated term SRI, LONG is entered, that portion of the author file shown in figure 109 would appear on the screen.

The desired term is again chosen by entering a line number, this time the number 5. This will produce the search display summary shown in figure 110.

Note that this summary not only shows the search term that has been entered but the number of documents (in this case 301) to which this term has been assigned in this system. The operator may select another author name by entering an S or another author from the search list (figure 109) by entering an L. Let us assume that the operator enters a G and is thus returned to figure 107 to select another file.

```
BIBLIOGRAPHIC SEARCH FUNCTION              AUTHOR            11/16/71
DISPLAY AUTHOR
1                          SPYERS-DURAN, PETER
2                          SQUIRES, EUAN J
3                          SRI
4                          SRI, INTERNATIONAL DEVELOPMENT CENTER
5                          SRI, LONG RANGE PLANNING SERVICE
6                          SRI, SOUTHERN CALIFORNIA LABORATORIES
7          AKADEMIIA NAUK SSSR
8          AKADEMIIA NAUK SSSR, INSTITUT ELEKTROKHIMII
ENTER  NUMBER  TO  SELECT  AN  ITEM  F = FORWARD  R = REVERSE  S = NEW
SEARCH TERM  G  =  NEW FILE
```

FIG. 109

```
BIBLIOGRAPHIC SEARCH FUNCTION         SEARCH DISPLAY        11/16/71
TOTAL COUNT OF UNIQUE DOCUMENTS:    301
1 AUTH: SRI, LONG RANGE PLANNING SERVICE                         301

                                                    I = INSTRUCTIONS
G = NEW FILE   S = NEW SEARCH TERM   L = SEARCH LIST   D = DELETE A TERM
```

FIG. 110

If the numeral 3 is entered, the descriptor file is called into play, and if the truncated term ELECTRONICS IND is entered as a search term, that portion of the descriptor file shown in figure 111 would be called forth.

```
BIBLIOGRAPHIC SEARCH FUNCTION            DESCRIPTOR          11/16/71
DISPLAY DESCRIPTOR
1                    SMALL ELECTRONICS BUSINESS
2                          ELECTRONICS DIAGRAM GRAPHIC SYMBOL
3                          ELECTRONICS DICTIONARY
4              BIOMEDICAL ELECTRONICS DIRECTORY
5                          ELECTRONICS INDUSTRY
6                          ELECTRONICS MAINTENANCE
7                  ADMIRE ELECTRONICS MAINTENANCE
8                   ATOMS ELECTRONICS MAINTENANCE
ENTER  NUMBER  TO  SELECT  AN  ITEM  F = FORWARD  R = REVERSE  S = NEW
                      SEARCH TERM  G = NEW FILE
```

FIG. 111

If line 5 is selected, the search display summary would again appear on the screen, this time as shown in figure 112.

Here the two selected search terms are displayed with the number of documents associated with each. Note that although the total number of documents is 308, the total count of unique documents

```
┌─────────────────────────────────────────────────────────────────────┐
│                                                                     │
│  BIBLIOGRAPHIC SEARCH FUNCTION        SEARCH DISPLAY      11/16/71   │
│  TOTAL COUNT OF UNIQUE DOCUMENTS:    303                            │
│  1 AUTH: SRI, LONG RANGE PLANNING SERVICE                   301     │
│  2 DESC: ELECTRONICS INDUSTRY                                 7     │
│                                                                     │
│     ENTER BOOLEAN REQUEST    AND    OR    NOT    I = INSTRUCTIONS   │
│  G = NEW FILE   S = NEW SEARCH TERM   L = SEARCH LIST   D = DELETE A TERM │
│                                                                     │
└─────────────────────────────────────────────────────────────────────┘
```

FIG. 112

is only 303. This indicates that 308—303 = 5, or the number of documents that have term 1 *and* term 2 in common. Other search terms could be added, but let us assume that the letter I is entered as a request for further instructions. This produces the display shown in figure 113.

```
┌─────────────────────────────────────────────────────────────────────┐
│                                                                     │
│  BIBLIOGRAPHIC SEARCH FUNCTION      SEARCH INSTRUCTIONS   11/16/71   │
│                                                                     │
│  ONCE YOU HAVE ASSEMBLED YOUR LIST OF DESIRED TERMS, YOU MAY        │
│  PERFORM A BOOLEAN SEARCH BY LINKING THE TERMS WITH LOGICAL         │
│  CONNECTORS. FOR EXAMPLE, YOU WOULD ENTER EXPRESSIONS SUCH AS:      │
│        1 AND 2                                                       │
│        1 AND 4 OR 2                                                  │
│        3 NOT 1 AND 2                                                 │
│  OPERATIONS ARE PERFORMED STRICTLY LEFT TO RIGHT. SPACES ARE        │
│  OPTIONAL.                                                           │
│                                                                     │
│  L = RETURN TO SEARCH SUMMARY   F = FORWARD TO DEFINITIONS          │
│                                                                     │
└─────────────────────────────────────────────────────────────────────┘
```

FIG. 113

If the letter F is entered, the display shown as figure 114 would appear.

```
┌─────────────────────────────────────────────────────────────────────┐
│                                                                     │
│  BIBLIOGRAPHIC SEARCH FUNCTION      SEARCH INSTRUCTIONS   11/16/71   │
│                                                                     │
│  THE LOGICAL OPERATIONS AVAILABLE ARE DEFINED AS FOLLOWS:           │
│  AND:    ALL DOCUMENTS DESCRIBED BY BOTH SEARCH TERMS               │
│   OR:    ALL DOCUMENTS DESCRIBED BY EITHER SEARCH TERM OR BY BOTH   │
│  NOT:    ALL DOCUMENTS DESCRIBED BY THE FIRST SEARCH TERM BUT NOT   │
│          THE SECOND                                                  │
│                                                                     │
│  L = RETURN TO SEARCH SUMMARY                                       │
│                                                                     │
└─────────────────────────────────────────────────────────────────────┘
```

FIG. 114

From this the letter L returns the operator to the display shown as figure 112. By typing in 1 AND 2, figure 115 appears on the screen.

```
┌─────────────────────────────────────────────────────────────────────────┐
│                                                                           │
│  BIBLIOGRAPHIC SEARCH FUNCTION          SEARCH DISPLAY        11/16/71     │
│                                                                           │
│  TOTAL OF 1AND2                                              IS  5         │
│  1 AUTH:SRI, LONG RANGE PLANNING SERVICE                       301         │
│  2 DESC:ELECTRONICS INDUSTRY                                     7         │
│                                                                           │
│         B = DISPLAY BIBLIOGRAPHY                                           │
│  L = RETURN TO SEARCH SCREEN   D = LIMIT BY DATE  T = LIMIT BY DOCUMENT TYPE│
│                                                                           │
└─────────────────────────────────────────────────────────────────────────┘
```

FIG. 115

It would be possible, of course, to further delimit the number of documents called forth by this bibliographic search. However, the entry of the letter B at this stage would produce on the CRT screen a listing of the five items in the library that fulfill this search request, including the author, title, date, and call number of each item, and because of other parts of the total ELMS system, a statement concerning the present location of each item. Upon request, the terminal operator may review the full citation of any document at the CRT.

Implementation and Future Support

Up to the present time the ELMS system has been considered as an experimental system, and in fact this is indicated by the title the IBM Corporation has given to the system. Nevertheless, it has been in operation at the Advanced Systems Development Division's Los Gatos Laboratory for over four years now, and from an operator's point of view it is well documented. In addition to several generalized manuals that describe the operation of the system, there is a Librarian's User Manual that provides complete instructions in nontechnical terms for anyone wishing to use the system.

As stated previously, the ELMS system is presently being modified and marketed as an installed user program, Library Access System. Anyone who acquires Library Access System for installation at some other location will receive the normal support for such programs from the IBM Corporation in the form of personnel and the documentation and experience that has grown out of several years of work with the system. Additional support such as for modifications for unique user requirements, as desired by any customer, may be contracted for from the IBM Corporation.

DESCRIPTION OF THE
W. H. Over Museum
Information System

Background

The information retrieval system used by the W. H. Over Museum is an example of what can be done in the preparation of a computerized catalog by means of special programming for a small-scale computer. There are a number of museums in the United States that have approached the cataloging problem in much this same way, utilizing the computing equipment and programming capabilities that were readily available (usually on a university campus) rather than attempting to acquire an information system as a complete package. Each of these systems, of course, is unique and not readily transportable from the location where it was developed to another computer center. However, there is a similarity of concepts that extends through most of these systems even though some are card oriented, some are designed to function through a remote terminal, some maintain the files on tapes, others maintain the files on magnetic disks, and they are designed for a wide variety of computer sizes, models, and brands.

The system in use at the W. H. Over Museum is written in a programming language called SPS (Symbolic Programming System) for the IBM 1620. It operates on an IBM 1620-1 with a core size of 40K, and the files are stored on IBM Model 1311 magnetic disks. The programs were written by Gerald Norby, a graduate student working under the direction of Lanny Hoffman, director of the computer center at the University of South Dakota. Mrs. June Sampson is director of the museum and the one most active in utilizing the computer catalog.

At the present time the computerized catalog file contains the records on 900 plus ethnographic specimens and 400 plus photographs. For these items the system is capable of providing: a listing of all records that contain any specified key word descriptor, an alphabetic index of the key words that have been recorded as such, catalog listings, and catalog cards for all or any portion of the file.

System Description

The structuring of the records is essentially free form, which means that a record can be of almost any length (there are some system limitations) and there are no predefined fields within the record, either created by the use of tags (see page 37) or through positional structuring of fields within the record. However, a record does consist of two parts: (1) key word descriptors that are used as record-finding devices and (2) descriptive text. The list of key words always precedes the descriptive text and is separated from it by a single asterisk. Two records in the computer file are separated by a double asterisk.

Records are stored on the disk in random order (i.e., in the order in which the punched cards are fed into the computer).

When a user of the system wishes to retrieve the records on all objects that contain a specific word as one of the descriptor terms, the system searches each record sequentially to determine the presence or absence of that term in the list of descriptors present (note that composite terms must be hyphenated; a space separates one descriptor from another). A search can be made in approximately the same length of time on a single descriptor term or on a combination of two or three descriptor terms since the list of descriptors in each record in the file must be completely examined in any search.

A modification of this search strategy is incorporated in some of the information systems that are similar to that at the W. H. Over Museum. For example, with MIRS (Meta Information Retrieval System), which is used at The Children's Museum in Boston, the record structuring is similar to this but at the time a record is entered, the location where it is stored is also recorded in an inverted index. When a user wishes to retrieve the records on a given descriptor term, the system goes first to the index and from there directly to each succeeding record that contains that term (i.e., making a *sequential* search of all the records unnecessary). In a large file this results in a much faster search and retrieval operation. This additional feature, though, requires a somewhat larger computer and more sophisticated programming than that which is available at the University of South Dakota.

As an example of a retrieval from the W. H. Over Museum files, let us assume that the photographic file is searched in accordance with the descriptor term MINER. The resulting record print-out would be as shown, in part, in figure 116. In the illustration the descriptor term has been underlined on each record for clarity. Note that each record is printed out in full, with the listing of all descriptor terms applicable to that object appearing first, followed by a blank line and then the full descriptive text.

A complete listing, in paragraph form, of all descriptor terms that have been used in recording the photographic file is shown, in part, as figure 117.

```
MINER *

POR3 PLAINS GUARD MINER CAMP DEADWOOD MORROW COLLECTION FRONTIER

MINERS FRONTIER OR3 GOOD CONDITION D3A SLIGHTLY TORN ON TOP CAT. R. SAWREY
1-30-70 PHOTO NO. D3A NEG. NO. 3 OR3 AND D3A ARE THE SAME SIZE**

POR4 PLAINS MORROW COLLECTION HUNTER CABIN BLACK-HILLS MINER FRONTIER

MINERS FRONTIER FAIR CONDITION PRINT QUALITY POOR D4A FAIR CONDITION SLIGHT
LY BENT AND TORN CAT. R. SAWREY 1-30-70 PHOTO NO. D4A NEG. NO. 4 OR4 AND D4
A ARE THE SAME SIZE**

POR5 PLAINS MORROW COLLECTION VIEW PLACER DIGGING FLUME DITCH DEBRIS MINER
FRONTIER

MINERS FRONTIER GOOD CONDITION D5A GOOD CONDITION D5B GOOD CONDITION CAT. R
. SAWREY 1-29-70 PHOTO NO. D5A D5B NEG. NO. 5 D5A IS SAME SIZE AS OR5 D5B I
S ENLARGEMENT OF OR5**

PN6 PLAINS MORROW COLLECTION FATHER-DESMET MINE MINER FRONTIER

MINERS FRONTIER GOOD CONDITION CAT. R. SAWREY 3-17-70 NEG. NO. 6**

PN7 PLAINS MORROW COLLECTION SMITH-ORIGINAL SHERMAN MINER FRONTIER VIEW VIL
LAGE VALLEY

MINERS FRONTIER VIEW OF SMALL VILLAGE IN A VALLEY GOOD CONDITION CAT. R. SA
WREY 1-29-70 NEG. NO. 7**

POR8 PLAINS MORROW COLLECTION BADLANDS VIEW SOUTH DAKOTA MINER FRONTIER

MINERS FRONTIER FAIR CONDITION CAT. R. SAWREY 1-29-70 NEG. NO. 8**

PN9 PLAINS MORROW COLLECTION BEAR-BUTTE BLACK-HILLS MINER FRONTIER

MINERS FRONTIER GOOD CONDITION CAT. R. SAWREY 3-17-70 NEG. NO. 9**
```

FIG. 116

In using this system the edit options for printed output are extremely limited (although the line length can be varied from the default option of 72 characters). File status information is provided by statistical options that give key word usage counts and average record length.

This information system is designed for and used exclusively at a single installation. Presumably, those who regularly work with the system know how to use it. Therefore, the matters of documentation and future support, which have been an important part of the other information system descriptions, are not appropriate here. Documentation is always desirable, but in a small, closely controlled system such as this, it may be an unnecessary embellishment that is not worth the cost.

```
AFRAID=OF=THE=BEAR AGENCY AGENT ALCOVE ALLIGATOR AMERICAN ANNUITY ANTONE
 ARASTER ARIKARA ARMOUR ARMY ARTILLERY ASSINABOINE AUTOGRAPH BACKGROUND
BADLANDS BANNOCK BARGE BARNES BARRACKS BATALLION=DRILL BATTLE BEAR=BUTTE
 BEAR=CLAW=NECKLACE BEAR=GULCH BEAR=ROCK BEAUREGARD BEAVER=TRAP BIG=HORN
 BIG=SNAKE BIRDS=EYE BLACK=EYE BLACK=HILLS BLACK=PRAIRIE=CHICKEN BLOCKED
BLOODY=MOUTH BOATING BOULDER BOX=CAR BRADY BRAVE=BEAR BREAST=PLATE BRIDA
L=VAIL BRIDE BROTHER BRULE BUCKSKIN BUFFALO=GAP BUFFALO=HIDE BULL=BOAT B
URIED BUSINESS=STREET CABIN CAMP CANTATA CAPITAL=STREET CAPITOL CAPTOR C
ARGO CAROLINA CARRYING CASCADE CALVALRY CEMETERY=HILL CHAPMAN CHARGE CHA
RLESTON CHEYENNE=RIVER CHICAGO CHIEF CHILDREN CHOIR CHURCH CHURCH=HILL C
ITY=POINT CIVIL=WAR CIVILIZATION COLLECTING COLLECTION COLONY COMMISSION
 COMPANY CONFEDERACY CONGREGATIONAL CONSTRUCTION CONTONEMENT CORPS CORRA
L COSTUME COULSON COUNCIL CRAZY=IN=THE=LODGE CRIB CRITTENDEN CROOK=CITY
CROSSING CROW CROW=CREEK CULPS=HILL CURING CUSTER CUSTER=CITY CUSTER=HIL
L CUT=HEAD CUTTING DAKOTA DARK=ROOM DAUGHTER DAVIS=JEFFERSON DEADWOOD DE
ADWOOD=GULCH DEBRIS DECORATING DELL=RAPIDS DEPOT DESCENDANT DESERTED DES
TRUCTION DEVILS=DEN DEVILS=GULCH DEVILS=LAKE DIGGING DIRT=ROOF DISCOVERY
 DITCH DOCK DOCTOR DOG=SLED DOME=SHAPED DONKEY DORM DRESS DRESSING DROWN
ED DRUM DRUMMER DRY=DELLS DUNLOP DUTCH=GAP DWELLING DYNAMITE EAST EAST=H
ALL EASTERN EAT=DOG ECHO=CANYON ECHO=ROCK EFFECT ELEVATOR ELK=TEETH EMIG
RATION ENGINE ENTIRE ENTRANCE EPISCOPAL EVARTS EXCELSIOR=MILLS FAMILY FA
RM FARMER FAST=BEAR FATHER FATHER=DESMET FAVORITE FERRY=BOAT FERRY=BOAT=
LIVINGSTON FIELD FIFTH FIGHTING FIRST FISHING FLAG FLOOD FLORIDA FLUME F
OOTE FOOTPRINT FORD FOREGROUND FORT=BENTON FORT=BERTHOLD FORT=BUFORD FOR
T=KEOGN FORT=NIOBRARA FORT=RANDALL FORT=SULLY FORT=TOTTEN FORT=WADSWORTH
 FORTIFICATION FOURTH=STREET FREAK FRENCH=CREEK FRONTIER FROST GALENA GA
RFIELD GATHERING GAYVILLE GOLD GOVERNOR=ARCHIBALD GRANDFATHER=STONE GRAN
DMOTHER=TREE GRANITE GRANT GRAVE GREENHOUSE GRINDING GRISLEY GROS=VENTRE
 GROSBY GUARD HABITATION HALFBREED HAND=TO=HAND HATCH HEADQUARTERS HEART
=ARCH HELENA HIGH=SCHOOL HIGH=WATER HOOKER HOPE=SCHOOL HORSE=MEAT HOUSE
HUDDLING HUNTER ICE=GORGE IDA=REEVES INDIAN INFANTRY INSTANTANEOUS IRON=
BRIGADE IRON=BULL IRON=CART ISLAND ISSUING JAIL JUNCTION KELLY KELLYS=TR
AIL KETCHUM=SARAH=ELDRIDGE KIDDER KILLING LABELED LANDING LINCOLN LITTLE
=HORN LOAFER LODGE LOG=CABIN LONE=ROCK LONGSTREET LOOKOUT=MOUNTAIN LOOKO
UT=VALLEY LOVER=RETREAT LOW=WATER LOWER=FALLS MA=TO=WA=CA MAIDENS=WHIRLP
OOL MAIN=FALLS MAIN=STREET MANDAN MARKET MARKET=STREET MARTYR MARYLAND M
ASSACRE MEDICINE MEDICINE=BEAR MEDICINE=TEEPEE MEETING=STREET MEXICAN=ST
YLE MILES MILES=CITY MILITARY MINE (MINER) MINNECONJEAUX MISCELLANEOUS MIS
SION MISSISSIPPI MISSOURI=RIVER MONTANA MONUMENT MORMON MORNING MORROW M
```

FIG. 117

One of the limitations that a person must face with a system such as this is the fact that it is not designed to interact with other systems, and in fact, such interaction would be almost impossible to achieve. It is possible, though, for the user to employ data categories and terminology that conform to industry and/or discipline data standards. This is done by means of a controlled, hierarchically structured list of descriptor terms, in which the first segment of each term contains the data category (perhaps, in numerically coded form) and a second segment the descriptor term itself.

What To Look for in Selecting an Information System

In practice, the information system that has been selected by each institution for the purpose of building and maintaining a catalog has been based upon the interaction of four factors:

1. Precedents that have been established by other institutions in the same discipline or area of interest.

2. Computer hardware that happens to be available (the particular brand, model, and storage capacity that is most readily and economically available).

3. The skills and biases of the persons who will be responsible for making the system work (systems analysts, computer programmers, etc.).

4. The budget available (*a*) to acquire a system and (*b*) to operate the system.

The way one or another of these four factors controls the selection can be illustrated by comparing the experiences of six different institutions that have recently been involved in the selection of an information system to accomplish a single purpose—namely, to create a catalog of archaeological sites—and then to look at a few other institutions unrelated to the field of archaeology.

In 1971 the Arkansas Archeological Survey made the decision to adapt the GRIPHOS system for the cataloging of archaeological sites. At that time there was no precedent of any system being used elsewhere for this purpose, the computer hardware available to the Survey at the University of Arkansas was an IBM 360 Model 50 (one of the models for which the GRIPHOS system was designed), the skills and biases of the persons who would be responsible for this system were not opposed to the use of the GRIPHOS system, and an adequate budget was available to both acquire and operate the system.

A short while later Mr. Frank Fryman from the Florida State Archeologist's office visited Arkansas, and on the basis of the then limited experience of the Arkansas Archeological Survey, elected to adopt the same system, virtually without change. Already a precedent had been established for archaeology.

At Arizona State University, however, Dr. Sylvia Gaines had two special problems: *(a)* she did not have any type of IBM equipment available and had to do any cataloging that was to be done on Honeywell (at that time GE) equipment and *(b)* her particular project involved processing data on the computer from a remote location—an archaeological site in the middle of the Navaho Indian reservation. In order to resolve this, Dr. Gaines was forced to develop a specialized information system of her own. The most recent version of this system is called ADAM-2.

The deciding factor or factors at three other institutions that have elected to establish computerized archaeological site files more recently have been as follows:

1. The Iowa State Archeologist's office has elected to follow the precedent of Arkansas in much the way Florida did and is recording sites for entry in the GRIPHOS system. So far they have been unable to obtain a budget that is adequate to acquire and operate the system.

2. At the University of Arizona the only computer available is a CDC/6600. However, the person responsible for setting up an information system on this equipment, Mr. Larry Manire, is well skilled in computer programming. Thus, the logical choice was to acquire the SELGEM program package and rewrite the COBOL programs to work on the CDC equipment.

3. In the Michigan State Archeologist's office the computer equipment available is manufactured by the Burroughs Corporation and the only feasible answer will be something similar to the experience at the University of Arizona.

In contrast to the varied factors that have determined the information systems selected by archaeologists, natural scientists (other than botanists) have almost unanimously followed the precedent established by the strong leadership of Dr. James Mello and his associates at the Smithsonian National Museum of Natural History. SELGEM has not been officially adopted as the information system of the Association of Systematics Collections, but the museums directed by the current ASC president and secretary (The Florida State Museum and the Museum of Natural History at the University of Kansas) have both established catalogs using SELGEM.

Turning to yet a third major class of institutions, the art museums that were a part of the initial (1967) Museum Computer Network experiment established, under the leadership of David Vance of the Museum of Modern Art, such a strong precedent that virtually all art museums that have done anything with computerized cataloging have used the GRIPHOS system.

Given enough time precedent would probably be the determining factor in any discipline that is involved with computerized museum cataloging. Where botanists have become involved with cataloging per se (the Flora North America project is a data bank of a different sort), they have followed the early work of Dr. David Rogers at the University of Colorado and used TAXIR; most of the limited work done by ethnologists followed the early lead of Dr. Alex Ricciardelli in using the GIPSY system for the same reasons; and so on. Of the four factors mentioned above as being the usual determinants in the selection of an information system, it is apparent that precedent in a particular discipline has been the most important, with the other three serving primarily as limiting factors that have forced an institution to go to some system when it could not use the system dictated by peer pressure.

Precedent, hardware, skills, and budget, of course, cannot be ignored. However, there are two other factors that are seldom adequately considered: the information needs of the institution and the probable future support that the user will receive from the developer of the system. Throughout this book an attempt has been made to place first priority on deciding what information is really needed, who needs that information, how often is it needed, and in what form. Admittedly anything is better than nothing (the present status in too many museums), but the starting point should be to determine your information needs rather than just to assume they will be met by any system that has been used by someone else in the same discipline. First consideration should seriously be given to questions such as the timing of answers that you would like to have when a request is put to the computer file (next week? tomorrow morning? five minutes?) and the extent of completeness you would like to have in your master file (i.e., the frequency with which new data is to be entered—every six months? every three months? once a month? the day after an object has been received and accessioned?). You may not be able to have everything you want in the systems that are presently available. However, *you should know what you want,* for computerized information systems—those described here and others as well—are changing rapidly, and the type of system that is available tomorrow will be based upon the information needs that are *expressed* by museum administrators today.

It is difficult to discuss probable future support without being both negative and critical. It is probably a fact that no established computerized catalog has ever ceased to exist solely because of inadequate support from the developers. It is equally true, though, that (1) it takes *some* measure of support to get the project off the ground in the first place and (2) it takes enthusiastic support, both from someone within the institution *and* from the developers, to bring a catalog up to the level of an efficient tool that is respected and appreciated by all the museum staff.

The extent of the support offered with any information system can be measured by asking three lines of questions:

1. What changes have been made in the programs within the last year? What changes are contemplated within the next year? What procedures are used to make sure that all users have these changes? The most important part of the answers here is not the specifics

of the changes as much as the fact that there is a conscious attempt being made to improve the system and to communicate improvements to users.

2. How adequate is the present documentation? When was the last documentation released? Is anything presently being written? Who does the actual writing? Again, the importance of this line of questioning is not the specific answers; it is the question of whether or not documentation is considered to be vital enough to have someone actually working on it in some systematic fashion.

3. How is the system supported? Is it dependent upon developmental grants or is the work being done by regular employees? What happens if *the* key individual moves to another job? Will the system continue to be sponsored by the company or institution or is it, either legally or because of his knowledge and enthusiasm, something that cannot grow and prosper without him?

In general, the most complete and reliable support will be provided for those information systems owned and distributed by well-established computer companies such as IBM. These are generally the most expensive systems as well, but the support is there and it will be in the future. Large, noncommercial institutions can provide good support. However, unpredictable policy changes can destroy tomorrow what seems to be indestructible today. Unfortunately, there have not yet been any museum information systems supported solely by the cooperative funding of a membership type organization. This kind of organizational support would appear to provide the best possible incentive for continued improvement of an information system and a reasonable level of support costs. Any system that is dependent upon one man for all new developments should probably be avoided if at all possible.

In summary there are six, not four, factors that should be considered in the selection of an information system:

1. The carefully defined information needs of the institution and the suitability of a particular system to meet those needs.

2. The experiences (precedent) of other institutions involved with the cataloging of similar types of objects.

3. The computer hardware that is available (but here look to commercial time-sharing organizations, banks, and other institutions in the community in addition to the equipment at the campus computing center).

4. The probable future support that can be expected from the developers of each system under consideration.

5. Budget restrictions or limitation.

6. The skills (and this time I am intentionally eliminating the word *biases*) of the persons who will be responsible for the system.

No mention has been made here of the techniques of data input and file maintenance as factors in the selection of an information system. These are the largest single cost factors involved in the operation of such a system. However, the techniques of preparing data for input and converting it to machine-readable form are largely (though not entirely) independent of the information system that is to be used. As pointed out in chapter 5, it pays to design forms carefully and to fully analyze the alternate ways of entering data that may be available. The cost of preparing data for computer entry, though, will not vary too much from one information system to another.

7

Putting It All Together:
How to Get Started

A GENERAL framework of the activities and key decisions involved in establishing a computerized museum catalog were set forth in table 2 (page 36), and the detailed information necessary to make these decisions has been provided (hopefully) in the last three chapters. However, any one of the key decisions set forth in table 2 interacts with all the rest to such an extent that expensive mistakes can be made unless there is a well-laid plan for the accomplishment of the overall objectives. In this chapter an attempt will be made to give a time perspective to the sequence of decision making so that at each step along the way the responsible individuals may be reasonably sure they have not forgotten anything important.

Shortly after World War II the systems analysts employed by the United States Department of Defense developed a series of program planning techniques that are variously known as CPM (Critical Path Method) and PERT (Program Evaluation and Review Technique). With both of these analytical techniques the objective is to set forth in diagrammatic form the time sequence in which a series of decisions must be made in order to accomplish some specific objective. Figure 118 is a CPM or PERT type diagram setting forth the sequence of key decisions that are involved in establishing a computerized museum catalog. This diagram may look complex but the only things the reader needs to know are that (1) the individual boxes represent activities (note that each box contains a verb) to be performed in a sequence reading from left to right and (2) under normal circumstances the activities in any one box cannot and certainly should not be performed before all activities in all boxes to the left have been completed.

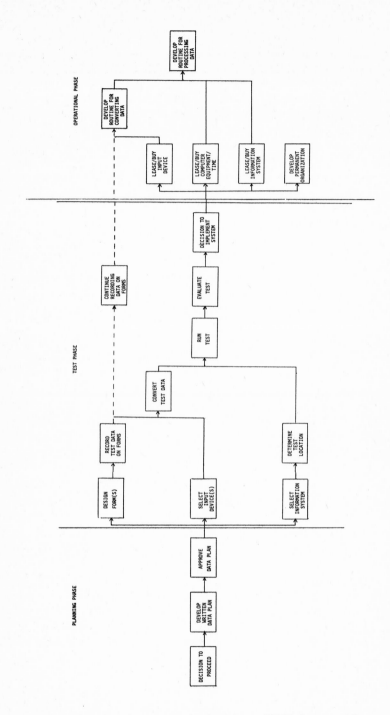

FIG. 118. Creation of a computerized catalog: a PERT diagram of the significant tasks

The diagram is divided into three major time phases corresponding to planning, testing, and operation of the system. Key points of approval are indicated immediately prior to the beginning of each of the latter two phases, and the only activity indicated as moving ahead regardless of these key decisions is the recording of catalog data on the forms for computer entry (note dotted lines both before and after this box).

The specifics of the activities involved on this diagram—those spelled out in previous chapters—will not be discussed again here. However, there are a number of important comments that need to be made concerning each of the three major phases.

Planning Phase

All too often a computerized cataloging program is undertaken by one or two individuals without adequate planning or support by their superiors and/or the governing board of their institution. Three separate boxes have been provided here for the planning phase and two of these are simply giving the responsible individuals authority to proceed—first, authority to proceed with the development of a comprehensive plan, and second, authority to begin implementation of the plan.

The data plan itself should be something much more comprehensive than just a statement about how to acquire a computerized catalog. Rather, it should be a total plan for the written information about the objects in the museum's collections. It should include a total review of all the information needs of all museum employees, whether or not the information should or can be entered in a computer and whether or not the information would logically be considered as a part of the museum's catalog. Suggestions on how to determine some of these information needs were provided in chapter 2.

The data plan should be in writing and should consist of at least four separate sections:

1. The data consideration per se. For this purpose each curator should prepare a written statement setting forth for each class of objects to be cataloged (a) the categories of data that would be necessary for a complete detailed description of the object, (b) the categories of data that probably would be necessary for display purposes, and (c) the categories of data that would likely be useful as finding devices (i.e., the data categories that probably should be contained in any kind of a computerized catalog). These written statements should be thoroughly discussed by all personnel. The

content of the museum's catalog, thus, is the first thing decided upon, and agreement on this should be reached before consideration is given to any kind of a cataloging system.

2. Plan of activities. Once the information needs of the museum have been determined, it is possible to move ahead with the development of an individualized flow chart for the particular institution patterned after figure 118. Each activity in the development of the catalog should be thoroughly discussed by the personnel involved, and once the sequence of activities is settled, the plan should be expanded to include target dates by which each activity is to be accomplished. In the development of CPM or PERT diagrams, this is sometimes done by estimating the number of man-days (or weeks or months) that it will take for each activity to be completed and entering these figures immediately above each connecting arrow. The procedure is not important but some time objectives should be established.

3. Establish responsibilities. Nothing ever gets done unless responsibilities for actions are clearly established. In a complex project such as this some work may be done by committees, other activities are best assigned to individual staff members, and yet other activities may require the specialized talents of an outside consultant (e.g., to assist in the selection of the information system and computer equipment that will best fill the institution's needs). If consultants must be selected, this of course adds yet another box to the list of activities to be performed.

4. Determine test data. It is desirable to include in the initial plan a statement concerning the class and number of objects that will be used in the initial testing of the system. Ideally this should be some part of the collections that are the responsibility of a curator who is sympathetic with the whole idea of a computerized catalog and willing to give it an objective test before everyone has become a slave to the machine.

Regardless of what is included in the data plan, the advantages of having such a plan, in writing, cannot be emphasized too strongly. Before any commitment is made to a consultant, to the sponsors of any information system, or to any supplier of computer time, the plan should be reviewed and approved, formally, by all the responsible museum administrators and the governing board or agency to whom the director is responsible.

Test Phase

Up to the present time almost all computerized cataloging that has been done in museums has been in the nature of experimentation or testing. Therefore, it may seem a bit presumptuous to talk of a "test phase" that precedes making a system operational. However, we are using the phrase here to mean a specific kind of testing, namely, a testing of data from your institution, using the information system that you plan to employ permanently, but prior to the time of committing yourself either to that system or to any particular input devices, computer equipment, and/or service bureau. The information systems described in this book are with one or two exceptions all being used at enough different locations to make it possible to run tests at some other institution in order to determine whether or not a particular information system will, in fact, accomplish the data needs of your institution in the best manner possible.

The procedures necessary to carry out a test such as that described are indicated in figure 118. It is, of course, necessary first to make enough of a preliminary investigation to select the system that will *probably* fulfill the information needs of your institution, and it is most efficient, ultimately, to design input forms and record catalog data on those forms with the selected information system in mind. Once this has been done, the other test activities shown on the PERT diagram can be undertaken in sequence.

As a part of the forms design activity it is well to carefully consider not only where the information will come from to enter on the forms but also the rules that will be followed in recording data. This should be formalized as a clear, unambiguous set of procedures that include precise statements of the recording conventions to be followed in entering data in every space, dictionaries and thesauruses to be used as authority files, and so on. You may find this to be one of the most difficult and time-consuming tasks in the whole program, but if it is carried out carefully, it will pay big dividends in minimizing the number of corrections, changes, and reentries of data later on.

Once the forms design and data recording procedures are under way and input devices and an information system have been selected, the sponsors of the information system will assist you in selecting a location where you can run tests with your own data. If the quantity of data to be run in the tests is not too large, one of the present users of the system often will be willing to run such tests for a potential new user without charge. In any case, a modest charge for computer time and possibly time of the personnel involved in running the tests will be compensated for both in terms of the secure knowledge that what you will eventually get out of the system is what you want and in terms of the sales value of having actual computer print-outs to show to the board when you are trying to convince them to include in next year's budget enough money to make the system operational.

Test runs should be made, if at all possible, with the individuals present who will eventually be responsible for the operation of the system, and the tests should include the running of all programs that are likely to be used at your institution—input programs, correction routines, file maintenance programs, and of course, all different forms of retrieval programs. Most of these information systems are relatively easy to use, but having your own people present when the tests are run, especially if you obtain some feedback from personnel at the computer center, will give you some assurances that the system will in fact work when you install it at your institution. The reason for running all the pertinent programs, of course, is to be sure that they will provide you the information you want and that your personnel know all the program conventions sufficiently well to make them run.

As with the planning phase, the final activity block shown for the test phase is a point of yes or no decision: "Yes, we move ahead to make the system operational" or "No, we scrap what has been done and go back to the drawing board."

Operational Phase

If the first two phases of the total activity shown in figure 118 are carried out adequately and a decision is made to make the system operational, the third phase becomes in some ways almost an anti-climax. Four things need to be acquired: a permanent organization, the information system, computer time, and suitable input devices. The development of an organization is, of course, beyond the scope of this book; the other three activities have been dealt with at length throughout the book. Making the whole thing operational is simply a matter of bringing these four things together and developing them into routines for the conversion of data into readable computer input and into routines for the processing of data on the computer.

In figure 118 the activity of recording data on the forms for computer entry is indicated as being a continuous activity once it is begun with test data. This is not an absolute requirement; it certainly would be possible to cut off the recording of additional data after the test data has been entered on the forms until such time as the test results are in and evaluated. However, it has been pointed out many times that the largest single expenditure of human energy in any computerized cataloging system is the time required to prepare data for entry, that is, to record data on the forms so that they can be converted to computer input. If by chance a decision is made not to employ the information system that was envisioned at the beginning of the test phase, the worst that can happen by continuing to record data for entry in that system is that a very small and inexpensive computer program will have to be written to translate the data into a form of input suitable for one of the other systems. This is a small price to pay in exchange for the time that would otherwise be lost waiting for a decision to be made and possibly a year or more in the budget cycle. If the initial planning has been well done, even this conversion becomes only a remote possibility.

In summary, the emphasis of this entire chapter must again be placed on the planning phase. If the project is thoroughly planned in advance and the plan is properly approved by all levels of administrative management, the carrying out of the plan, even through the test phase to say nothing of the operational phase, becomes almost a routine operation. In this sense the development of a computerized museum catalog is no different from the development of any other program for a museum. If the planning is well done, very little can happen to surprise anyone in carrying out the plan.

8

Computer Networks and Catalogs of the Future

AT THE beginning of this book the doubts of one museum director were expressed concerning whether or not computerized museum catalogs could ever be prepared as inexpensively as manual catalogs are prepared today. Subsequently, a lot of information has been presented about how to put together a computerized catalog, but nothing has been said that would in any way change the skeptic's mind about whether it is all worth it. It is not our purpose in this final chapter to defend the largely experimental work that has been done to date; rather it is our purpose to be frankly critical of it and to suggest the nature of the changes that will have to occur before computerized museum catalogs can become the kind of tools that museum administrators and boards cannot afford to be without.

Up to the present time it is safe to characterize the experience of most museums with computerized catalogs as being directed solely toward serving the information needs of the individual institution in the same way that card catalogs were supposed to have served those needs in the past. Little attention has been given either *(a)* to the need for shared data or *(b)* to the many creative new ways of developing and disseminating information that the computer makes possible once the "card catalog syndrome" is laid to rest.

The individualism, perhaps, was to be expected. After all, the important immediate cataloging need of most museums is just to create a finding device of some kind and to do this as cheaply and quickly as possible. To the analyst or administrator responsible for developing a computerized cataloging system, this need has been interpreted as a clear-cut set of instructions: obtain the least expensive information system that will work on equipment that is available and adapt that system to the apparent information needs of the institution. If the results happen to meet some interinstitutional need as well, this is fine, but the important objective has been to create some kind of a catalog for the institution being served.

The Museum Computer Network, of course, is an important exception. When this organization was first begun in 1967, it was assumed (perhaps correctly at least for art museums) that one major objective would be to ultimately make it possible for any member to retrieve data on any art object in the country. To accomplish this, the developers knew that certain constraints would have to be built into the system. Thus, the user of the GRIPHOS system does not have the freedom either to modify the computer programs or to establish his own data categories. The programs, for example, are distributed to members of the MCN in a form that prevents the user from changing them. Each module (i.e., each edition of the program package) has an expiration date, which means that every user has to have the current version—the same version that every other user has—or he cannot operate. There is no way at the present time that a user of the GRIPHOS information system can get inside the programs to modify them in any way. Also, through the Museum Computer Network, Inc., definitions of data categories are controlled so that all users are employing the same tag numbers to mean approximately the same thing. The developers of GRIPHOS may be criticized because the constraints and standards were established by a small group of people largely associated with art museums and without regard for all the needs of the many disciplines now interested in using the system. However, they should be commended for the farsightedness that is implicit in their basic approach. Even today, the Museum Computer Network, Inc., is the only organization to offer both *(a)* a generalized information system (GRIPHOS) and *(b)* a user organization (MCN) that is concerned about the need for shared data.

Any generalized information system that is used for purposes of museum cataloging should (indeed it *must*) accomplish the cataloging needs of individual museums. But in addition to this it can do a great deal more if a sincere attempt is made to integrate the work at any one institution with the work that is being done in similar institutions elsewhere. Suggestions as to organizations that will prevent this individualism from getting out of hand are included later on in this chapter.

The second characteristic of almost all computerized museum catalogs that have been developed so far is that they have basically been attempts to prepare on a computer something similar in type to the card file catalogs that previously have been created manually. This does not mean that the output of all cataloging so far has been in the form of cards, although one of the most complete files, that at the Museum of Modern Art, is in card form (see figure 50). Rather, it is a reflection of the fact that *curators and administrators have demanded that anything done on the computer should result in some kind of hard copy, printed output to replace the card catalog.* There are at least three reasons why this card catalog syndrome has been something less than satisfactory:

1. It is expensive. It is true that the cost of storing large quantities of data on computers is going down at a rate of about 20 percent per year. However, I am convinced that there is no way we will ever really save any money by trying to duplicate the production of card catalogs on a computer. Even at the Museum of Modern Art, where they have had more experience and are probably more efficient than anywhere else in the production of a computerized catalog, David Vance estimates that it costs just about the same amount to prepare the present card files on a computer as it cost previously to prepare the card files manually. It is true that accuracy and consistency have been greatly improved, and there is a bonus in being able to prepare, when required, specialized arrangements of selected data quickly and easily. However, no one has yet made a claim that our present computerized cataloging procedures will save you any money.

2. It utilizes available technology only to a limited extent. Unfortunately, most museums view their catalogs as dead repositories of information somewhat analogous to the view that many people have (e.g., as expressed by Henry Miller in *The Colossus of Maroussi*) of museums as dead repositories for useless objects. When all the information in catalogs such as this is transferred into a computer file, the result is still a dead repository of information, and the only way the computer is used, in most cases, is to rapidly sort and reproduce the overly large catalog entries. No museum has yet dared to explore the whole concept of cataloging to include multiple files of carefully selected information integrated to serve all the information needs of the various individuals and groups who are in any way associated with the museum, that is, to create a true "information system." This is possible with present computer technology, but it will not happen so long as a card catalog is all that is wanted.

3. It has never worked anyway. One has only to ask how often a card catalog has effectively been used as a finding device to begin to question whether or not there ever has been a card catalog in

a medium-to-large-sized museum worth the time and effort that went into its preparation. In the first place, card catalogs have usually broken down through sheer weight of numbers if a museum contains more than ten to fifteen thousand objects. Beyond that, they always seem to be organized according to some cataloging scheme other than the one the user needs in order to find what he wants conveniently. Nevertheless, the thought that two, three, or four sets of card files may not comprise the best kind of a finding device has so far not occurred to most museum administrators.

If computerized catalogs are ever to become viable museum tools that are sufficiently attractive to be salable to directors and boards, they must *(a)* be attainable within a completely different dimension of cost than anything so far available and *(b)* be capable of truly serving the *real* information needs, not only of museum registrars but also of curators, exhibit specialists, researchers, the museum visitor, various disciplinary groups, and on an even larger scale, the information needs of the museum profession as a whole. This is a large order. However, it can be achieved. Before it is, though, several things will have to happen:

1. There will have to be some radical changes in the thinking of museum people at all levels concerning what a catalog is, what it should and should not contain, and how it can be used most effectively.

2. There will have to be new organizational emphases (and in some cases new organizations) to deal realistically with the information needs of different kinds of museums and different types of collections.

3. The content of computerized catalogs will have to be modified if the real information needs of museums are to be served.

4. There will have to be some major changes made in the information systems that are used by museums, particularly changes in the techniques of indexing, retrieval, and display. Present information systems serve some of the needs of museums, but they are not adequate for the expanding role that computers will probably play in museums of the future. This does not mean that the structuring of data for entry into existing systems (those described in chapter 6) will need to be modified, but it does mean that the present information systems will have to be greatly expanded or they will be replaced in time by systems such as that described later in this chapter.

Before we describe the kind of catalogs that will probably be developed to serve the needs of museums in the future, let us first look at the structure of the organizations that I think will be needed to bring these catalogs into existence.

Computer Networks

With most computerized museum catalogs there is an implication—this is made explicit in the work of the Museum Computer Network—that ultimately all museums will be linked together in some kind of network of computers so that any institution will have access to what has been recorded anywhere in the network. The lure of computerized information networks is readily understandable when one reads quotations such as the following: [22]

> A medical researcher sits at an on-line terminal in Honolulu searching an index to the world's medical literature stored on a computer in Bethesda, Maryland, over 5000 miles away. His request passes across a radio network of the University of Hawaii; the telephone network of the Hawaiian telephone company; the Pacific Ocean via an international satellite; a nationwide research network in the continental United States; and, finally, a commercial time-sharing network, before reaching the medical information system in Bethesda. By mail the request would have taken several days. By computer-communication networks it takes less than 5 seconds. The response to the request, a set of literature citations, starts printing out at the terminal back in Honolulu within 15 seconds from the time the request was dispatched. Numerous other remote users of the medical information system receive service simultaneously.
>
> This example of what is happening now may seem dramatized, but it does illustrate the daily use of a variety of communication networks that are currently providing efficient-interconnection between computer systems for their users. Domestic usage of the on-line medical information system through the commerical time-sharing network has been doubling every 6 months. This fact plus countless other important uses of networks in many areas proclaim the growing significance of information and computer networks.

To most of us networks such as this still seem to be almost in the realm of science fiction. However, EDUCOM (The Interuniversity Communications Council, Inc.) has been concerned since its founding in 1964 with fostering the collaboration of colleges and universities in the use of computer and communication technologies. It has given the subject of networks special emphasis, beginning with its July, 1966, summer study in Boulder, Colorado, and continuing with the open conferences it recently has been holding twice each year at the request of and with financial assistance from the National Science Foundation. In a recent *Science* article [23] and a comprehensive book being published by the M.I.T. Press,[24] the men responsible for these meetings in recent years summarize the results and recommendations that have emanated from them. Much of the following is adapted from these sources.

Today there are an estimated seven thousand computers in the United States whose primary business is processing information for research and education. Their combined annual operating budget runs into billions of dollars. These computers represent a nation asset of considerable importance by virtue of the magnitude and nature of the work they perform. Because of the similarity in programs they run, one might expect their operation to be concentrated in a relatively few places or at the very least to be well integrated, yet the overriding pattern is quite the opposite. These seven thousand computers are distributed in a large number of autonomous centers and laboratories that are separately staffed and managed.

The majority of these computers have until recently been directly or indirectly supported to a great extent by grants. Now that grant money is becoming more difficult to obtain, it has been necessary to include the operating budgets for these installations as part of the regular institutional budgets. In seeking ways to cut these budgets, a number of institutions have found that they could operate just as well by being part of a time-sharing system (where one computer serves many simultaneous users) as they did previously with a single access computer (where one computer serves a single user). Now many of the large universities and research organizations are exploring the possibilities of computer networks—where there are both many suppliers and many users—as yet a further step toward improving the power and capability which emanate from their local computer center or terminal without the costs that previously would have been considered inevitable in order to obtain such powerful computing services.

The functions and even the definition of a computer network are not firmly established. Some consider any time-sharing system a network. However, those who are involved with multiple user–multiple supplier systems (e.g., the ARPANET, developed to serve defense contractors, TUCC, MERIT, UNI-COLL and other systems designed to serve multiple university complexes, the Ohio College Library Center, and the National Library of Medicine's MEDLINE service) all have realized that the complexity of the operation goes up geometrically as one moves from a single supplier time-sharing service to a multiple supplier network. Networking presents special problems because of the involvement of many vendors, systems, and supplying organizations, and not everyone is convinced that it is worth the trouble.

In order to clarify some of the basic problems involved, EDUCOM conferees have delineated three functional categories of networks: user services networks, transmission networks, and facilitating networks.

> The user-services network includes the users and suppliers of services, along with the resources from which the services derive. The users and suppliers are joined not necessarily by physical links but by their mutual desire, commitment, and capability to share resources. To achieve a user-services network may require considerable change in attitudes, training, development of interpersonal contacts, and refinement of resources. The user-services network is fundamentally people-directed and task-oriented.[25]

By contrast, a transmission network consists of a set of communication facilities by which machines can pass data to each other. Mediating between the transmission and user-services networks are facilitating networks that create and enforce standards as for transmission codes, establish and implement user protocols, perform centralized accounting and billing, etc.

The user services network is given primary consideration here, for it is this type of networking that museums and museum-related disciplines should be developing. With some kinds of museums, transmission networks may eventually become a reality, and of course, facilitating networks will be necessary in order to make them work. However, it is not likely that museums will ever have sufficient funds available to be the initial developers of transmission networks. In the meantime, while others are doing this developmental work, user services networks are necessary even to determine how far museums should go with this type of activity.

What do we mean by user services networks for museums? In one sense the Museum Data Bank Coordinating Committee is such a network, for one of its basic goals is to determine the information needs of museums and possible common denominators of data (standards, if you wish) that *may* eventually serve as a basis for interinstitutional communication (computerized or not) in the future. The MDBCC, though, simply because it serves as a point for the generalized focus of all computer related problems, cannot be the only network of this type. Additional organizations can and should be formed *(a)* to determine information needs and *(b)* to establish standards of data content, conventions, and terminology for any museum related group that has in fact similar needs. Examples of the types of organizations needed are the special committees being formed by the Association of Systematics Collections and by the individual disciplines within ASC. Similar organizations and/or committees should be formed by art museums, archaeological museums, and any other group that appears to have a uniformity of data needs.

It would be relatively easy to say that these organizations should be set up along disciplinary lines. Unfortunately, though, the disciplines established by academic institutions do not automatically bring together all groups having common data needs. In some cases disciplines must be split apart for this purpose, and in other cases it can be a multidisciplinary effort. The following are examples in which the commonality of data needs can and should bring together parts of different disciplines into separate user services networks:

1. The institutions that are involved with cultural inventories of various kinds can well be served by a single network. These include various organizations such as that portion of the National Museum of Canada devoted to the development of a centralized data bank of Canada's cultural resources, the National Register of Historic Sites in the United States, the Registry of Archaeological Sites being developed by many states, and probably all art museums. With all these organizations there does seem to be a need for some kind of central file or transmission network that connects a number of computer files so that a user can locate (and count, describe, or whatever) individual objects that possess certain common denominators of information—artist's name, temporal period, geographic location, and so on. This, however, does not describe the primary information needs of most historical agencies and it certainly does not describe the kinds of information needs expressed by most natural sciences. The difference is not just in the categories of data used; there are differences in the ways this information is brought together and disseminated.

2. In the natural sciences the apparent need (and in some disciplines this is even to the exclusion of individual institution catalogs) is for an authority file or a clearinghouse of information. The Flora North American Program, for example, was designed to provide an authority file on botanical type specimens. Among botanists there is serious doubt as to whether a computerized catalog of the specimens in any institution would be used to any great extent. Similarly, Dr. Frank Seymour, in a recent letter provided me with several specific examples of the way field research in the natural sciences is often duplicated simply because there is no convenient way to know what collections have previously been made in a given area.

3. The term *historical agencies* may be used to define yet a third type of data need, but the nature of the collections included must be carefully defined. It does include museums that are concerned with historical objects and it includes most archaeological museums as well, but classes of unique objects that would be considered a part of a cultural inventory (i.e., archaeological or historic artifacts which are particularly important for their artistic or intrinsic value) should be excluded along with both historical and archaeological sites. Here the primary information need seems to be for the systemization (standardization?) of techniques, terminology, and recording conventions that are used for cataloging, simply as a means of bringing massive quantities of data under control. Ultimately, of course, this would permit the interchange of information between institutions by means of transmission networks, but networking per se is not the prime goal that it seems to be with institutions concerned with cultural inventories.

Different kinds of computer projects are required in order to completely satisfy the different kinds of information needs expressed above. To a greater or lesser extent, the idea of *a* museum data bank system or *a* network, thus, is impossible of attainment. There is a commonality in the structure of the requirements to meet the information needs of all museum-related disciplines, and the Museum Data Bank Coordinating Committee now is functioning as a user-services network to assist *all* museums in defining that structure and pointing out the nature of the decisions that must be made at some lower level. However, user services networks that are organized specifically to determine and coordinate the information needs of specific interest groups are also required. *Some* of these user services networks may eventually be expanded to include the functions of facilitating networks and transmission networks, but the catalogs of all museums probably will never be (probably will never need to be) integrated into either a single massive data bank or a single network of computerized museum catalogs that allow everyone to retrieve data on any collection in any type of museum.

Catalogs of the Future

The description of a medical researcher sitting at an on-line terminal in Honolulu (page 246) may sound like something out of the twenty-first century. If some of the more esoteric aspects of this illustration are eliminated, though, it may not be as remote from the needs of museums as it appears to be. For example, let us eliminate the radio and international satellite communication linkages and assume that this is a computer file that is located across campus, down the street, across town, or perhaps a hundred miles away. The difference between this and half a world away are entirely a matter of transmission techniques. The storage and retrieval or cataloging principles and problems are identical.

Catalogs of the future in some respects will not be a great deal different from what has been described in this book. Data needs will probably be determined much more explicitly than they are now by user services networks such as those discussed in the preceding section. However, within each institution each item in the collections will have to be examined by a curator or a curatorial assistant, much as it is now, and the information recorded on forms in the manner we have described in chapter 5. There will be some advances made in the methods by which the information is taken off the forms and entered into the computer, but there are not very many alternatives, other than those we have described, for the functions listed on table 2 as recording for entry, input to the computer, data verification, and error correction. The computer operations of sorting, merging, indexing, and storing data will become somewhat more efficient and less expensive in the future. However, even here I do not expect to see any monumental breakthroughs that will drastically alter the whole process of computerized museum cataloging.

The two areas where computerized museum catalogs of the future probably will be most dramatically changed from what has been done to date are in Phase I and Phase V (in table 2), namely, the function of data determination and the entire process of file inquiry.

As pointed out previously, the data presently contained in most computerized museum catalogs suffers from the "card catalog syndrome." An attempt is usually made to place all the information that is available about each object into the computer file so that listings of any desired information can be readily prepared on the high-speed printer. This, of course, defeats the purpose of the catalog as a finding device. In the future the *documentation* about each object will be prepared in manual or typed form and filed by registration number. The computerized *catalog* will contain only selected and carefully controlled types and quantities of data, such as *(a)* key word indexes to those categories of data considered significant finding devices and *(b)* textual data that is developed in connection with specific exhibits. This latter class of information will be maintained in separate files, accessible through the object indexes or by separate retrieval methods. Some of these files may contain information on specific objects, but others will be descriptive of classes of objects, temporal periods, geographical areas, biographical data, and so on. *The content of the computerized catalog files, though, will not duplicate the documentation that is available on every object.*

The change in file inquiry methods that *must* come about in catalogs of the future can be described in a few words although the reasons for this suggested change and the implications of it cannot be stated so simply. Briefly, I believe that CRT (cathode-ray tube) terminals will be used almost exclusively in catalogs of the future for file inquiry and in many cases for data entry and file maintenance as well. So far as data entry and file maintenance are concerned, the change is not too significant, but as a matter of convenience CRT terminals often will be used as the sole basis of communicating with the computer.

To the best of my knowledge the CRT terminal has not been used in any museum except as an exhibition of computer technology. Remote *teletype* terminals can be used to retrieve catalog data in the GIPSY system; the ADAM system at Arizona State University uses a teletype terminal with paper tape attachment for both entry and retrieval of data; the MIRS system, used experimentally at The Children's Museum in Boston, uses a teletype terminal for both entry and retrieval of data; and several kinds of remote terminals have been employed for entering data in both the SELGEM and the GRIPHOS systems. In all these cases a CRT terminal probably could have been used in place of the teletype terminal. However, none of these systems allows the user to employ the CRT terminal to scan index files in the search for particular records of significance, and none of them permits the integrated use of multiple files in the manner that is envisioned here for catalogs of the future. The reason for including a description of the ELMS system in chapter 6 is to give the reader some idea of the sort of information system which I believe it will be necessary to employ when museum catalogs consist solely of indexes and exhibit displays.

The logic of using a CRT terminal for the retrieval of data from a computerized catalog has several facets. It is perhaps obvious that this is one of the most convenient ways there is of looking at a large file. Beyond this, though, the generalized use of CRT terminals will ultimately permit even the moderate-sized museum to develop a computerized catalog for a price that is commensurate with the rest of their budget, and it will make it possible for the aggressive larger museum to use computer technology as a part of their exhibits program and for all kinds of information purposes not yet dreamed of.

The use of CRT terminals implies that somewhere there is a computer that is maintained on-line and ready to answer questions whenever someone sits down in front of the terminal and begins conversing with it—i.e., there is the implication of real-time processing (see page 26). Very few museums would be willing to invest the time and money that is required to maintain their own computer on-line for this purpose, even if they could afford it. However, if the programming for a system such as this were once set up in a time-sharing system—that is, with one computer *and one information system* serving many simultaneous users—it would bring the cost for each user down to the point where most museums could afford to be a part of the system.

It would not matter whether the time-sharing system was actually an expansion of a user services network into a cooperative consortium where the organization itself rented computer equipment and hired its own personnel, or whether the time-sharing system was operated by a commercial service bureau company. In many instances a reliable service bureau can save far more than what they charge for administrative overhead and profit.

A time-sharing system with its one supplier and many simultaneous users stands midway between a single access computer with its one supplier and one user and a network with its many suppliers and many users. In both a time-sharing system and a network the goal is to give each user the illusion of having his own single access system and at the same time to give him the cost benefit of sharing the system. In actual practice it has been demonstrated repeatedly that a time-sharing system is substantially less expensive for the user who has only occasional and normally brief demands for computer services than it is to acquire programs and someone to operate them, even when the computer time can be shared with others. The reason for this is that the only *fixed* costs (i.e., the costs that must be paid whether the system is used or not; costs other than for actual operating time) the user has are:

1. The rental of the terminal or terminals.

2. A small charge by the computer center for keeping a certain amount of space available on rapid access devices for each user's files and keeping these devices on-line.

3. Any fixed charges made by the telephone company (or an equivalent private company) for line service.

All other costs are variable costs, which means that they are incurred only as and to the extent that the computer is actually used. These normally include a flat rate "connect" charge, made by the computer center each time you sign on; a charge (prorated to the nearest 1/100 of a second) for the computer time used; and long-distance line charges if the computer center is located other than within reach of a local telephone call.

We have a chicken-and-egg situation here as far as costs are concerned: the individual museum cannot afford to operate a computerized catalog in the manner I have described until there are enough others who are a part of the same consortium or service bureau to make the fixed cost to each relatively small; and yet the consortium or service bureau cannot be organized until there is some assurance that there will be enough interested museums to make it worthwhile. I firmly believe that once user services networks (whatever they may be called) reach the point of development where they can state with some confidence the data needs (including recording conventions, authority files, etc.) of different user groups, venture capital will be willing to enter the scene to finance commercial time-sharing organizations as necessary to serve those needs. Beyond this, I am convinced that it will be a paying proposition for those on the ground floor who can actually demonstrate their capability of serving the various museum-oriented data needs, and that the volume alone will eventually bring this kind of service within reach of any museum with a full-time staff of more than three or four persons.

For the larger museum, the use of a system such as this (and why not the same time-sharing system that the smaller museum uses?) opens the door to an entire new range of computer applications that have not been discussed elsewhere in this book. The same principles of computerized storage and retrieval that are applicable to object documentation can be applied to a wide range of membership, promotion, and other applications as discussed in chapter 3. In addition, with only a moderate amount of individualized programming and the addition of more terminals, it is possible to think of an exhibit as the beginning point of a free-flowing educational experience for any museum visitor. After viewing the exhibit briefly, for example, the museum visitor of any age can turn to a CRT terminal to obtain "Additional Information" on anything that is related to the exhibit: for example, in an art museum, biographical data about the artist, information about the art style represented, catalog entries concerning other paintings by the same artist or of the same period, etc. There are several reasons why a CRT terminal is considered to be an essential here even though remote teletype terminals are less expensive: *(a)* the CRT terminal displays an entire tube of data as an immediate response to any query—the data must be typed out on the teletype terminal, *(b)* the CRT terminal is noiseless—a teletype terminal is in fact a typewriter, *(c)* a file can literally be "scanned" on a CRT terminal in the same way that one might scan an alphabetic index in the back of a book, and *(d)* because of the immediacy of response of a CRT terminal, the cost of computer time is somewhat less than that required when operating a teletype terminal, although this is not a major difference.

Finally, the stage is set for the eventual communication of the different computing centers in the form of transmission networks when, as, and if the organization and facilities are available for network operation and if the appropriate user services network organization has determined that this is desirable. Note, however, that the actual transmission network under circumstances such as this comes about as a logical outgrowth of meeting the information needs of individual museums in the most inexpensive way possible.

The computerized museum catalog or data bank can be an effective and economical tool. As with any other tool, though, it is the human factor in the man-machine equation that determines *how* effective and *how* economical. I can do no better than to end this with the admonition expressed recently by Stanwyn Shetler: [26]

Advocates of computerized information retrieval have tended, perhaps unwittingly, to exaggerate the role and the relative importance of the hardware/software component at the expense of the human factor. We have stroked terminals, sparred over input media, and dueled elegantly or fiercely over computer models and software packages as though these were the elements that will make or break a data-banking system. The implied message is: "The software is the system, and the system is the data bank;" or, in more prosaic terms, the means are the ends. The consequence has been a field day for the peddlers of hardware and software who have not got a clue as to the real ingredients of data-banking success. The unsuspecting user is led to think that, if only he could find the right do-it-yourself hardware/software black box, which he could plug into his system as simply as a new battery into his car, his data-banking problems would be solved, with the data bank virtually creating itself.

In truth, the point cannot be overemphasized that data-banking, like writing books and papers, is tedious work that can consume enormous amounts of professional manpower. Computers notwithstanding, the human factor is and always will be the critical factor in the data-banking equation. Whether a data bank will succeed depends entirely on whether the human factor can be met and whether the all-important man/machine interfaces can be elaborated strand by strand. Once these interfaces exist and a system is functioning, every effort should be made to protect and to reinforce them to keep the system functional. These delicate strands should not be ruptured lightly to chase the rainbow of utopian hardware or software in the usually illusory hope that costs can be cut and the human factor reduced.

Notes

1. George Santayana, *Dialogues in Limbo* (London: Constable & Co., 1925).

2. Attributed to Mary Baker Eddy, *The Christian Science Monitor,* 8 November 1963.

3. *Museum Accredition* (Washington, D.C.: American Association of Museums, 1970).

4. *The American Heritage Dictionary of the English Language* (New York: American Heritage Publishing Co., 1969), p. 864.

5. Carl E. Guthe, *The Management of Small History Museums,* 2nd ed. (Nashville: American Association for State and Local History, 1964), pp. 35–36.

6. A widely used system, recommended by the American Association of Museums in its publication *Museum Registration Methods,* provides for the numbering of objects and related documentation with three sets of digits separated by periods or hyphens: a two-digit number for the year the object was accessioned, a number corresponding to all objects in a single accession, and a registration number to establish the individual identity of each item.

7. Guthe, *Small History Museums,* p. 36.

8. George Bowditch, *Cataloging Photographs: A Procedure for Small Museums,* American Association for State and Local History, Technical Leaflet 57 (Nashville, 1971), p. 2.

9. Guthe, *Small History Museums,* pp. 42–43.

10. Guthe, *Small History Museums,* p. 35.

11. The flow-charting symbols and explanations shown in figures 2A and 2B have been adapted from several sources in order to explain, as simply as possible, the symbols used elsewhere in this book. This is not a complete list, and the explanations are in no sense "official." However, they conform to the recommendations of both the International Organization for Standardization (Recommendation R1028) and the American National Standards Institute, Inc. (Subcommittee X3.5-1970).

12. Carl E. Dauterman, "Sèvres Incised Marks and the Computer," in *Computers and Their Potential Applications in Museums* (New York: Metropolitan Museum of Art and Arno Press, 1968), pp. 177–194.

13. B. L. Gerken, *An Approach to the Evaluation and Selection of Data Management Systems* (Bedford, Mass.: The Mitre Corporation, 1972), p. iii. Distributed by

257

National Technical Information Service, U.S. Department of Commerce, 5285 Port Royal Road, Springfield, Va. 22151.

14. In the strictest sense, of course, this statement is a *non sequitur,* for it is only after one or more of the second level detailed observations have been made that there is any basis for the preliminary classification. These initial observations, however, are most often made at the subconscious, intuitive level for the purpose of deciding what other observations might be meaningful.

15. It is suggested that all dates except those used to record temporal origins (i.e., paragraphs 25, 26, and 27) be recorded in a way that will facilitate computer sorting from left to right, with two digits for each year, month, and day (yymmdd) and no intervening punction or space. The symbol "ƀ" is used to designate a blank space. The alert computer scientist will recognize that this suggestion prescribes a precise recording convention to handle repeating groups of data categories (actually, this is what might be called "linked pairs," but this in turn is only one example of a repeating group). Another example of the same problem occurs with the contents of paragraphs 84-87 and the concept of "type status" which is basic in systematic biology. The whole problem of repeating groups is not adequately handled by most information systems in use today. Here the problem is avoided by special recording convention or syntax, but it is recognized that this is not a satisfactory long-term, general-purpose solution.

16. Since this category is normally used only by archaeologists, the term they use, *provenience,* has been substituted for the term used in the art world, *provenance.* The meanings are similar.

17. Terms are taken from John Buettner-Janusch, *Origins of Man* (New York: John Wiley & Sons, 1966), p. 35. Terms in parentheses are the corresponding words used primarily by botanists. (Personal communication, Dr. Edwin Smith, University of Arkansas, Department of Botany.)

18. George P. Murdock, Human Relations Area Files, Yale University, 1961.

19. Record and field lengths and address fields in the record are recorded in a packed code form to permit their values to be larger than the number of field positions indicate in figure 58.

20. George F. Estabrook, "The Theory of TAXIR Accessioner." *Mathematical Biosciences* 5(1969): 330,338.

21. These instructions are for the IBM 2260 terminal; with a 2741 a single key replaces the SHIFT/ENTER instruction and another key replaces the SHIFT/NEW LINE instruction.

22. Martin Greenberger, Julius Aronofsky, James L. McKenney, and William F. Massey, "Computer and Information Networks," *Science* 182 (1973): 29.

23. Ibid., pp. 29-35.

24. Martin Greenberger, Julius Aronofsky, James L. McKenney, and William F. Massey, *Networks for Research and Education* (Cambridge, Mass.: M.I.T. Press, 1974).

25. Greenberger, "Computer Networks," p. 32.

26. Stanwyn G. Shetler, "Demythologizing Biological Data Banking," *Taxon* 23, no. 1 (February 1974), p. 85.

Index